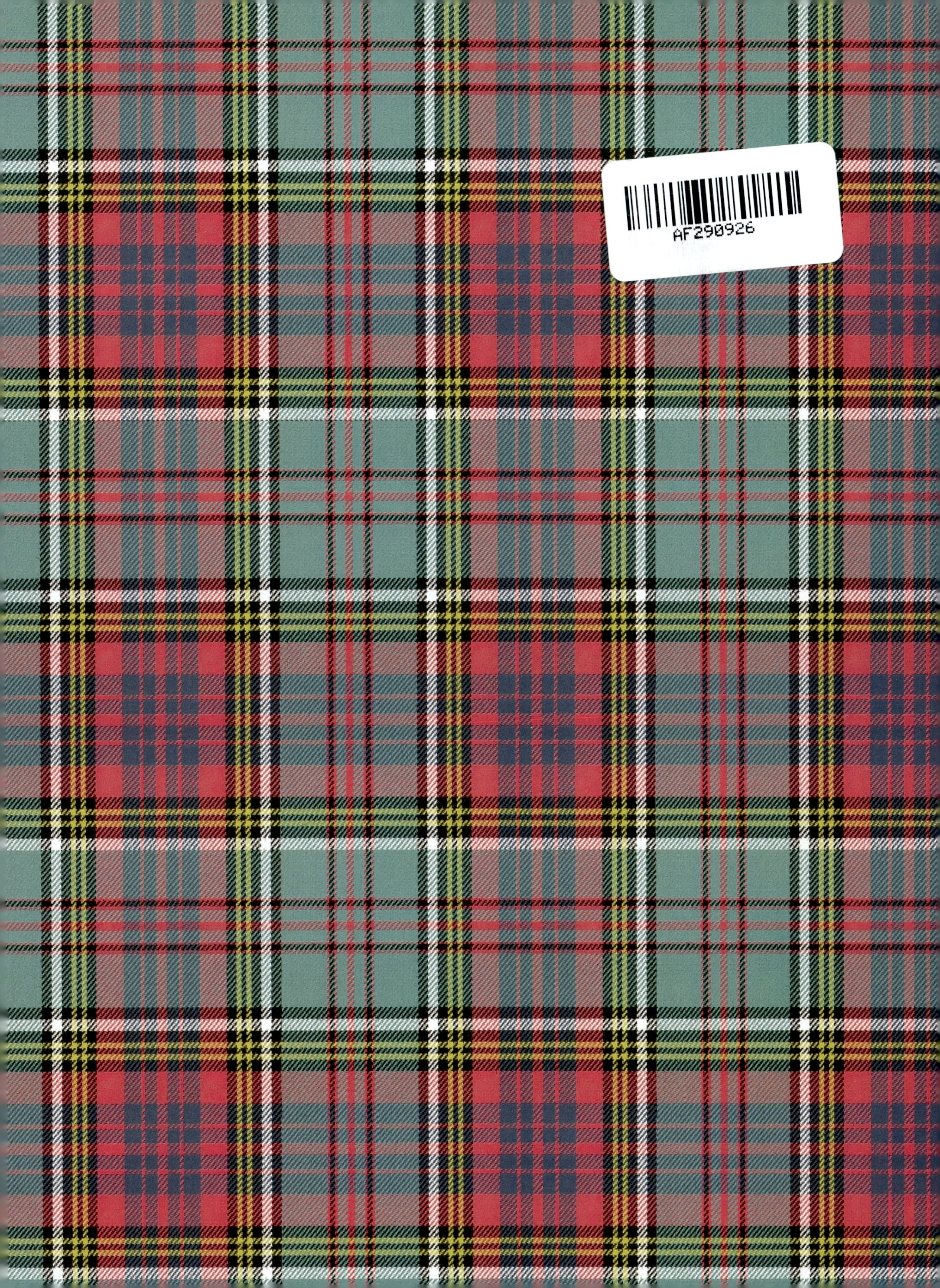
AF290926

THE FASHION ICONS

VIVIENNE WESTWOOD

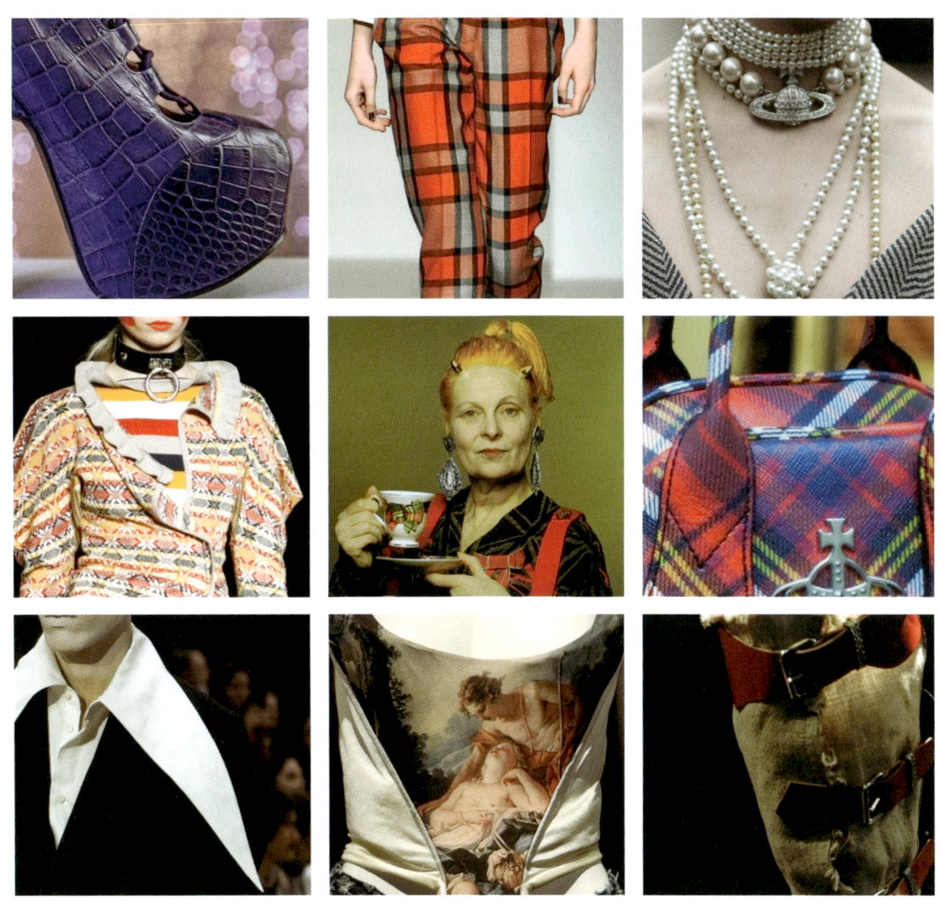

Alison James

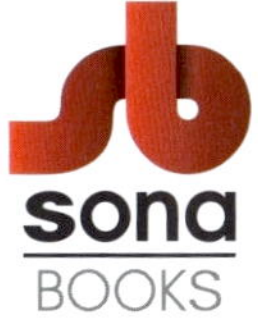

sona
BOOKS

CONTENTS

INTRODUCTION: THE GODMOTHER OF PUNK   8

ROOTS OF REBELLION 1941-1965   10

MEETING MALCOLM 1965-1971   16

PARADISE LOST AND FOUND 1971-1973   24

NEW YORK AND CHICKEN BONES 1973   32

SEX AND RAGE 1974-1975   40

ANARCHY IN THE U.K. 1975-1978   44

"VIVE LA REVOLUTION!" 1979-1980   54

PIRATES AND SAVAGES 1981-1982   64

LAST DANCE WITH MALCOLM 1983   74

"I MAY BE A REBEL, BUT I'M NOT AN OUTSIDER" 1984-1986   82

THE BRITISH INVASION 1986-1988   92

THE STUDENT BECOMES THE TEACHER 1988-1994   100

THE END OF THE ROAD 1994-2000   108

NEW BEGINNINGS 2000-2005   114

JACK OF ALL TRADES 2006-2010   120

VIVIENNE WESTWOOD X 2014-2021   124

LONG LIVE THE QUEEN 2022   130

A LIFE IN DATES   136

INTRODUCTION:
THE GODMOTHER OF PUNK

"The only possible effect one can have on the world is through unpopular ideas."

Vivienne Westwood

Revered for her revolutionary designs and unrelenting vision, Vivienne Westwood's legacy is one of bold defiance and unapologetic individuality. Yet, beneath the surface of this celebrated fashion icon lies a story woven with plenty of contradictions and profound depth.

Her journey from a working-class girl with a disdain for corruption and global injustice, to a pioneering force in haute couture, was nothing short of remarkable.

Emerging from the British punk rock scene of the 1970s, Westwood's provocative designs shattered conventions and redefined the fashion landscape forever. Vivienne Westwood's creations were emblematic of her fearless approach to life and unwavering determination to challenge the status quo. The safety pins, pirate shirts, bondage trousers, and the audacious use of traditional tartan she championed were not mere stylistic choices, but radical statements that blended art with social commentary. For Vivienne, fashion was a weapon.

Her capacity to merge the personal with the political, the past with the present, cemented her place as a vanguard of the fashion world and a catalyst for change. She urged women to embrace their individuality and reject societal expectations, embodying the spirit of rebellion that defined her brand.

During her career spanning nearly 50 years, Vivienne Westwood gave birth to punk, conquered high-fashion, and built a global empire. She invented New Romantics style, sent Naomi Campbell down the catwalk wearing her iconic platform heels, and turned

OPP PAGE TOP: Vivienne Westwood shop sign
OPP PAGE MAIN: Vivienne Westwood backstage ahead of her show during the London Fashion Week, June 2017

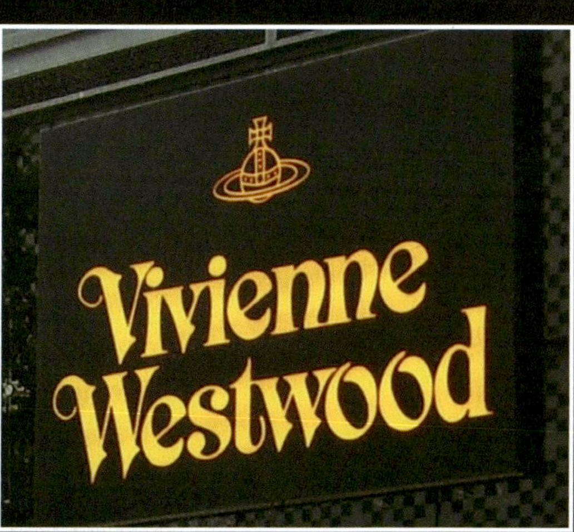

up to meet the Queen having forgotten to wear underwear. Through her work and unique persona, she managed to influence an entire generation of young designers such as John Galliano and Alexander McQueen.

Despite her outward bravado and public persona, Vivienne Westwood remained an enigmatic figure in every aspect of her life. Celebrated as the godmother of punk fashion, she was also, less famously, a teacher, a mother, an environmental activist, and a provocateur with a penchant for anarchism.

The story of how Vivienne Westwood, a woman of immense contradictions, orchestrated her rise from humble beginnings to global fame is, of course, fascinating and full of twists and turns.

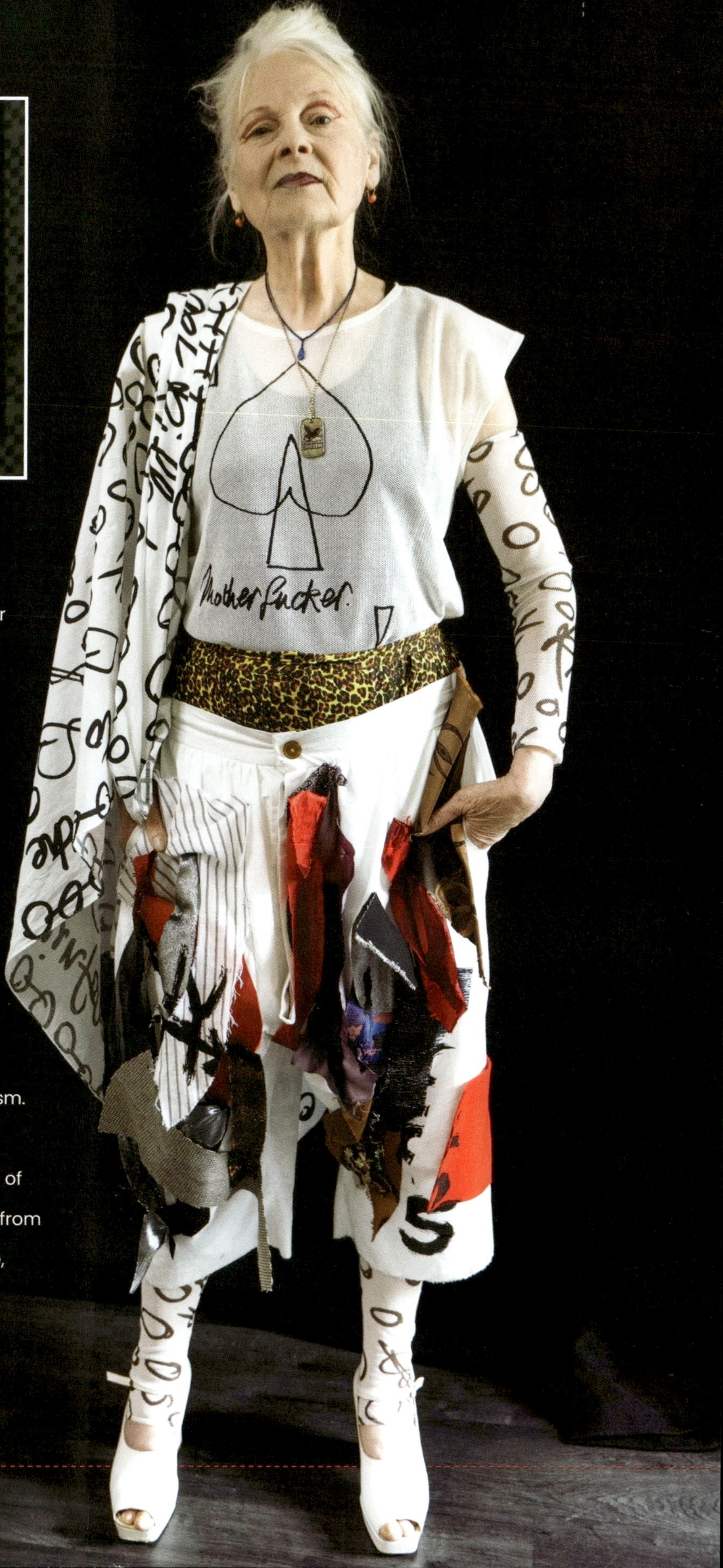

ROOTS OF REBELLION

1941-1965

"I was born during the war and grew up in a time of rationing. We didn't have anything. It's influenced the way I look at the world."
Vivienne Westwood

On August 19th, 1939, two weeks before the outbreak of the Second World War, Dora Ball and fruiterer Gordon Swire married in Tintwistle's Christ Church, in county Cheshire. After a short honeymoon in Scarborough, the young couple settled into their first marital home, a small stone cottage close to the village of Hollingworth. It was in this home that the Swires welcomed their first-born child, Vivienne Isabel Swire, on the 8th of April 1941. During the war, Vivienne's father worked as a storekeeper at an aircraft factory near Manchester, while Dora took employment as a cotton weaver to help supply materials for the war effort. A couple of years later, the family expanded with the arrival of Vivienne's little sister, Olga, in January 1944. Young Vivienne was outraged by the new addition, and her desire to be the centre of attention was once again squashed by the birth of her second and last sibling, a baby boy named Gordon, born in 1946. The family eventually moved to the village of

Glossop, in Derbyshire. Though both of her parents were employed, growing up in post-war Britain was challenging, with economic hardships shaping much of daily life. The government was pushing frugality, with rationing set to continue until 1951. The austerity of post-war Britain, combined with her working-class upbringing, inculcated in Vivienne the necessity of thriftiness, a trait she would carry into later life. Vivienne demonstrated early on a keenness for literature, which nourished her imagination and led her to fantastical worlds beyond her family and hometown.

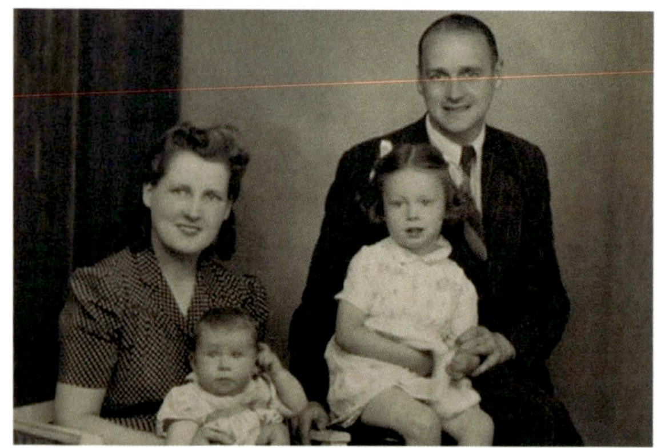

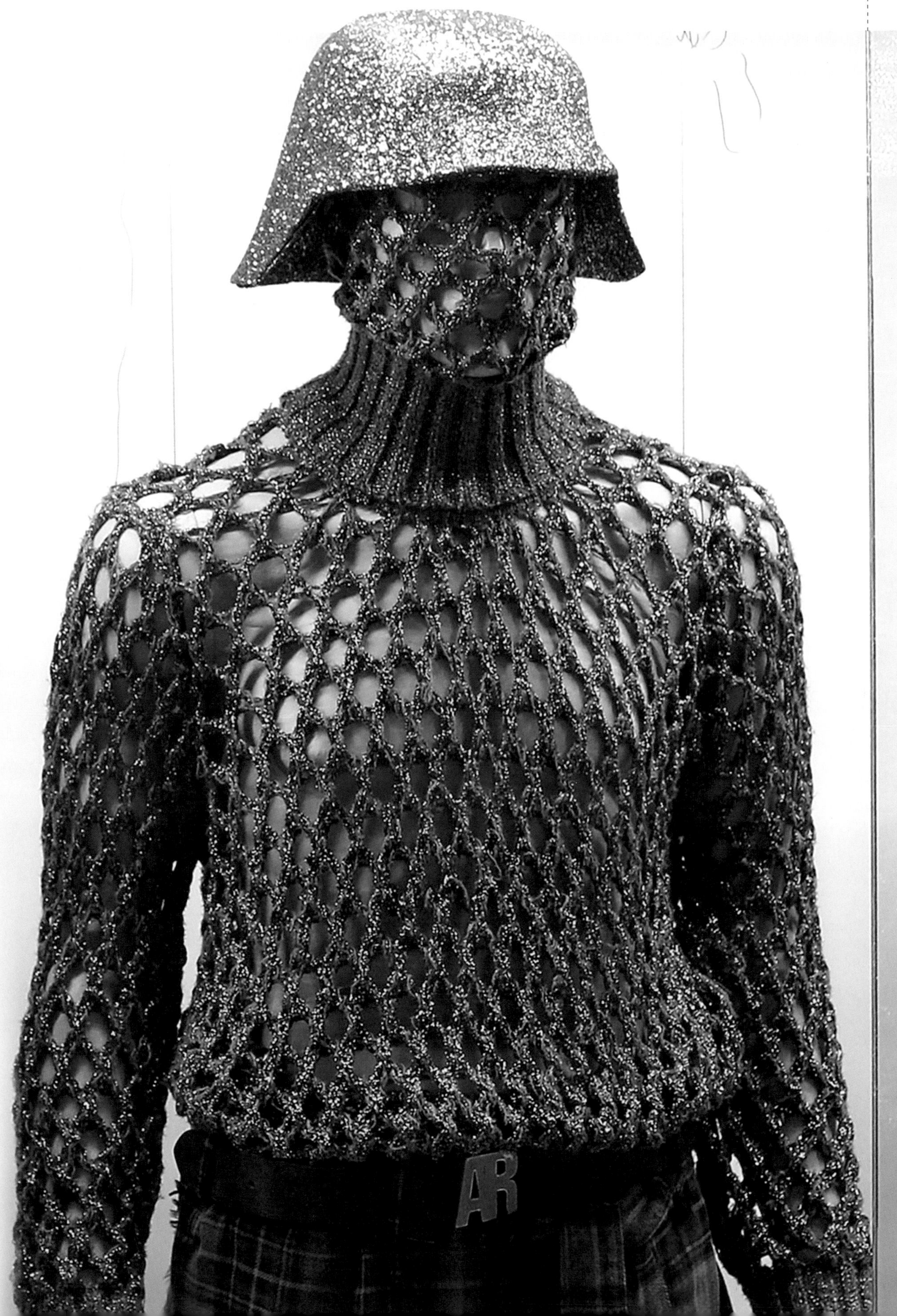
AR

THE CORONATION OF QUEEN ELIZABETH II

The coronation of Queen Elizabeth II in 1953 marked a pivotal childhood memory for Vivienne. Growing up in a small village in Derbyshire, the grandiose event was in stark contrast to her everyday surroundings. The nationwide celebration, steeped in tradition and pageantry, captivated the young girl, igniting her fascination with history, royalty, and the power of symbolic imagery. The vibrant colours, the elaborate costumes, and the sheer spectacle of the coronation stirred her imagination and sowed the seeds of her future in fashion design. This experience also instilled in Vivienne an understanding of the profound impact that clothing and ceremony can have on culture and identity.

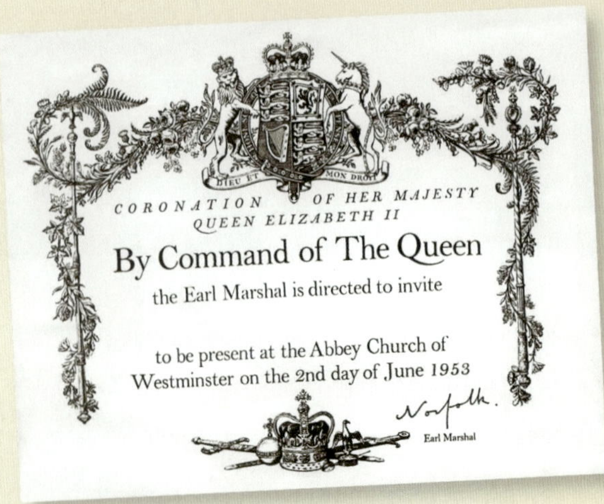

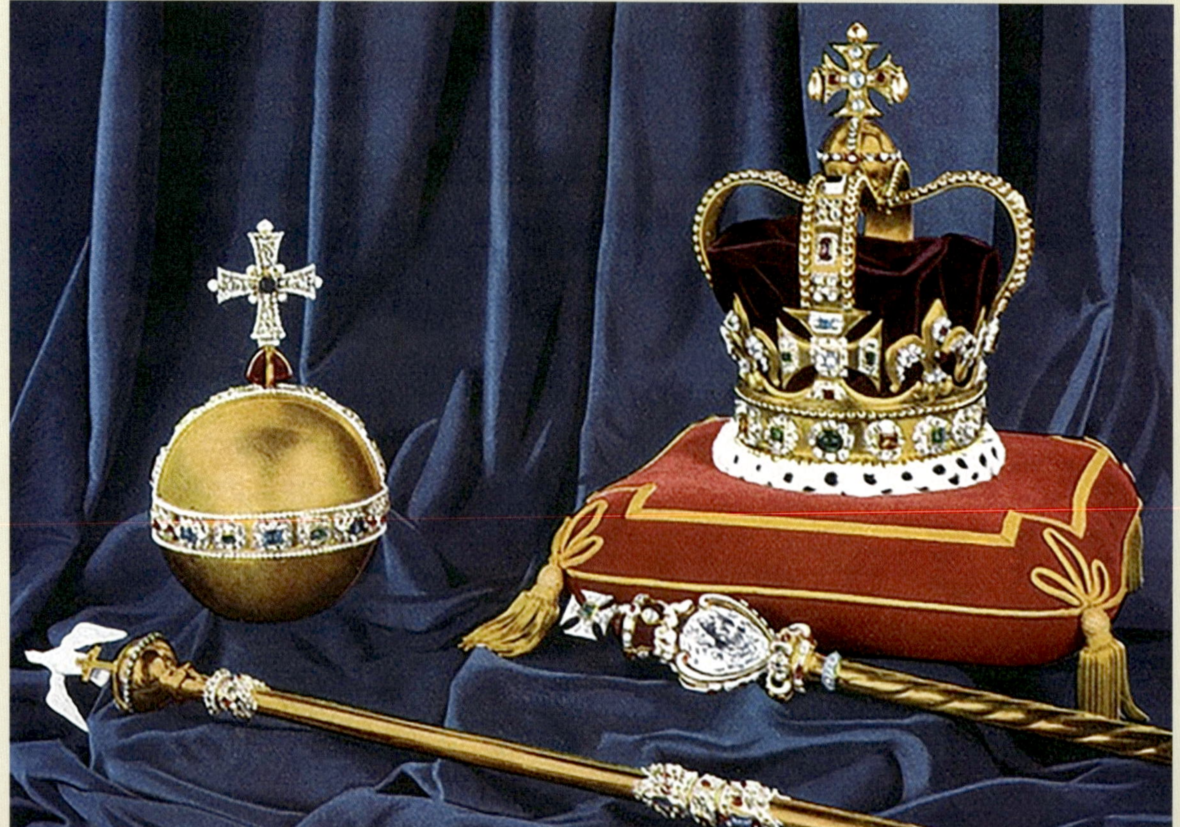

TOP: Coronation invitation designed by Joan Hassall
ABOVE: St Edward's Crown, the Orb, the Sceptre with Cross, and Sceptre with Dove
OPP PAGE: Coronation portrait of Queen Elizabeth II, June 1953, London, England

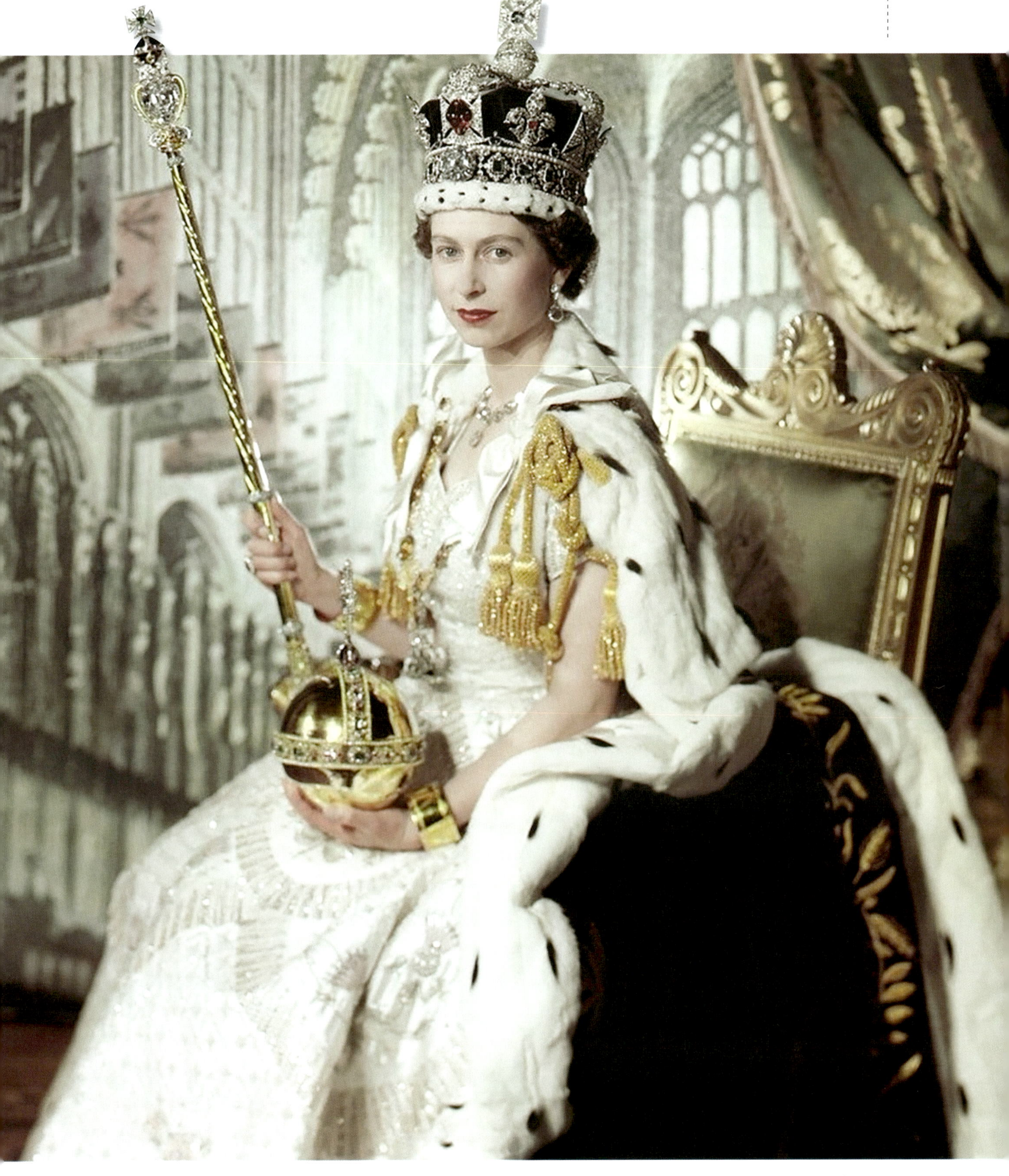

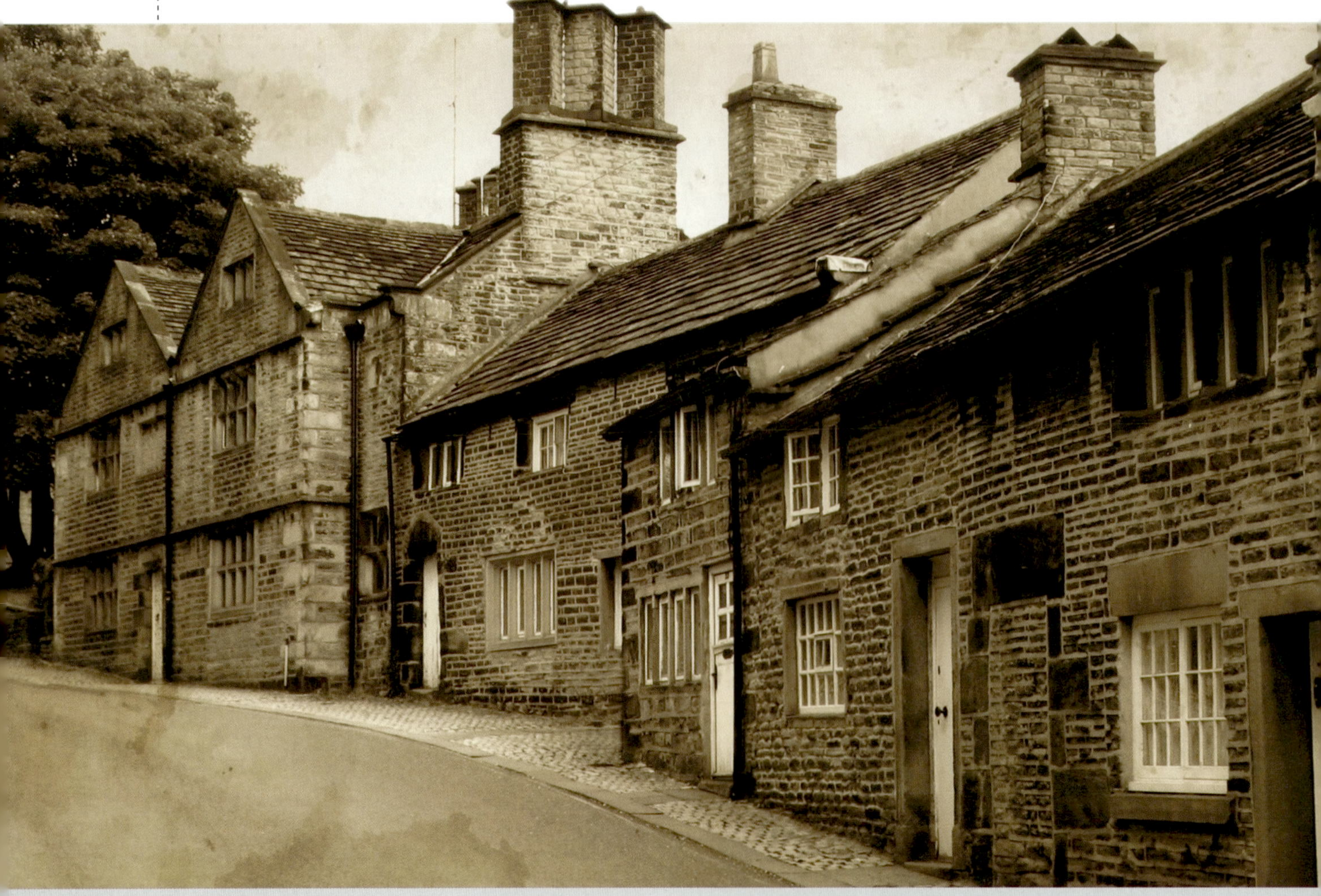

Vivienne's life in Glossop was marked by a blend of conventionality and burgeoning rebellion. She often found herself at odds with the provincial expectations of her community. She was accepted into Glossop's Grammar School and was determined to make her mark. Past classmates recall a young Vivienne as being loud and unashamed, boasting constantly about her various suitors. It was during this time that her budding interest in fashion started to grow. She became obsessed with the women featured in the glossy pages of upmarket magazines such as *Vogue, Harper's Bazaar,* and *Vanity Fair.* Vivienne Westwood found herself captivated by the glamour and allure of iconic Hollywood stars such as Marilyn Monroe, Grace Kelly, and Elizabeth Taylor, and even tried to emulate them. At school, Vivienne wanted to dress like a woman, not a girl, and opted to don a tight pencil skirt with a pair of heels, as both items felt very sensual to her. She soon began to garner attention by simply putting together eclectic and provocative outfits, further deepening her love of fashion.

In the summer of 1957, Vivienne's life changed dramatically. She left school, aged sixteen, and

ABOVE: Church Street, Glossop
OPP PAGE: Magazine covers from the 1960s

her dad became unemployed, leading the family to relocate to the more affluent South to take over a post office in Harrow, just outside London. Vivienne struggled, at first, to integrate into her new surroundings, due in particular to her pronounced northern accent. She decided to attend a silversmithing and jewellery making course at Harrow Art School, but promptly dropped out after just one term, famously stating: "I didn't know how a working-class girl like me could possibly make a living in the art world". After that, she took a job as a typist for an advertising company, before starting training to be a schoolteacher.

Vivienne was a lifelong fan of dancing, and spent countless hours in her youth attending local dances. During a dance in late 1961, Vivienne met her soon-to-be first husband Derek John Westwood. The couple bonded over their shared love of rock'n'roll music and were instantly smitten with one another. The couple married a year later in a large Edwardian church near her parents' family house. Due to economic constraints, the young bride made her own wedding dress, the first of a long tradition of Vivienne Westwood bridal wear. The following year, Vivienne gave birth to her first son Benjamin Westwood. Despite her stable family life and her new job as a primary school teacher, Vivienne couldn't help but feel bored. Her younger brother Gordon attended Harrow Art School, and she would often envy his new circle of friends. She started spending time with Gordon's artist friends, and would eventually make the acquaintance of someone who would change her life forever.

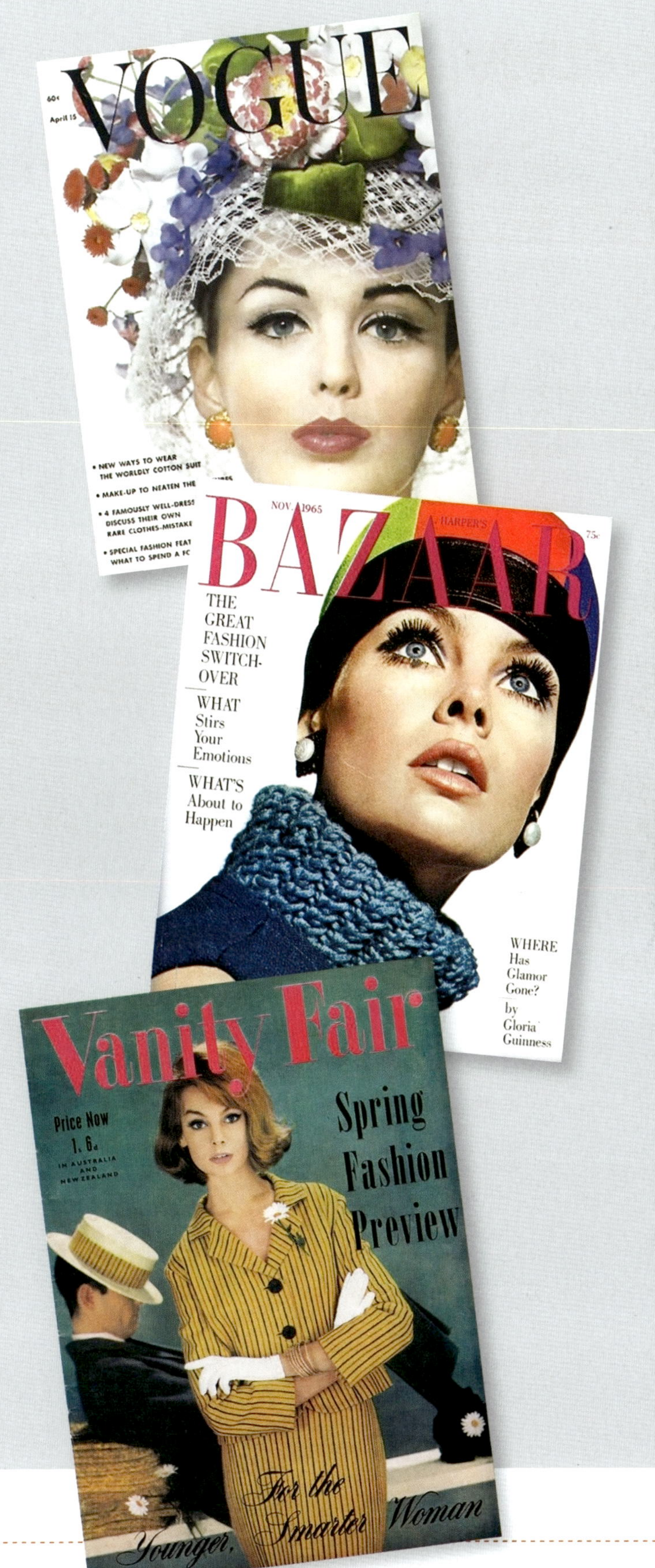

MEETING MALCOLM
1965-1971

"He influenced the way I dressed and thought about clothes too. He began to spend most of his student grant on clothes for me. He cared passionately for clothes and transformed me from a dolly bird into a chic, confident dresser."

Vivienne Westwood

By 1965, Vivienne felt trapped within her marriage. "We were living the American dream, but the dream ended with me in the kitchen", she later recounted about her relationship with her first husband. Despite Derek Westwood's kindness and good looks, she didn't share his simple interests and resented the fact she "was not learning from staying with him".

The rift between the young couple was further accentuated as Vivienne became more and more enthralled with the world being opened up to her by Gordon, five years her junior, and his friends. Gordon often brought his friends from art school home to visit, where Vivienne would occasionally cross paths with them. She quickly understood that these visits were more than just casual get-togethers; they were vibrant exchanges of ideas, creativity, and cultural critique. Vivienne, who was well into her twenties at the time, found herself captivated by the artistic and intellectual discussions that surrounded her. She was introduced to a world of avant-garde art, radical literature, and unconventional lifestyles. This exposure was in stark contrast to Vivienne's more conservative upbringing.

After several attempts to leave, Vivienne finally broke away from Derek, taking her then three-year-old son Ben to live with her parents. She felt that in order to fulfil her full potential, she had to separate from her husband. The couple officially divorced the following year, though Vivienne decided to keep his surname.

Whilst she was living in her parents' flat above the post office, she would make the acquaintance of

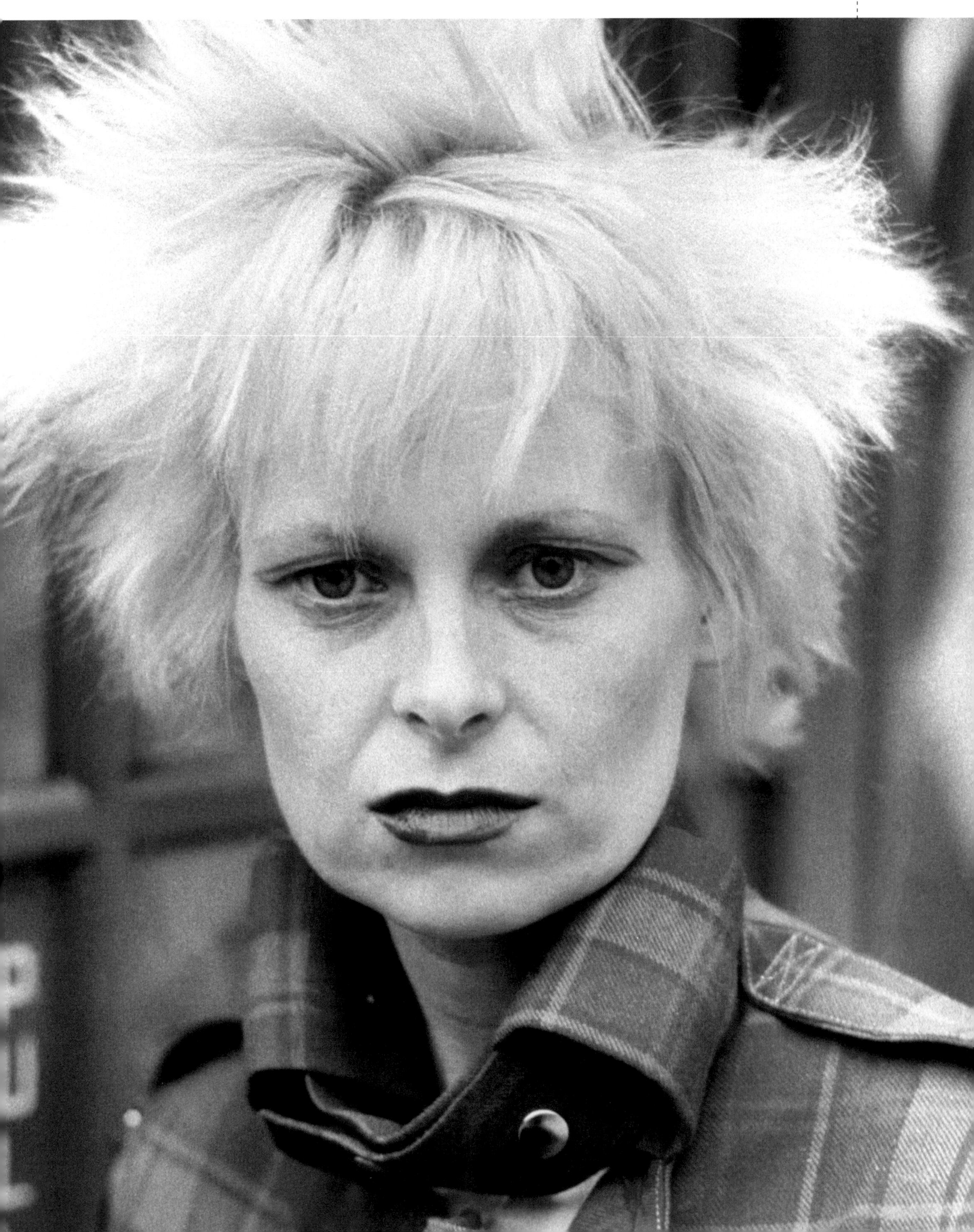

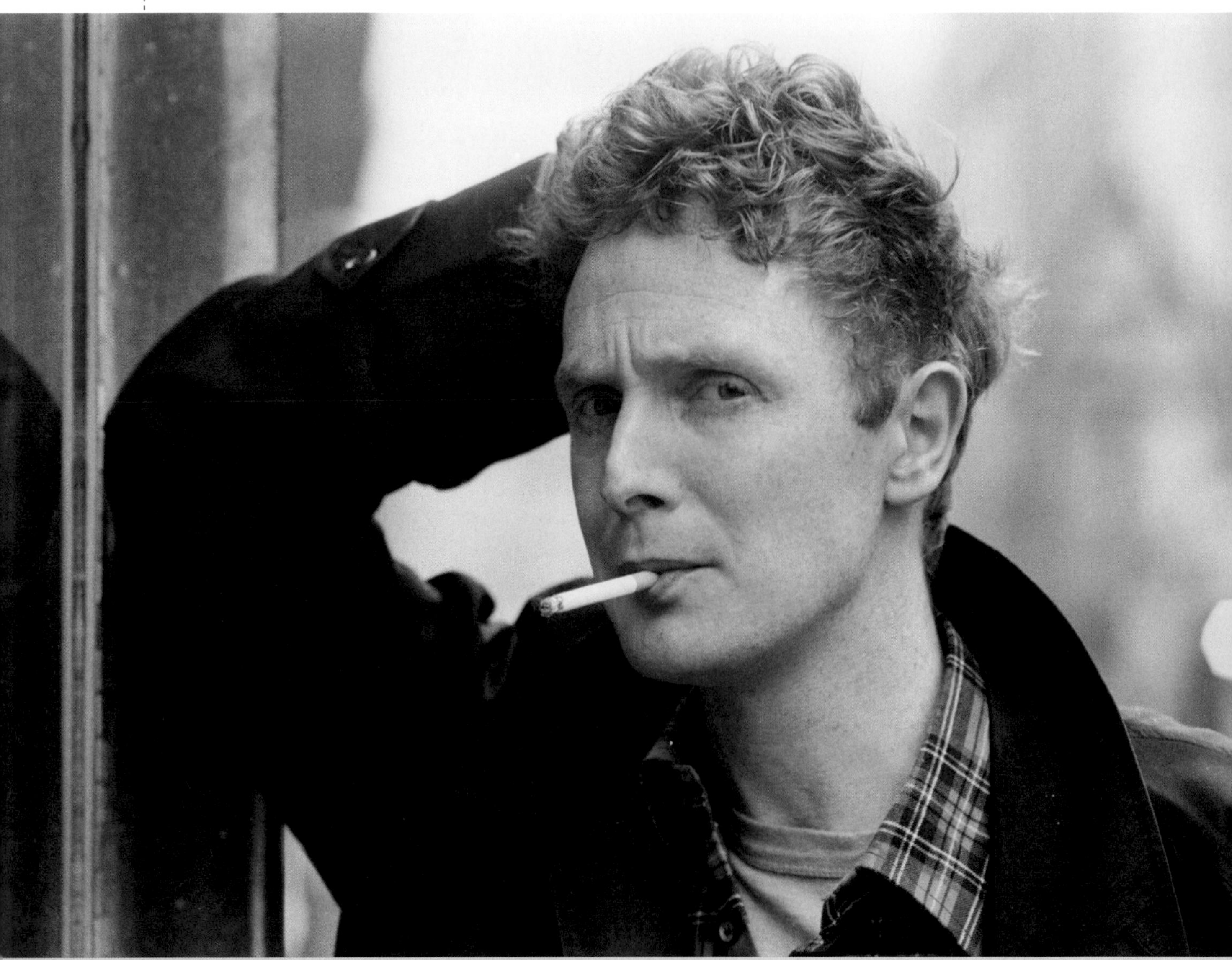

somebody who would change the entire trajectory of her life. One night, Gordon brought a couple of friends to their home in Harrow, including a 19-year-old fellow art student. He had red hair, and a face whitened with talcum powder. His name was Malcolm McLaren, a self-declared genius and future manager of the Sex Pistols. Vivienne's relationship with Malcolm McLaren was not a story of instant infatuation, but rather a slow burn that developed over time. When they first met, Vivienne was still grappling with the aftermath of her divorce from Derek Westwood and was focused on providing for her young son, Ben. Malcolm, on the other hand, was a charismatic and provocative teenager with a penchant for anarchism. His radical ideas and rebellious spirit resonated with Vivienne, but the attraction was intellectual and creative rather than romantic.

ABOVE: Malcolm Mclaren, 1983
OPP PAGE: Old Compton Street, Soho in 1960

GODFATHER OF PUNK: MALCOLM MCLAREN

Born on January 22nd 1946 in London, Malcom was the son of Peter McLaren, an upper-middle-class Scottish engineer who was at that time serving with the Royal Engineers, and Emily Isaacs, the daughter of Jewish tailor Mick Isaacs and the independently wealthy Rose Corré Isaacs.

As young children, he and his older brother, Stuart, were dragged around London by their mother, as she visited various lovers. Their father soon left the family, having grown tired of his wife's serial infidelities. The couple divorced when Malcolm was only two, marking the end of his relationship with his dad, as the divorce agreement stipulated that Peter could have no contact with his sons until after Emily's death.

McLaren's early years were marked by familial instability and a deep sense of abandonment. This desertion had a lasting impact on Malcolm, fostering a rebellious streak and a lifelong disdain for conventional authority figures.

Emily struggled as a single mother, balancing the demands of raising Malcolm and Stuart while managing her own personal and professional challenges. Seeking stability and support, she relied heavily on her mother, Rose Corré Isaacs, a formidable figure in Malcolm's life. Rose, who owned a successful chain of women's clothing shops, became a surrogate parent to Malcolm, offering him a glimpse into the world of commerce and fashion. Rose was an eccentric in her own right. She would routinely tell her grandson "To be bad is good, because to be good is simply boring", a mantra that he would live by. Malcolm was close to his grandmother, even going as far as sharing a bed with her.

McLaren was more interested in exploring radical ideas and engaging in acts of defiance than conforming to the expectations of formal education, and Rose enabled him. When his school head complained about his poor behaviour, she would shrug and tell him "boys will be boys" – a refrain that McLaren would parrot later whenever his punk protégés, the Sex Pistols, got into hot water.

During the 1960s, Malcolm became deeply involved in the counterculture movements that were reshaping London. This exposure to radical thought reinforced his belief in the power of subversion and the role of creativity in challenging societal norms.

Encouraged by Rose, Malcolm consistently defied his mother, who disapproved of his habit of staying out all night prowling the streets of Soho. At 18, his mother, frustrated by his rebellious behaviour, threw him out, leading to a 25-year estrangement. McLaren subsequently set up home in a friend's car. That friend was Gordon Swire, whose sister was Vivienne Westwood.

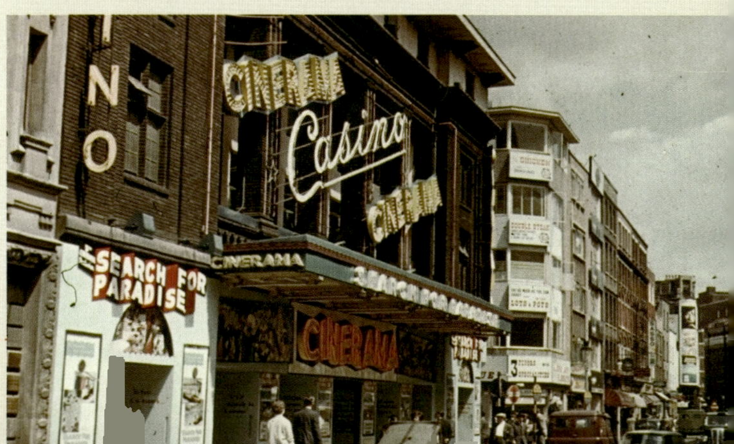

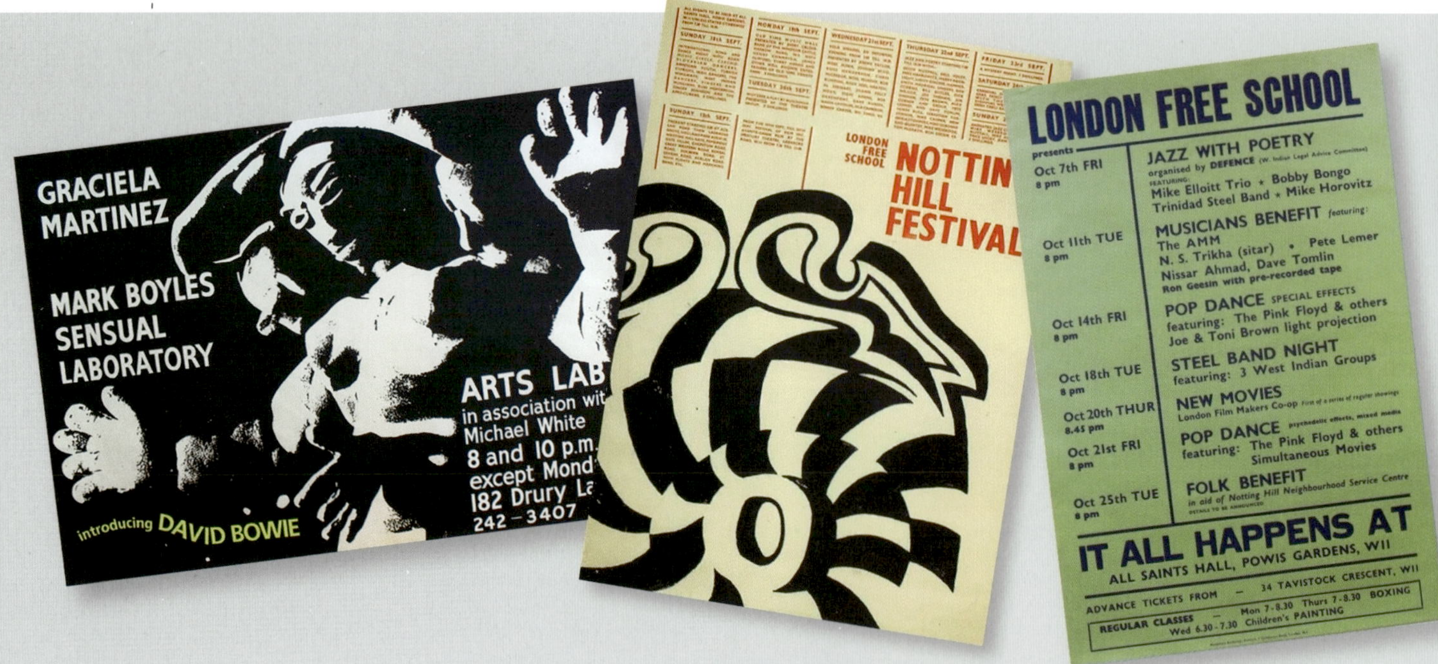

Gordon left Harrow to study at London College of Film Technique and took up residence with two schoolmates, including Malcolm, in a rundown house at 31 King's Avenue, near Clapham North underground station in South London. To McLaren's complete horror, Vivienne and her son moved in following the dissolution of her marriage. He saw this addition to the household as a compromise to the 'boys club' he had established, and allegedly considered Vivienne as a threat. Though Malcolm's attraction towards the young mother was obvious from the start, the feeling wasn't mutual. She was famously into 'pretty boys', whereas McLaren was rail thin with a head of unkempt ginger hair. Despite his lack of conventional good looks, McLaren was very charismatic. He charmed Vivienne with his endless lectures on the political power of art and the appeal of cult fashions. Newly inspired by the radical and avant-garde ideas she had absorbed from her interactions with Malcolm, Vivienne decided to channel her creativity into making jewellery. Thus began one of Britain's greatest creative partnerships, one that would go on to launch a cultural revolution that shook, and sometimes frightened, the world.

The duo began creating unique, handmade pieces of jewellery that reflected their burgeoning rebellious spirit. Vivienne's designs were bold and unconventional, incorporating elements that defied the traditional aesthetics of the time. Malcolm, with his flair for promotion and eye for the subversive, saw the potential in Vivienne's creations and supported her in bringing these pieces to market. They chose Portobello Market on Notting Hill as the hub for their rapidly growing enterprise. The market stalls of Notting Hill provided the perfect backdrop for their edgy and distinctive jewellery. Here, they could reach an audience that was more likely to appreciate and embrace their avant-garde designs.

ABOVE: Flyers for avant-garde events in London
OPP PAGE: World famous Alice antique shop on Portobello Road

NOTTING HILL: THE BOHEMIA OF LONDON

By the 1960s, Notting Hill had established itself as a vibrant and eclectic area of London, known for its bohemian atmosphere and bustling market scene. It became a magnet for all those seeking to break away from societal norms and express their individuality.

The neighbourhood's affordable housing attracted a young, creative crowd who were often at the forefront of cultural and social change. Communal living arrangements and shared artistic spaces became commonplace, fostering a sense of community among the residents. The area was home to numerous squats and artists' studios, where experimentation and creativity thrived.

The Portobello Road Market, a landmark in Notting Hill, became a focal point for this bohemian enclave. Known for its antiques, vintage clothing, and eclectic stalls, the market embodied the district's spirit of individuality and rebellion against the mainstream. It was a place where artists and musicians could find inspiration, and where the latest trends in fashion and music were often born.

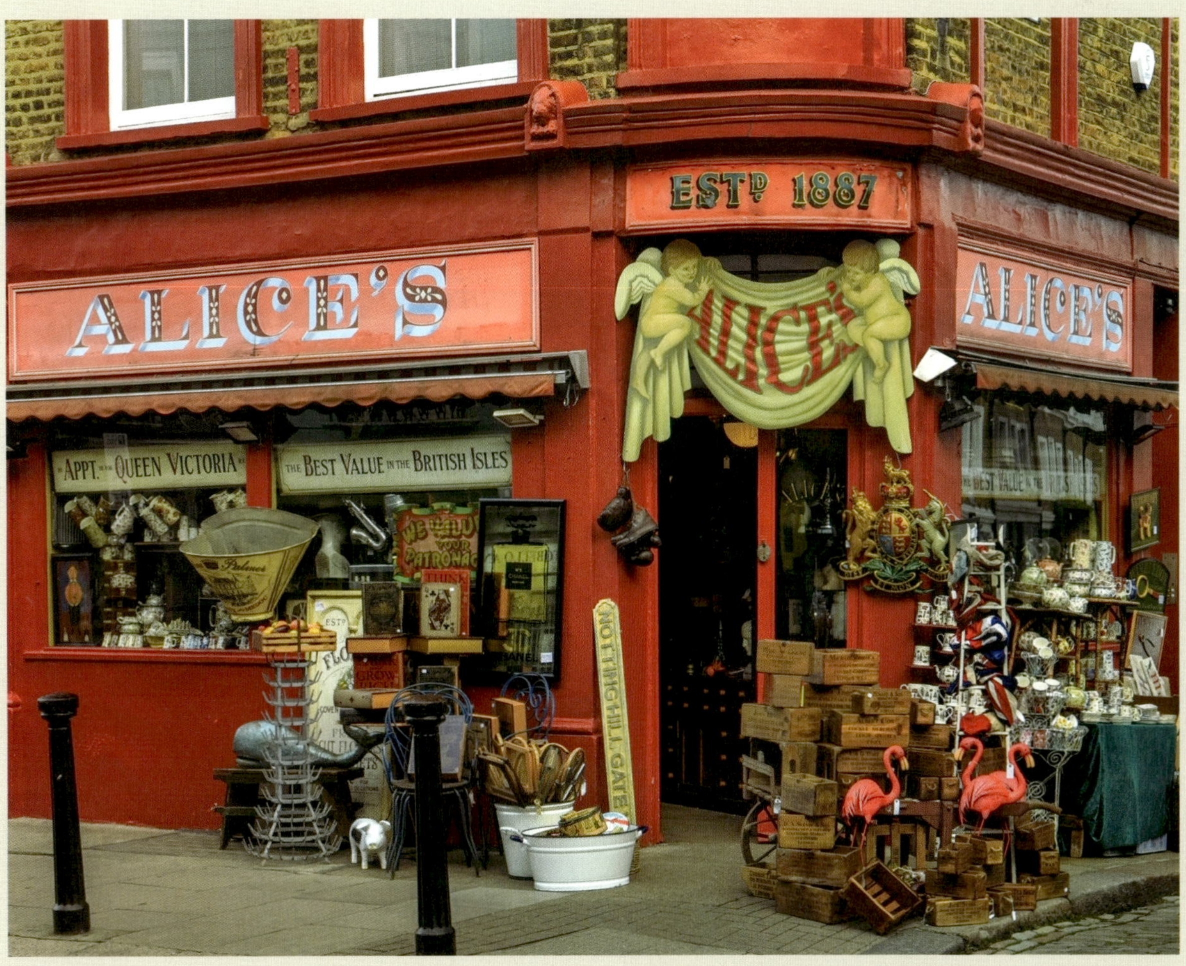

During this time, their roles were established and set for the next decade: she as the student craftsman, he the opinionated art director. Their success in Notting Hill gave them the confidence and experience to take on more ambitious projects, but trouble was right around the corner, and threatened to disrupt the duo's plans.

Vivienne and Malcolm were spending an increasing amount of time together, and although their relationship was exclusively platonic up until that point, the forced proximity brought the pair closer together. Finally, their relationship turned intimate after two years of friendship. At the time of their fling, Malcolm developed a deep emotional tie to Vivienne, often acting possessive and resulting in a few temperamental 'fits'.

Within the weeks following their initial get-together, Vivienne found out she was pregnant with McLaren's child. His attitude towards her completely shifted, and he encouraged her to seek an abortion, though the practice was still illegal in 1967 Britain. His grandmother Rose, who had always disapproved of Vivienne, also pushed to terminate the pregnancy. She allegedly showed up in front of a doctor's office with her cash in hand, trying to persuade Vivienne to undergo the procedure. In true Westwood fashion, the burgeoning fashion designer took the money and went to Bond Street to buy herself a coat instead.

On the 30th of November 1967, Vivienne gave birth to her second son, Joseph Ferdinand Corré, his middle name deriving from Malcolm's favourite Velasquez painting, *Archbishop Fernando de Valdés y Llanos,* and his surname being the same as his paternal grandmother's. Malcolm took six days to visit Vivienne in hospital after the birth of their son. He refused to be called 'Dad', and threatened to send the child away when he was asked to pitch in.

Despite McLaren's apparent disdain for becoming a father, the couple decided to move in together in a ground floor apartment near the Kennington Oval, to raise their family. However, this would prove to be a short lived episode.

The deterioration of their relationship prompted Vivienne to move back with her parents, who now resided in a small cottage in Oxfordshire.

Malcolm would occasionally take the train to visit Vivienne and his son in Oxfordshire, but for the most part they lived separate lives. He went on to study at Goldsmiths College of Arts in South London, while Vivienne focused on raising her two sons, reading Thomas Hardy novels and teaching. In her absence, Malcolm married another woman, a Turkish-French student, though Rose Corré quickly paid the couple to secure a divorce. During this time, Malcolm's visits to see Vivienne became more and more frequent, resulting in the couple's reconciliation.

Her childhood had been happy, but a cultural desert. Creatively, Malcolm was an awakening, introducing

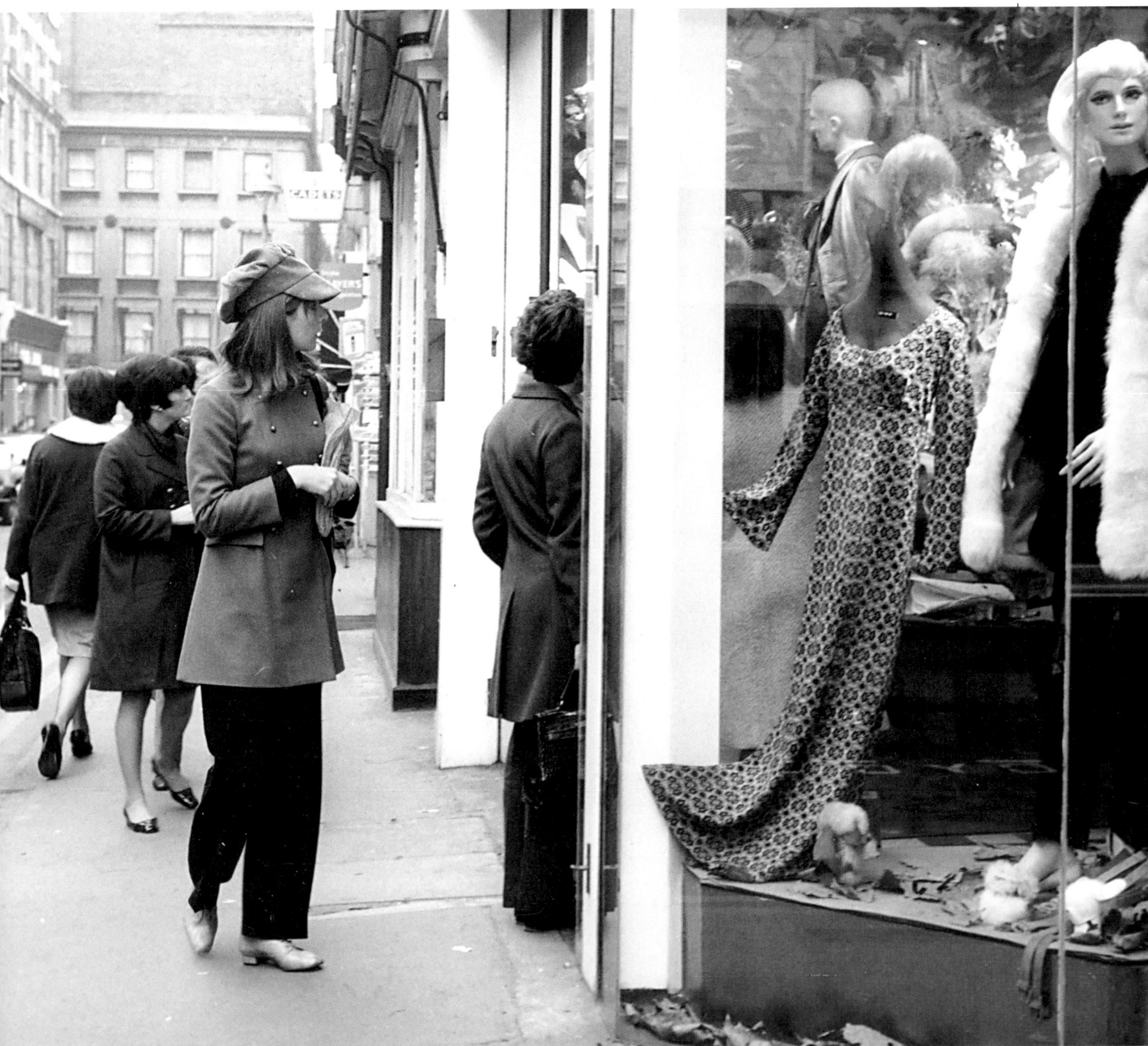

her to art, music, and helping her transform "from dolly bird into a chic, confident dresser". "I latched onto Malcolm as somebody who opened doors for me," Vivienne said. "I mean, he seemed to know everything I needed at the time".

Malcolm and Vivienne moved in together once again, into a small flat on Nightingale Lane, down the street from Rose and only four miles away from the shop that would turn this unconventional couple into one of Britain's most notable partnerships.

PARADISE LOST AND FOUND

1971-1973

"Be childish. Be irresponsible. Be disrespectful. Be everything this society hates."

Malcolm McLaren

Vivienne's last vestige of provincial conformity was eliminated in 1971 when she dramatically cut and bleached her hair. At twenty-nine years of age she relinquished her long hair, convinced by McLaren that having it cropped would look more sexy, cool, and urban. That same summer, Malcolm, then aged 25, finally ended his student days by graduating from Goldsmith's, prompting him to fall into a deep depression. With money being tight and a family to provide for, Malcolm had to come up with a solution to his financial woes. At the time, he had no interest in pursuing fashion, despite his family's background, and instead chose to follow his true passion, which was music. Perhaps he could even make a living from it. He decided he would start out by setting up a stall and selling his collection of rock'n'roll records and memorabilia. Malcolm was totally obsessed with the idea that the 1970s needed a new, revolutionary sound with which to push forward anti-establishment notions, and was convinced he was the man for the job.

Malcolm sought out Vivienne's expertise to help kickstart his new endeavour, as she had an extensive background in shopkeeping. Vivienne, being very practical, was sceptical at first about the whole business venture, but after some convincing from Malcolm, she agreed to his wishes. The couple then joined forces with one of Malcolm's friends from art school, Patrick Casey, creating an eccentric and dynamic trio that would soon take London by storm. Now that they had found their business plan, the next step was to find the perfect location to launch it. In October 1971, dressed in a teddy boy jacket and lurex draped trousers, which Vivienne made for him, he stepped out down the Kings Road, in search of a chance encounter that would determine his and Vivienne's future.

OPP PAGE: Malcolm McLaren with his assistant Addie Chase outside the Let It Rock Shop on King's Road, 14th March 1972

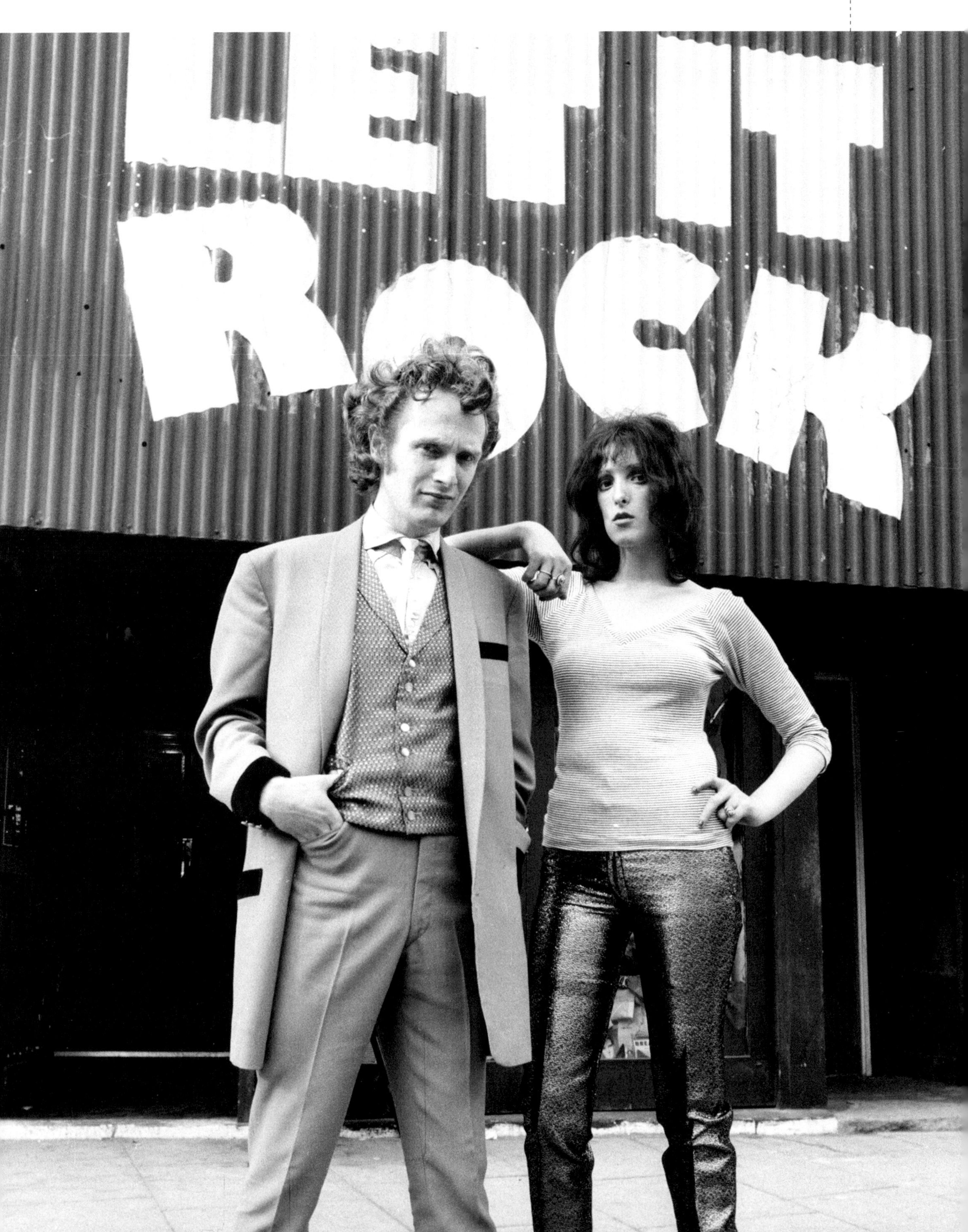
LET IT
ROCK

LET IT ROCK ON KING'S ROAD

Built in 1694, King's Road was created to provide King Charles II with a private road, exclusively to be used by monarchs and their privileged companions. The idea was supposedly given to him by his mistress Nell Gwynn to facilitate his travels between his palaces in St James' and Kew.

The King's Road remained privatised until 1830, transforming the relatively sedate street into a hotbed of countercultural activity. Located in the heart of Chelsea, the now iconic road seamlessly combines its origins, steeped in royal history, with a unique status as the birthplace of the 20th Century's most iconic cultural and fashion movements.

The 'Swinging Sixties', a term used to describe the cultural change happening in Britian, was actually first coined in an American *Time* magazine article in 1966 by Piri Halasz – '*London: the Swinging City*'. In the article, Halasz wrote that every decade has had its city: Paris in the twenties, Berlin in the thirties, New York in the forties, and Rome's 'la dolce vita' in the fifties. But the sixties were all about London, "a city steeped in tradition, seized by change, liberated by affluence".

The Swinging Sixties was a youth-driven cultural revolution that took place during the mid-to-late 1960s, emphasising modernity and fun-loving hedonism. This was a period marked by significant social change, characterised by a break from the conservative norms of the post-war era.

The neighbourhood of Chelsea was particularly 'swinging', with King's Road at the centre of it, becoming a haven for art, fashion, and music, spearheaded by the influential British designer, Mary Quant.

Boutiques like Mary Quant's Bazaar became hubs for the popular mod culture, introducing revolutionary

ABOVE: Bazaar, Mary Quant's boutique, King's Road
OPP PAGE: Punk helping passerby on King's Road, Chelsea, London in the 70s

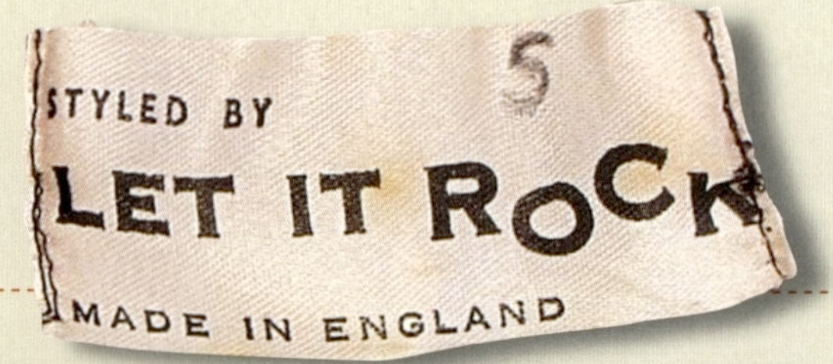

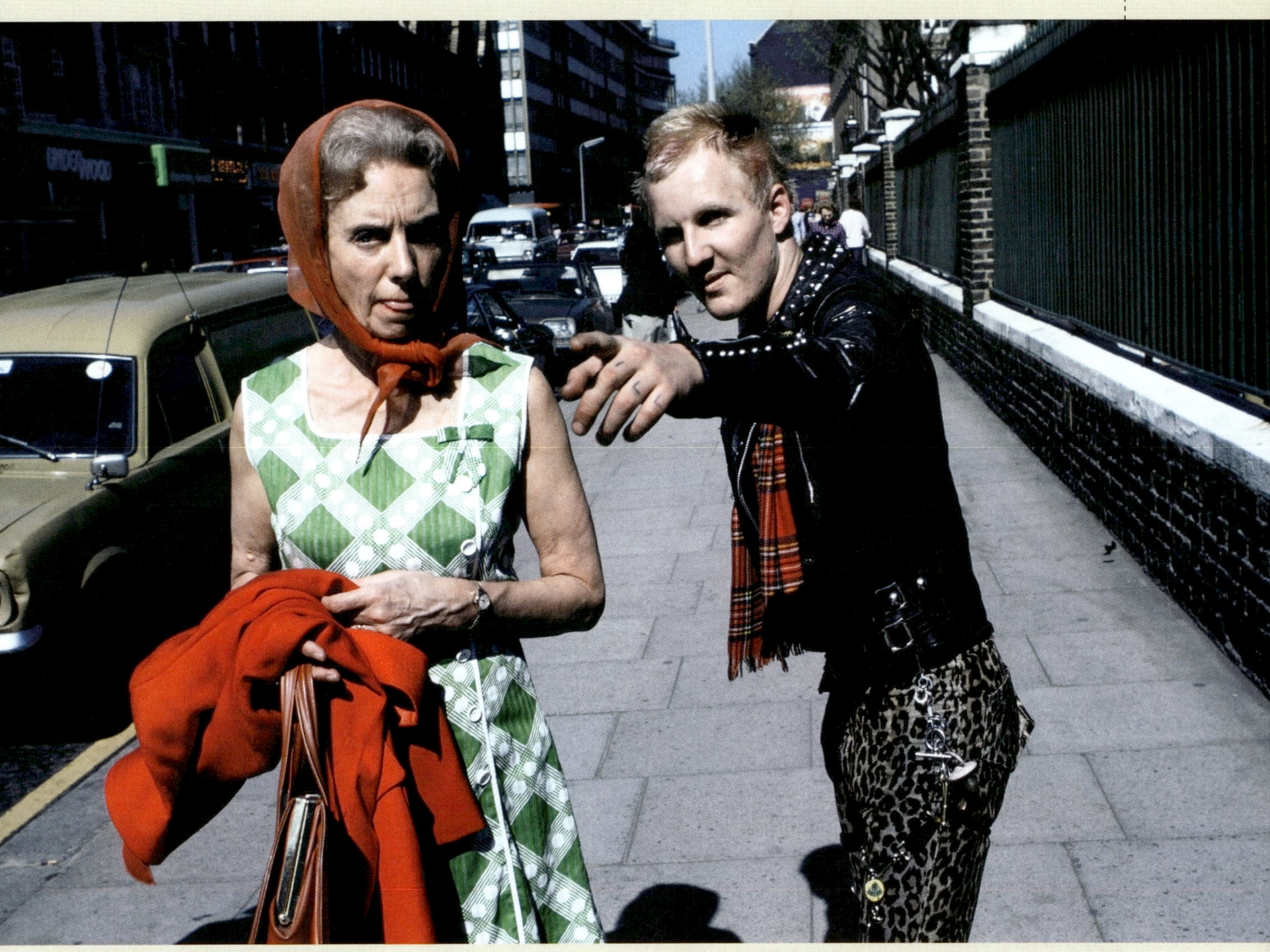

fashion trends that celebrated youth and rebellion. Quant popularised the mini skirt, which became a symbol of the liberated spirit synonymous with the decade. A magazine at the time described the street as "an endless frieze of mini-skirted, booted, fair-haired angular angels".

Independent boutiques sprang up everywhere, captivating the world with the latest fashion trends and musical movements. King's Road became a global hotspot, attracting artists, musicians, and free spirits from near and far.

As the 1970s dawned, the mood on King's Road shifted. The optimism of the 1960s gave way to a more cynical and rebellious energy. Economic challenges and political unrest contributed to a feeling of disillusionment among the youth. This discontent found expression in the punk movement, which would come to define the decade.

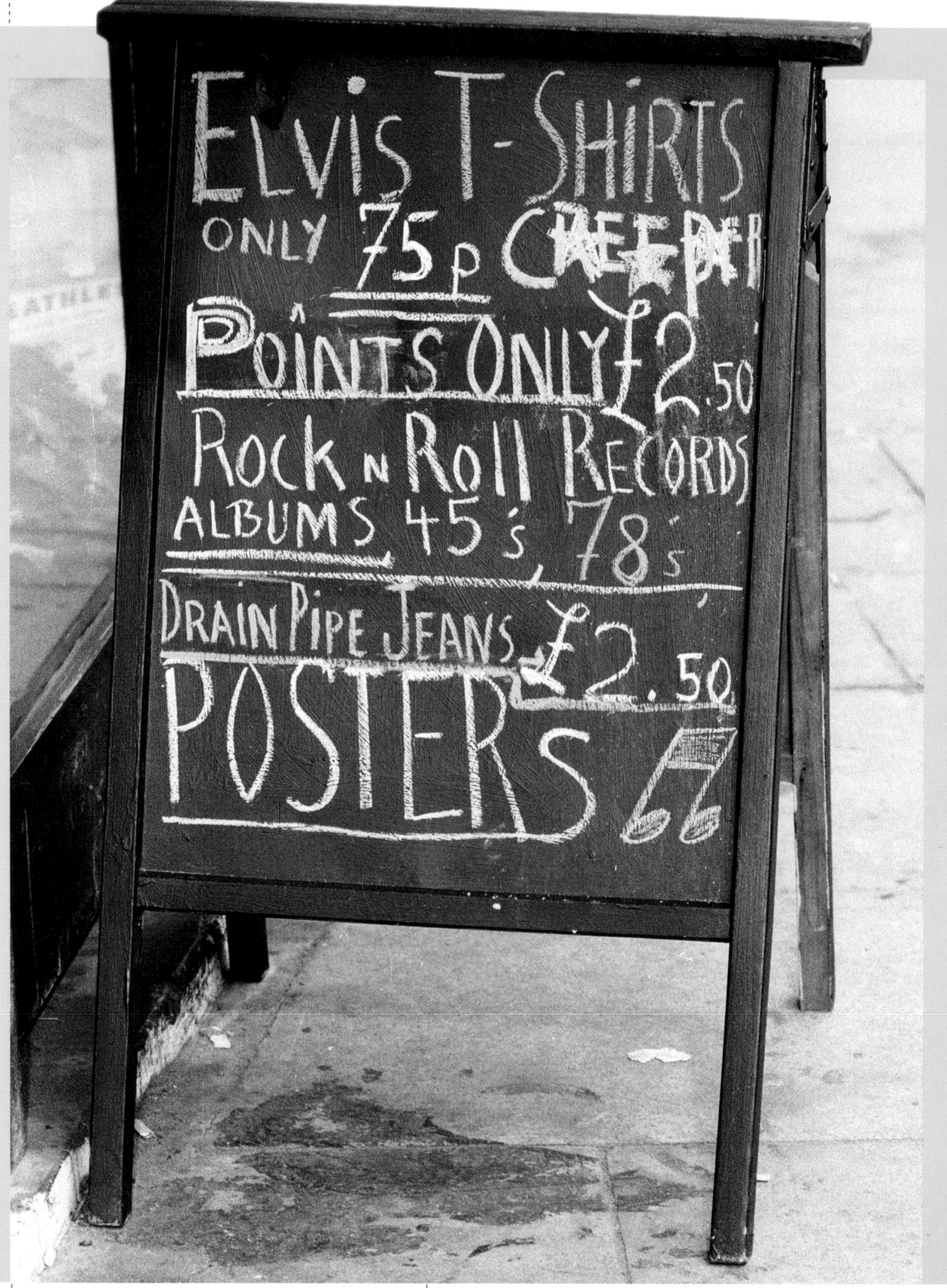

ABOVE: A sign outside the newly opened shop 'Let It Rock' on King's Road, Chelsea, 14 March 1972

As Malcolm passed by number 430 on King's Road, Bradley Mendelssohn, the manager of the store 'Paradise Garage', struck up a conversation with the young entrepreneur. "Where are you going man? I dig the drainpipes!", said Bradley, referring to Malcolm's eccentric pair of trousers. McLaren explained that he was looking for a space to set up his rock 'n' roll merchandise shop and by the end of the conversation, Bradley suggested he use the back half of his shop.

By November 1971, the store opened as 'Let It Rock', named after a Chuck Berry song. The words *Let it Rock* were painted onto a black corrugated façade in fluorescent pink letters, encapsulating the rebellious spirit of the rock 'n' roll era.

The store specialised in Teddy Boy clothing, featuring drape jackets, brothel shoes, and rockabilly records. The interior, furnished to look like a 1950s living room, was littered with porno mags, 50s memorabilia and a vintage jukebox, creating a nostalgic yet defiant atmosphere. Vivienne later spoke about the décor of the shop saying, "We chose the 50s as our inspiration because that seemed a time when youth rebelled against age: See you later, Daddy, you're too square!". 60s rock'n'roll was too polished for Vivienne and Malcolm; they strived for a grungier and more rebellious aesthetic. 'Let It Rock' quickly became a hub for those disillusioned with the mainstream, attracting a diverse clientele drawn to its subversive style.

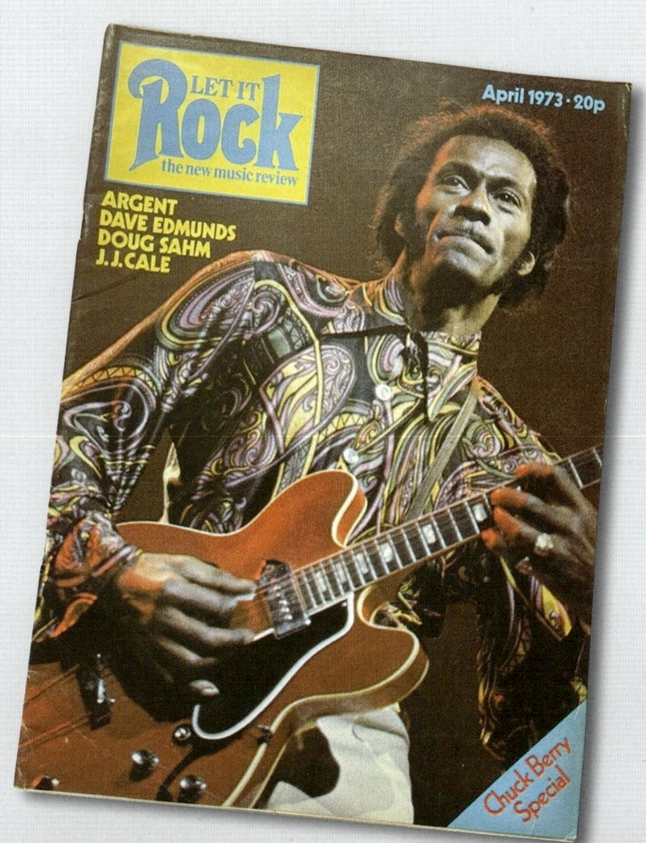

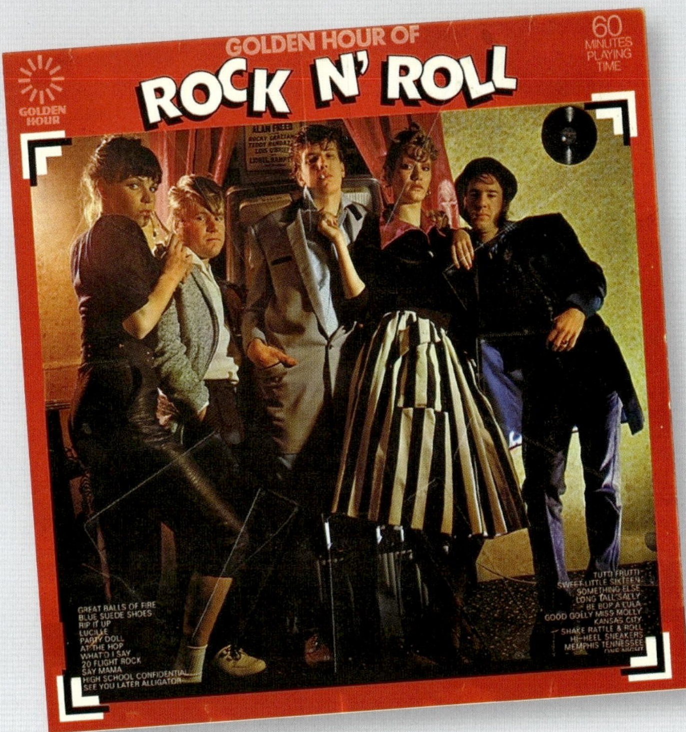

TOP: Let it Rock music magazine featuring Chuck Berry who had a song of the same title that was the inspiration behind the Let it Rock shop name
ABOVE: This LP cover image was taken in Let it Rock

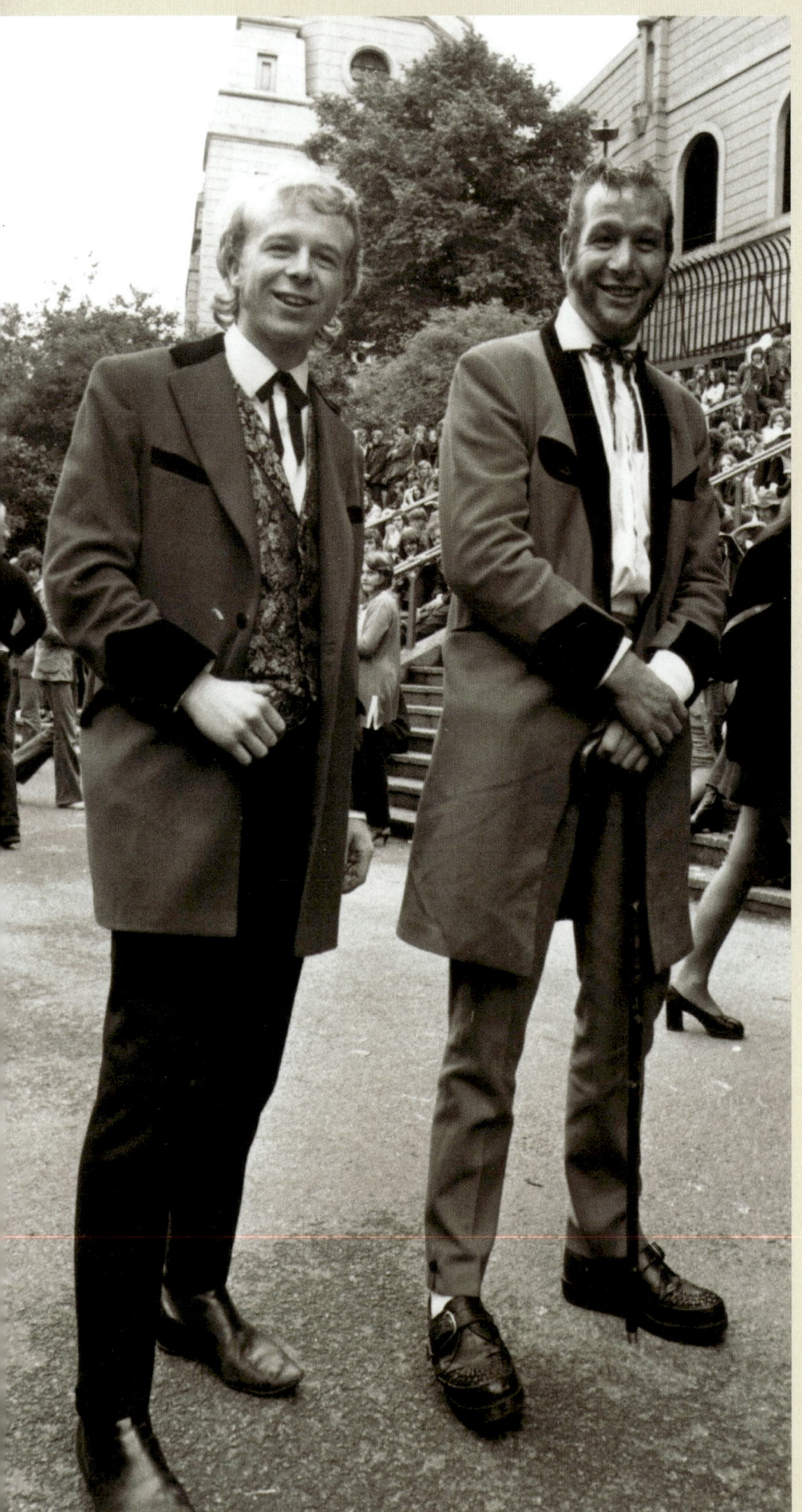

THE TEDDY BOYS

The Teddy Boy, or Ted, style has its roots in the early 1950s, a period of significant social and economic change in Britain. The end of World War II had brought about a sense of renewal and a desire for a fresh start among the youth, who were eager to break away from the austerity of the post-war years. This coincided with young people generally having more disposable income. In defiance, they adopted a grand style inspired by the Edwardian dandies of the early 20th century, repurposing elements of this elegant, upper-class look into something bold and rebellious.

Key features of the Teddy Boy style included drape jackets, reminiscent of 1940s American zoot suits, usually in dark shades, sometimes with a velvet trim collar. The jackets were then paired with 'drainpipe' trousers, narrow and tight-fitting in shape often exposing the socks. The outfit also included a high-necked, loose-collared white shirt, coupled with accessories like a 'Slim Jim' tie or western bolo tie. Brothel creepers were also a staple of the Teddy Boy style. Originally worn in the North African deserts, the thick-soled crepe boots were ideal for dealing with the hot and sandy terrain of the area. There is some speculation as to how the shoes inherited the nickname of 'Brothel Creepers', with one prominent theory postulating that, upon their

RIGHT: Two 'Teddy Boy' fans come to Wembley for the Rock and Roll Festival 1972
OPP PAGE: Teddy boys walking on a busy street in the 70s

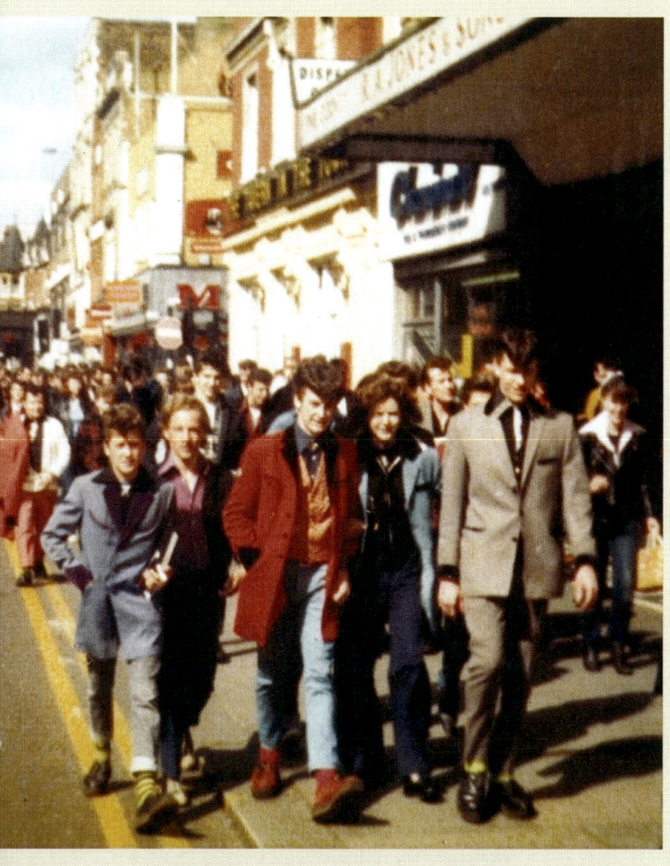

return from war, soldiers wanted to experience some fun after years away fighting and found themselves in the backstreets of Soho.

The revival of the Teddy Boy influence in the late 60s and early 70s was pivotal in the evolution of the punk movement. The defiant spirit of the Teds, their rejection of mainstream culture, and their distinctive, often shocking, fashion choices resonated deeply with the emerging punk ethos. Vivienne and McLaren's reinterpretation of Teddy Boy style laid the groundwork for punk fashion, which would explode by the mid-1970s.

Within a few months, 'Let it Rock' began running out of original teddy boy clothing, so McLaren convinced Vivienne, who had made her own clothes since she was a teenager, to run up copies.

Left undistracted in Nightingale Lane, Vivienne began laying the groundwork for her new career by repairing, altering, and eventually replicating rock'n'roll clothing. She meticulously unpicked and duplicated original Teddy Boy garments, while Sid Green, an East End tailor she frequently consulted, crafted the drape jackets in neon colours with faux fur or lurex collars selected by her.

Vivienne had been introduced to the fashion business by Malcolm, but it became (in her words) "a baby I picked up and never put down". Although McLaren was the frontman, Vivienne gradually became the stronger personification of 'Let it Rock', where she was spending an increasing amount of time. For her, the shop represented a commitment to a lifestyle, whereas for McLaren it served as a backdrop for a profitable business.

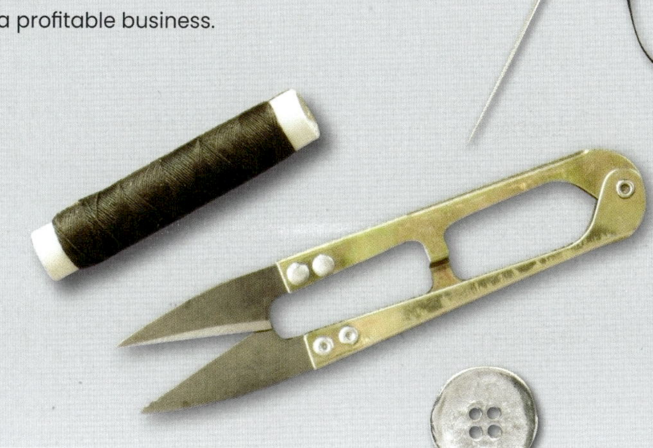

NEW YORK AND CHICKEN BONES

1973

"At one time, I was very angry. I even treated fashion like a kind of crusade: you were either with us or against us, that kind of feeling. Now I know we need ideas, not kicking down a door."

Vivienne Westwood

Vivienne and Malcolm's journey into the heart of British counterculture took a significant turn with the rebranding of their shop at 430 King's Road.

Two years in and business at 'Let It Rock' was booming; the shop quickly became the place to be and be seen, and even managed to attract many high-profile shoppers such as Ringo Starr and David Essex. Despite this obvious success, familiarity with the Teddy Boys quickly bred into contempt, and by early 1973, Vivienne and Malcolm had grown tired of this. Patrick Casey had left

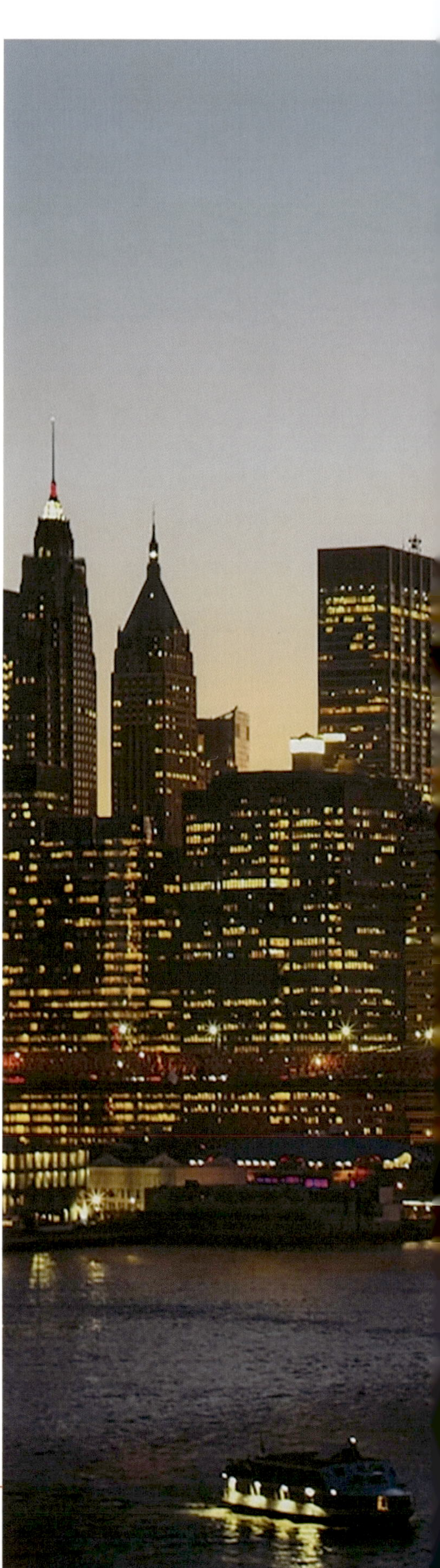

RIGHT: New York at sunset

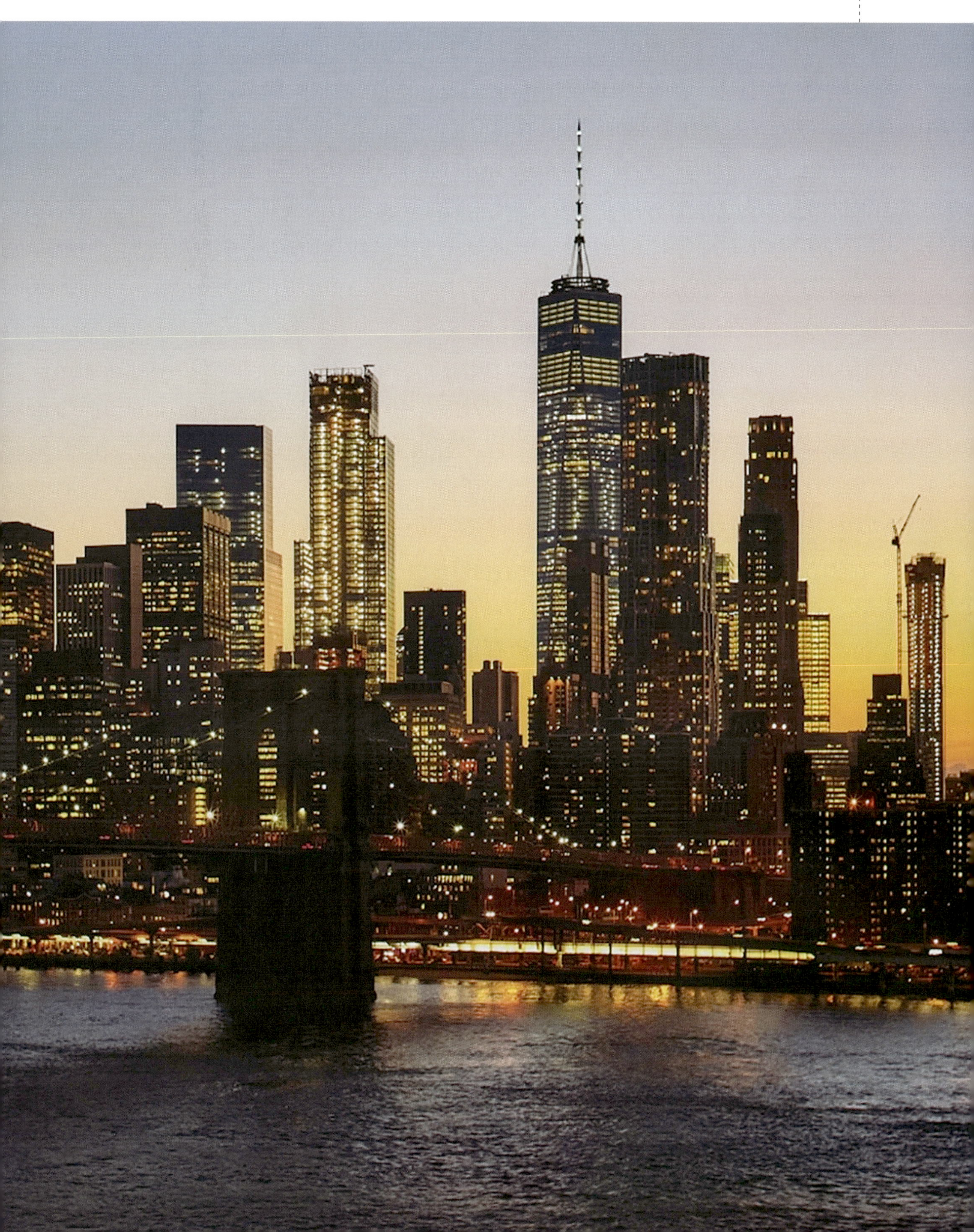

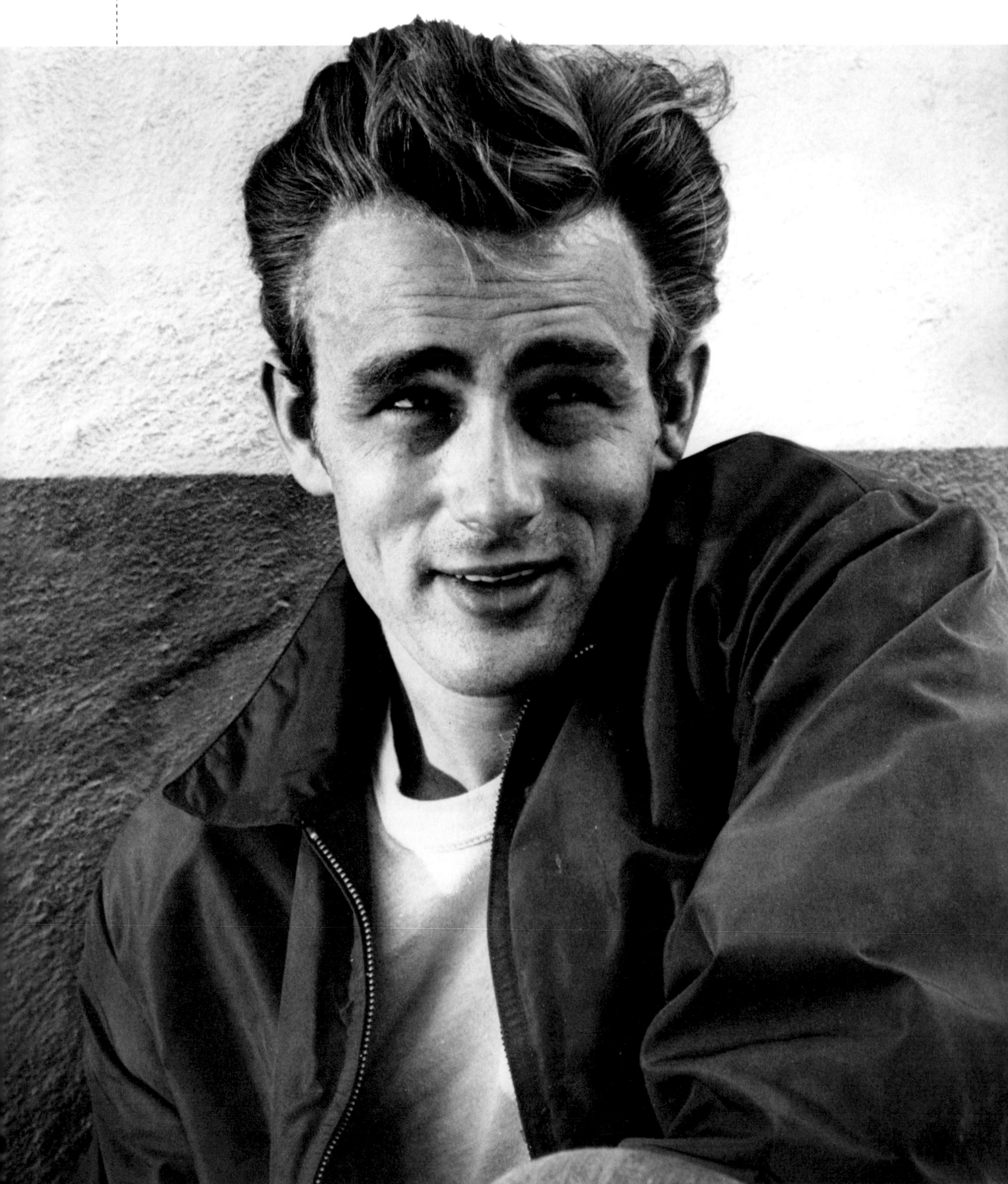

ABOVE: James Dean, 'Rebel Without A Cause'
OPP PAGE: Too Fast to Live, Too Young to Die
screenprint and T-shirt

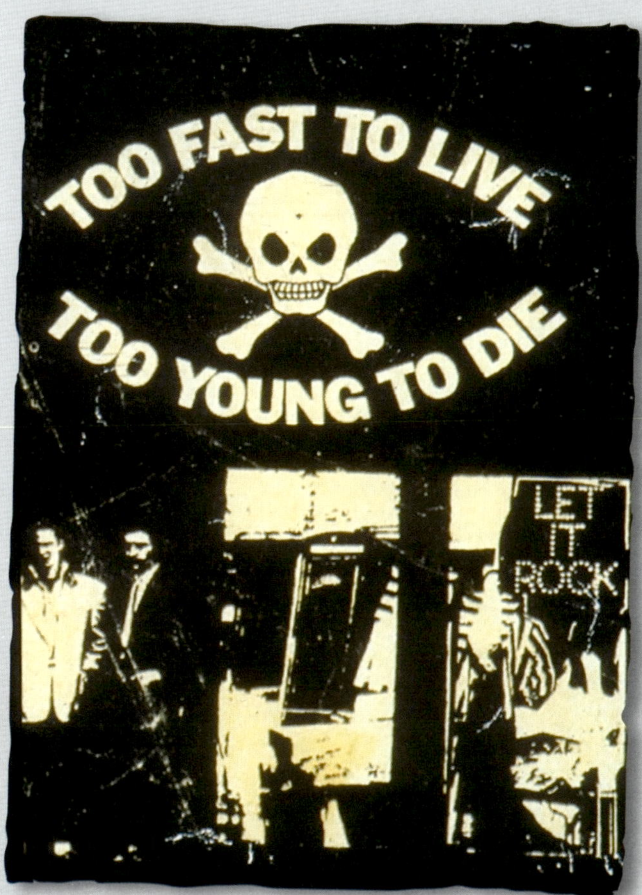

punk movement and setting the stage for their future influence on fashion and music. The store's façade, now adorned with a menacing skull and crossbones, signalled a deeper, darker dive into the rebellious rocker aesthetic, embracing a more nihilistic tone compared to their previous nostalgic 50s-style store.

During this shop-period Vivienne began to design printed T-shirts. The first iterations of her tees were quite unremarkable, as they simply advertised her and Malcolm's various idols such as Buddy Holly, Elvis Presley, and Marlon Brando. Clearly, Vivienne needed to make her designs more memorable. Inspired by

the business by this point, and the couple announced, much to everyone's shock, that they would be temporarily closing 'Let It Rock'.

A couple of months later, unable to sit on their laurels for too long, Vivienne and Malcolm reopened their store with the new and provocative name, 'Too Fast to Live, Too Young to Die'. Named after an epithet worn on the motorcycle jackets of American bikers to honour the death of James Dean, the rebranding marked a bold shift in the shop's aesthetic and cultural impact, aligning it more closely with the burgeoning

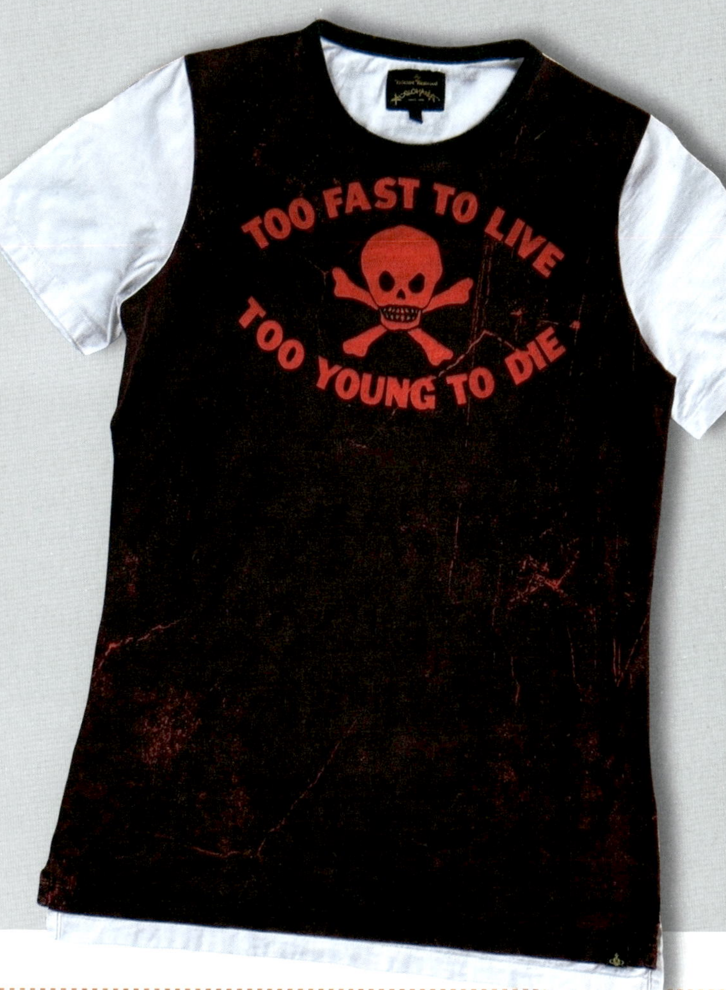

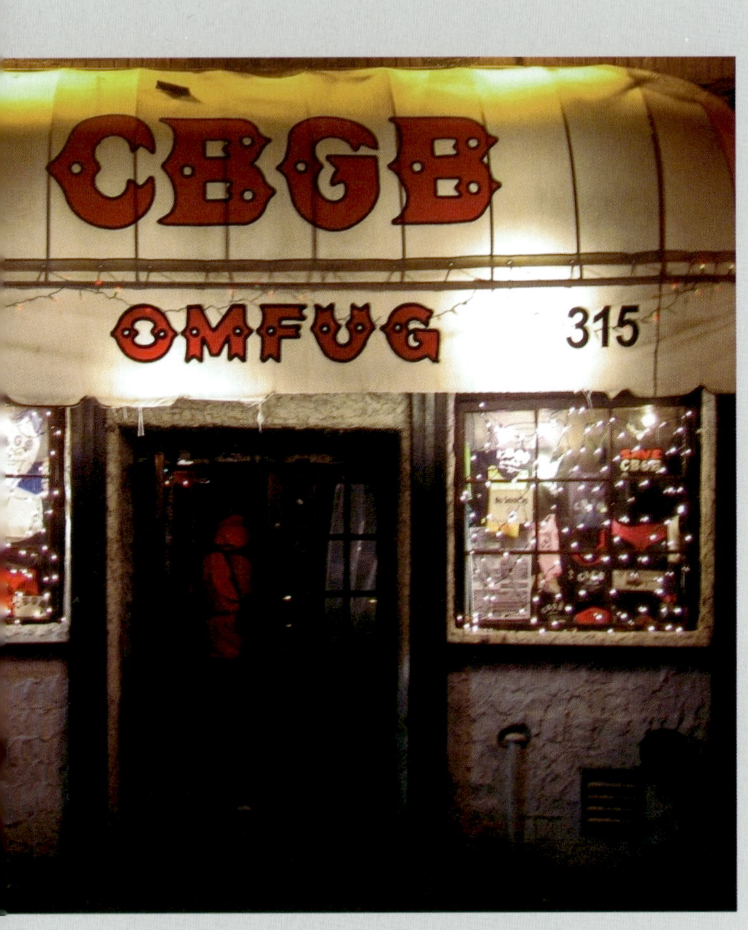

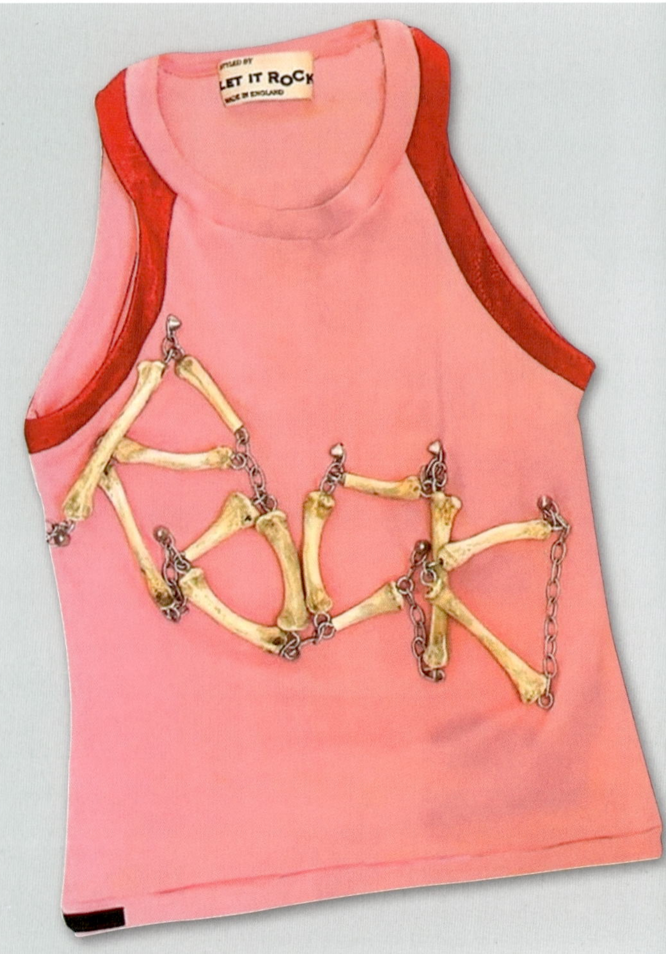

McLaren's anti-capitalist and Situationist politics, she began customising sleeveless black T-shirts with inflammatory slogans, spelt out in safety pins, glitter glue and sometimes with more unusual items, like bleached chicken bones. Vivienne would acquire discarded chicken carcasses and boil them, to strip them of their flesh. She would then drill holes and manoeuvre the bones to spell out various anarchist slogans. 'PERV', 'ROCK' and 'SCUM' T-shirts were all stocked alongside their classic black drainpipe jeans and vests covered with zips. Vivienne also famously used horsehair and bike tyre sleeves to create her iconic 'Venus' tee.

The budding designer's new do-it-yourself approach to fashion design was sending shock waves through London. Her customisation of various clothing items such as biker jackets, featuring studs, chains, bones, and feathers would become an enduring motif of her future fashion collections.

The former schoolteacher meticulously crafted each of her creations with the intention to 'instruct' society. The perverseness of her political messages and designs attracted youthful customers, the more shock and offence they caused to the public, the greater the demand was.

ABOVE: CBGB club in New York

ABOVE RIGHT: Let It Rock chicken bones 'Rock' T-shirt

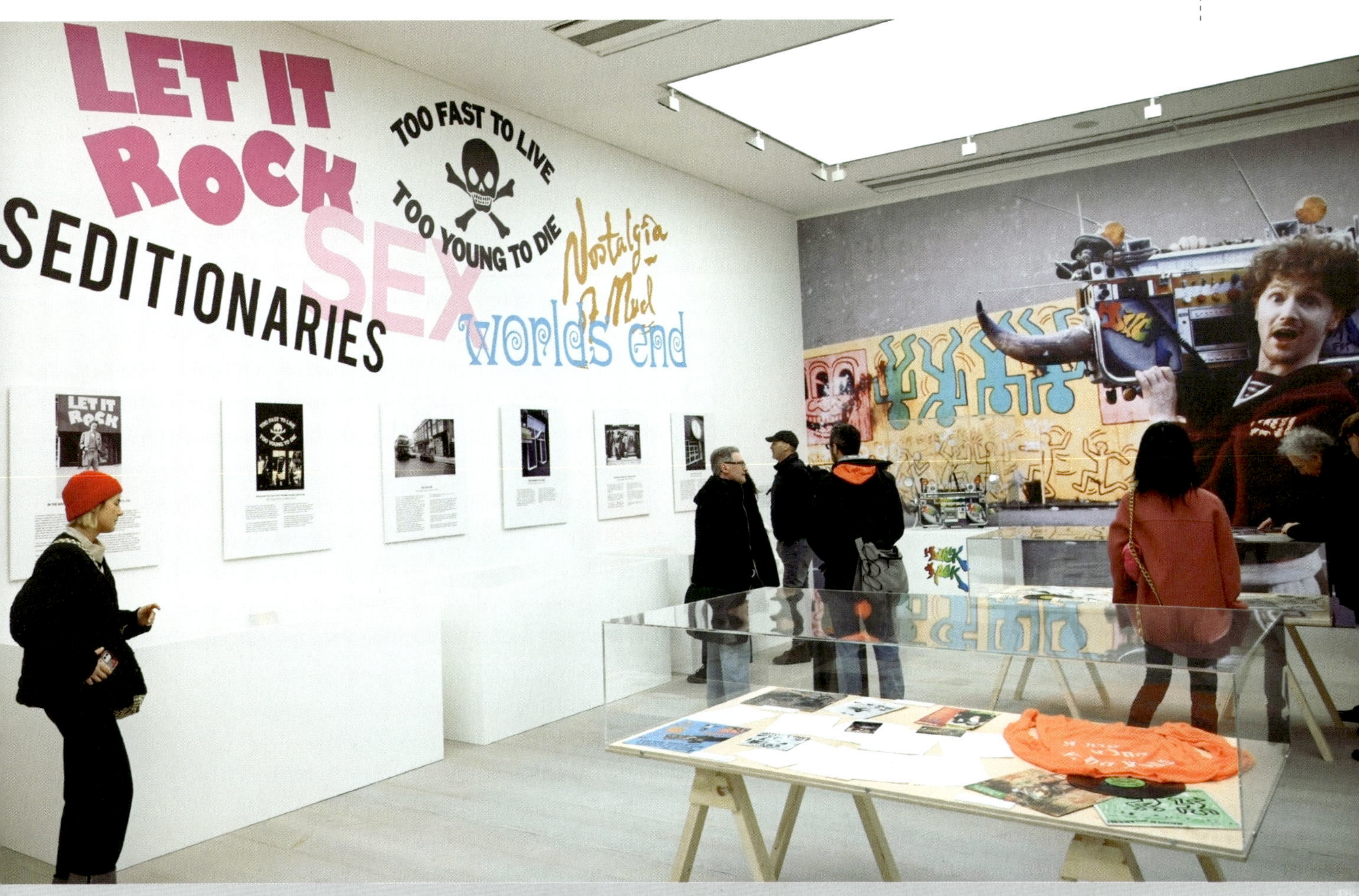

Vivienne's creations were beginning to gain visibility and acclaim, with big celebrities like Alice Cooper purchasing her clothing items. In August 1973, several shops on King's Road were invited to show their merchandise at the annual National Boutique Show in New York, including their store: 'Too Fast to Live, Too Young to Die'. Excited by the prospect of escaping domestic life for a bit, Vivienne and Malcolm jumped at the opportunity to travel to New York City. The event was being held at the McAlpine Hotel, located in Midtown. Vivienne and McLaren set up their stall in one of the hotel bedrooms, showcasing their collection of slogan tees, rocker clothing, and rock 'n' roll memorabilia. It was here that a member of the cult band the New York Dolls paid a visit to the eccentric duo. The Dolls' band members introduced Malcolm and Vivienne to the heart of New York culture, initiating them into the punk scene of the Big Apple. They visited venues like CBGB's, a hotbed of creativity and rebellion where bands like the Ramones, Patti Smith, and Television were pioneering a sound and style that was raw, unpolished, and full of attitude. McLaren, always with his finger on the pulse of cultural shifts, was deeply inspired by this burgeoning movement.

ABOVE: The shop names and slogans Vivienne and Malcolm had created would become legendary - Pictured here being honoured 50 years on in 2023 at the 'Beyond The Streets London' exhibition

THE NEW YORK EFFECT

In the early 1970s, New York City's socio-economic conditions were no better than London's. Local rock groups were reinventing music and style in protest against what had become perceived as the star-centred, showy, and elitist mentality of 60s super-groups such as The Rolling Stones and The Beatles. These local bands, like the New York Dolls and performer Richard Hell, were breaking down barriers at the infamous proto-punk club, Max's. Hell was well known for his nihilistic lyrics and self-styled ripped T-shirts bearing slogans like "Please Kill Me."

The DIY ethic of New York punk, characterised by ripped clothing, safety pins, and provocative graphics, had a direct influence on Vivienne's designs. She was fascinated by the way New York's youth culture used fashion as a form of rebellion, drawing a rich tapestry of inspiration from the city's gritty streets, underground music venues, and avant-garde art scene.

Vivienne was quick to absorb and reinterpret these influences through her own unique lens, and began to create pieces that reflected the anarchic spirit of punk, utilising unconventional materials and techniques.

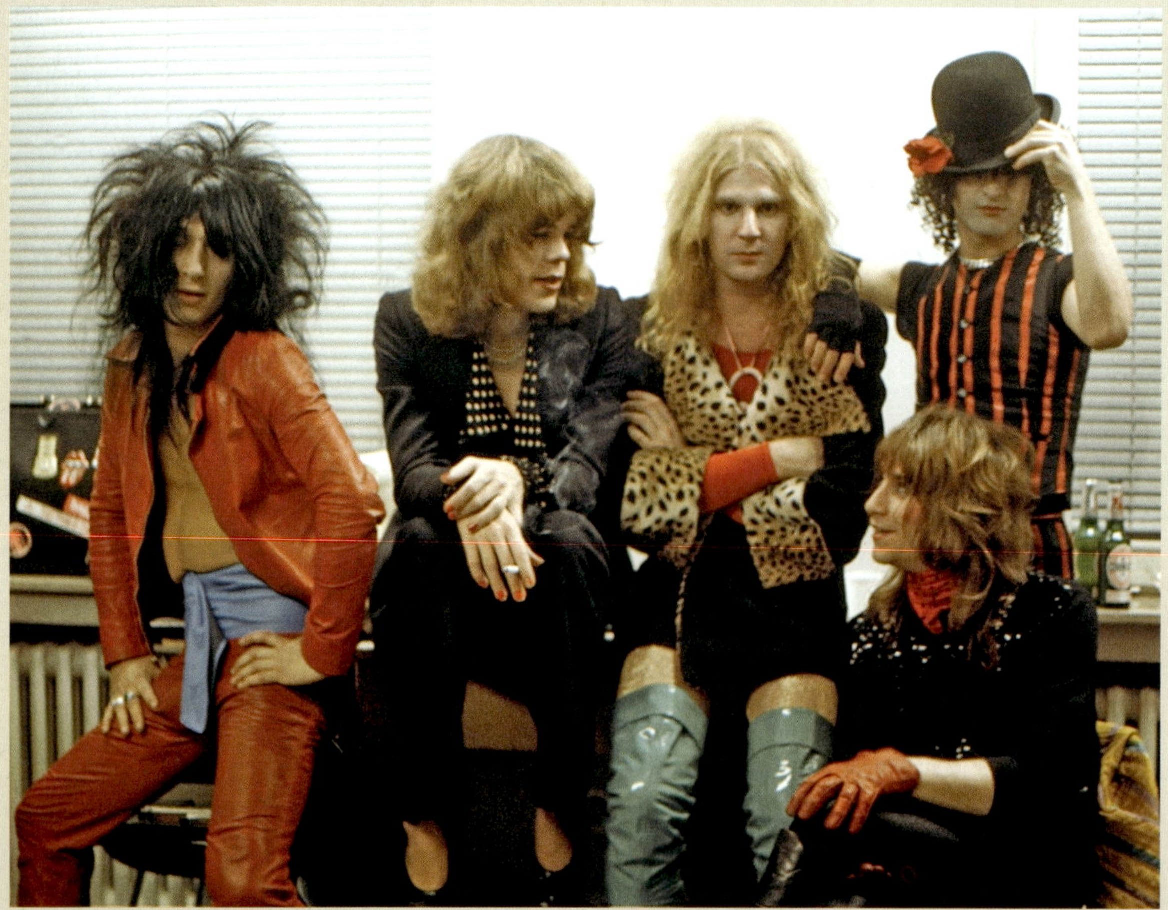

ABOVE: New York Dolls, 1970s
OPP PAGE: View of New York and New York Dolls concert poster

Vivienne and Malcolm's trip to New York proved to be very fruitful, and while Vivienne greatly enjoyed her time in the Big Apple, upon her arrival back in London she brazenly declared she hated the United States and would not return to the country for another two decades. McLaren, on the other hand, was completely smitten with the city and decided to split his time living between New York and London, determined to bring the radical aesthetics of New York back to London. He also became 'the New York Dolls' biggest groupie'.

Punk might have only been in its infancy, but it was soon going to take the world by storm, and Malcolm was going to be one of its facilitators.

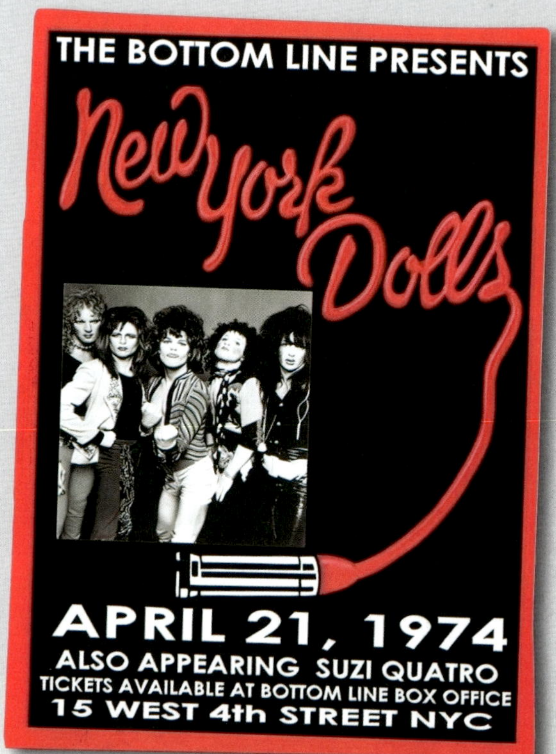

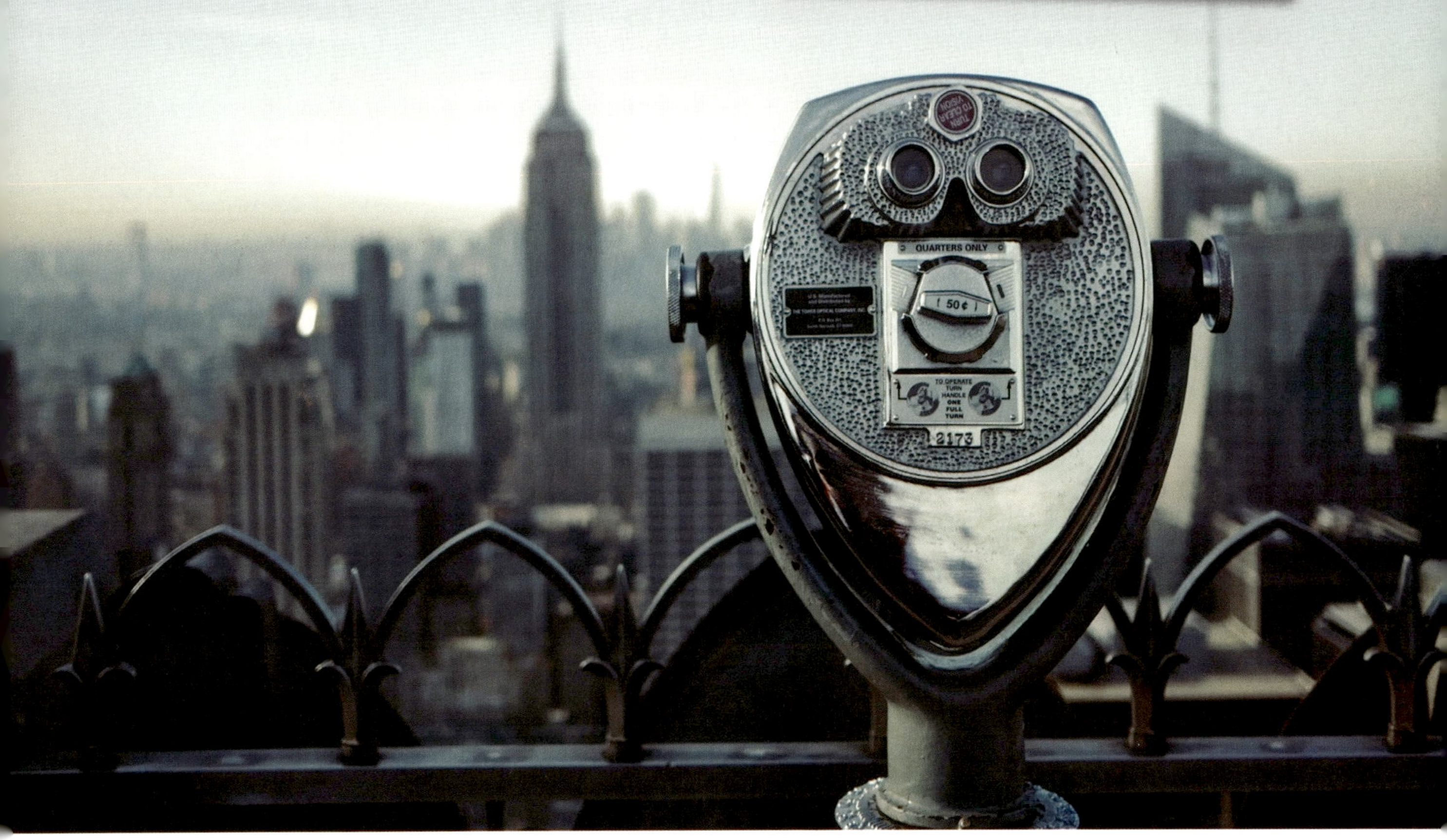

SEX AND RAGE
1974-1975

"There was no punk before me and Malcolm. And the other thing you should know about punk too: it was a total blast... what I do now is still punk – it's still about shouting about injustice and making people think... I'll always be punk in that sense."

Vivienne Westwood

Back in London, McLaren and Vivienne took advantage of the changing tides and the increased liberalisation happening in the city to channel their newfound New York-inspired ethos into their own creative ventures.

Their boutique, previously known as 'Let It Rock' and 'Too Fast to Live, Too Young to Die', underwent yet another transformation in April 1974. After an extensive renovation, the store reopened later that summer under the new and provocative name 'SEX'. Journalist Andrea Tuzio wrote about the historic opening in the magazine *Collater*, saying "When the store was renamed 'SEX' in 1974, the rich and bigoted community of Chelsea expressed their indignation at Westwood's bold move, which consolidated her anti-establishment

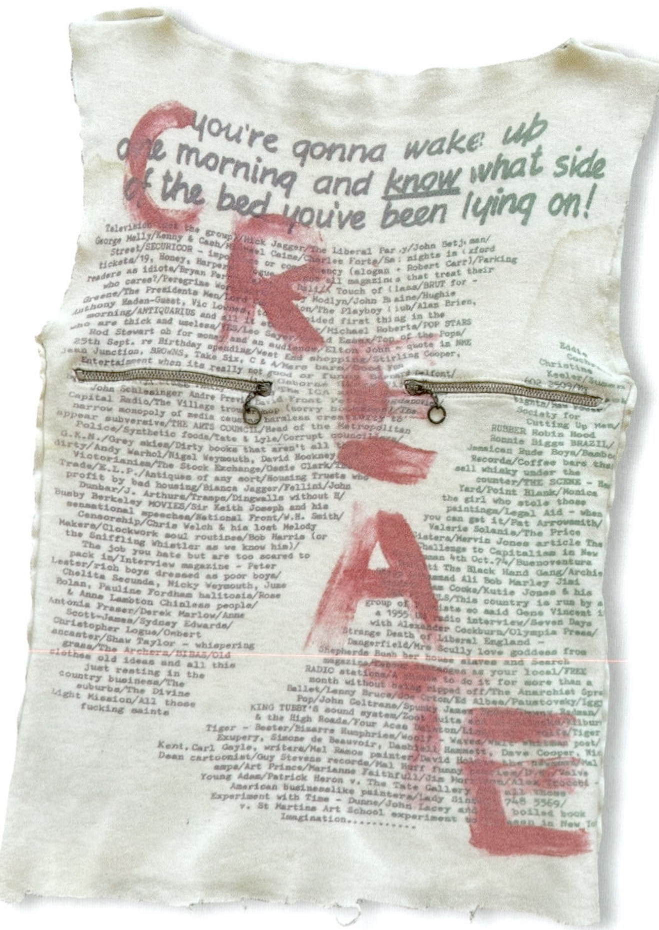

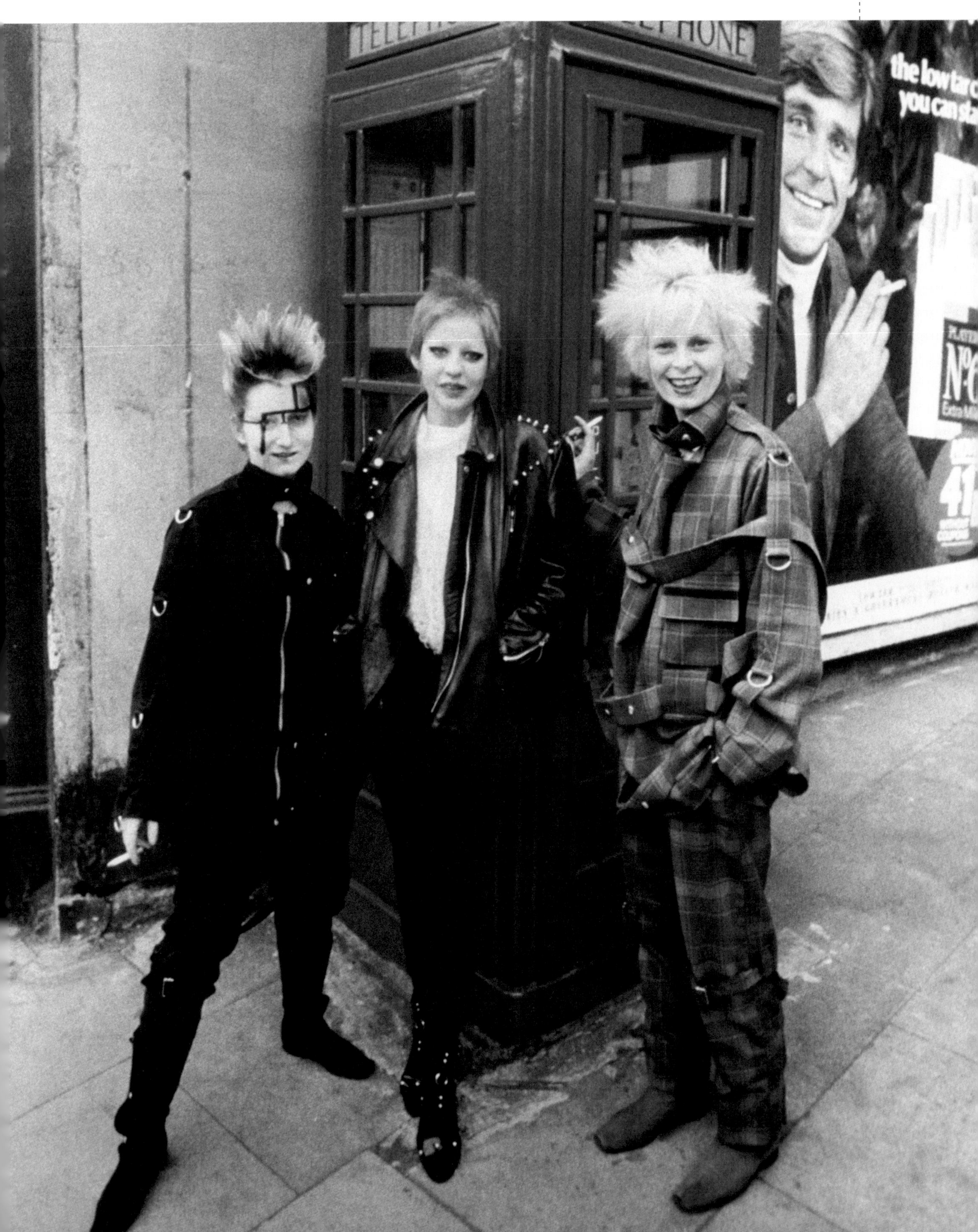

position" and placed her as a landmark in the up-and-coming punk movement.

McLaren and Vivienne were provocateurs by nature, and their latest clothing venture was created to shock and undermine the puritan attitudes surrounding sex. The pink inflatable letters spelling out the word 'sex' was sure to grab any passerby's attention. The opaque shop windows, inspired by actual sex shops, prompted curious window shoppers to enter the store to find out what was being sold inside. The shop's interior, designed with a spongy, womb-like material and decorated with anarchic graffiti, further underscored this rebellious spirit.

SEX wasn't simply a clothing boutique, but a meeting point for the thousands of young Londoners who couldn't stand capitalism, British materialism, and the strongly pro-monarchic public opinion that only saw punks as 'young thugs'.

The shop's taboo-confronting fashion, labelled as 'anti-fashion,' resonated with the young generation's desire to push back against the bleak economic stagnation, social strife, and the looming threat of nuclear war hanging over Britain. "Vivienne and Malcolm used clothes to shock, irritate, and provoke a reaction but also to inspire change", Viv Albertine of The Slits recalled in her memoir. Vivienne's designs, such as mohair jumpers knitted so loosely that they were transparent and slashed T-shirts with seams and labels on the outside,

mirrored the punk ethos of embracing imperfection and authenticity.

Vivienne took her now iconic slogan tees and made them even more punk. One of the earliest SEX T-shirts, devised in the autumn of 1974, was a tribal manifesto entitled "You're gonna wake up one morning and know what side of the bed you've been lying on!" It listed over a hundred 'Hates' on the left and their 'Loves' on the right.

In a 2002 interview with the *Independent*, Vivienne articulated her vision: "I was messianic about punk, seeing if one could put a spoke in the system in some way. I realised there was no subversion without ideas. It's not enough to want to destroy everything." Her designs, imbued with a higher purpose of subverting the status quo, used fashion as a conduit for social and political commentary.

During this tumultuous time, McLaren grew increasingly tired of Vivienne and started an affair with Addie Isman, the wayward daughter of a wealthy New Jersey family and employee at their store. Their fling would be short lived however, as Addie moved back to the States only six months after striking up a relationship with Malcolm.

Shortly after, Malcolm would move to New York full-time York to manage the New York Dolls, though this brief stint in band management would prove to be short lived.

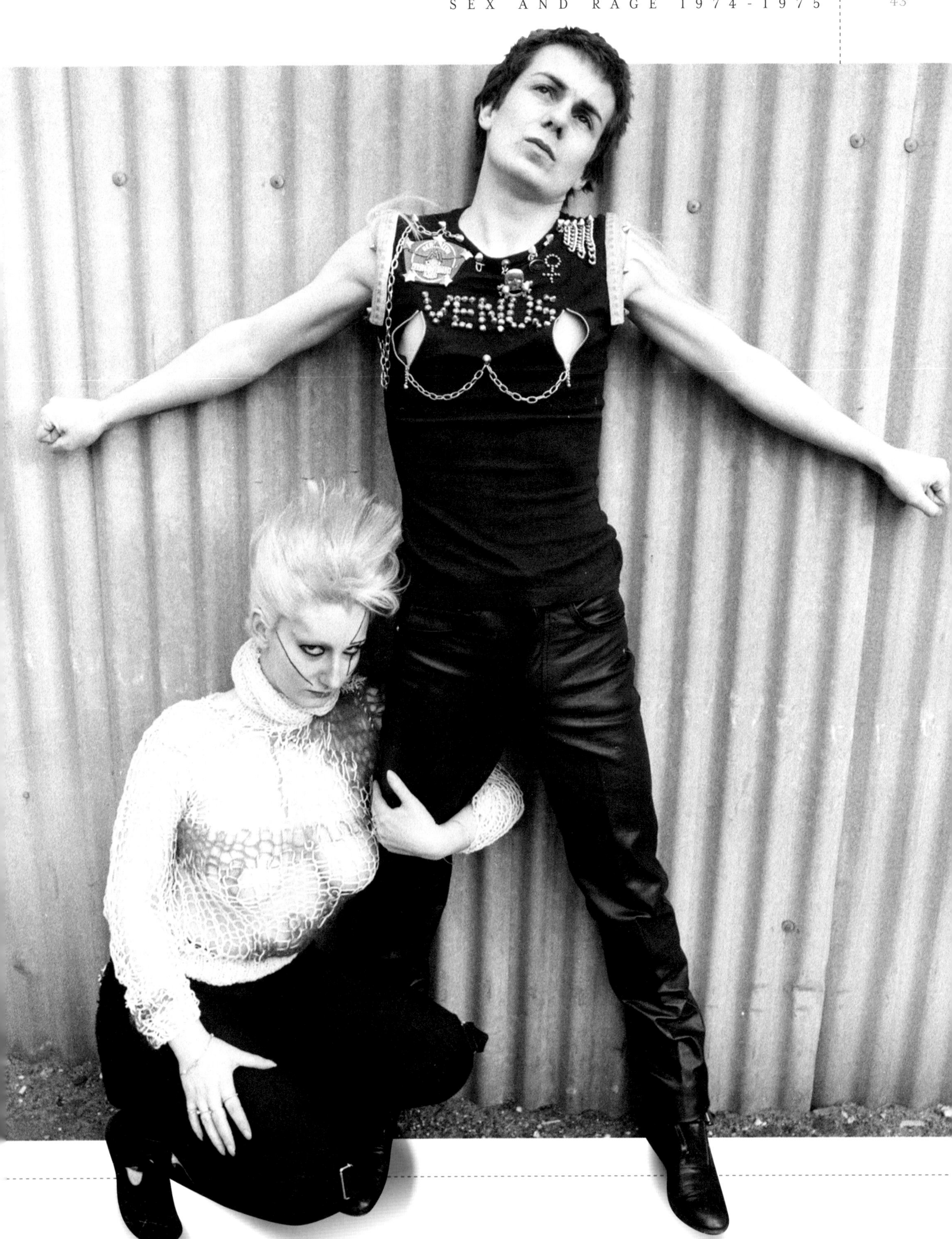

ANARCHY IN THE U.K.

1975-1978

"When music moves from the music section to the front page of a newspaper, you're in trouble."

Vivienne Westwood

In the mid-1970s, London was a city on the edge. The glitter of the swinging sixties had faded, replaced by a grim reality of economic stagnation, rising unemployment, and social unrest. Against this backdrop, a new subculture began to emerge from the depths of the city's youth. It was raw, angry, and unapologetically rebellious. It was punk.

Punk has had the greatest impact on Western popular culture of any youth-led movement since the hippies in the 1960s. From fashion to music to politics, there seemed to be no area untouched by the power of punk. Yet, despite its enduring impact, the hard-core punk movement, or 'punk-tide' as it is often referred to, was short-lived, lasting only 30 months, with most of its influence spanning from the end of 1975 until 1978, before officially fizzling out by early 1980.

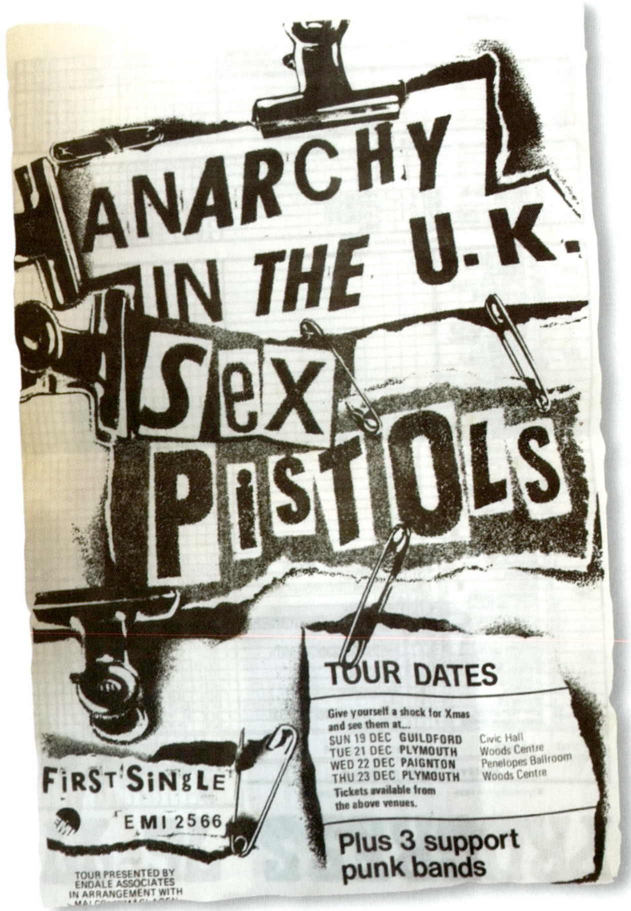

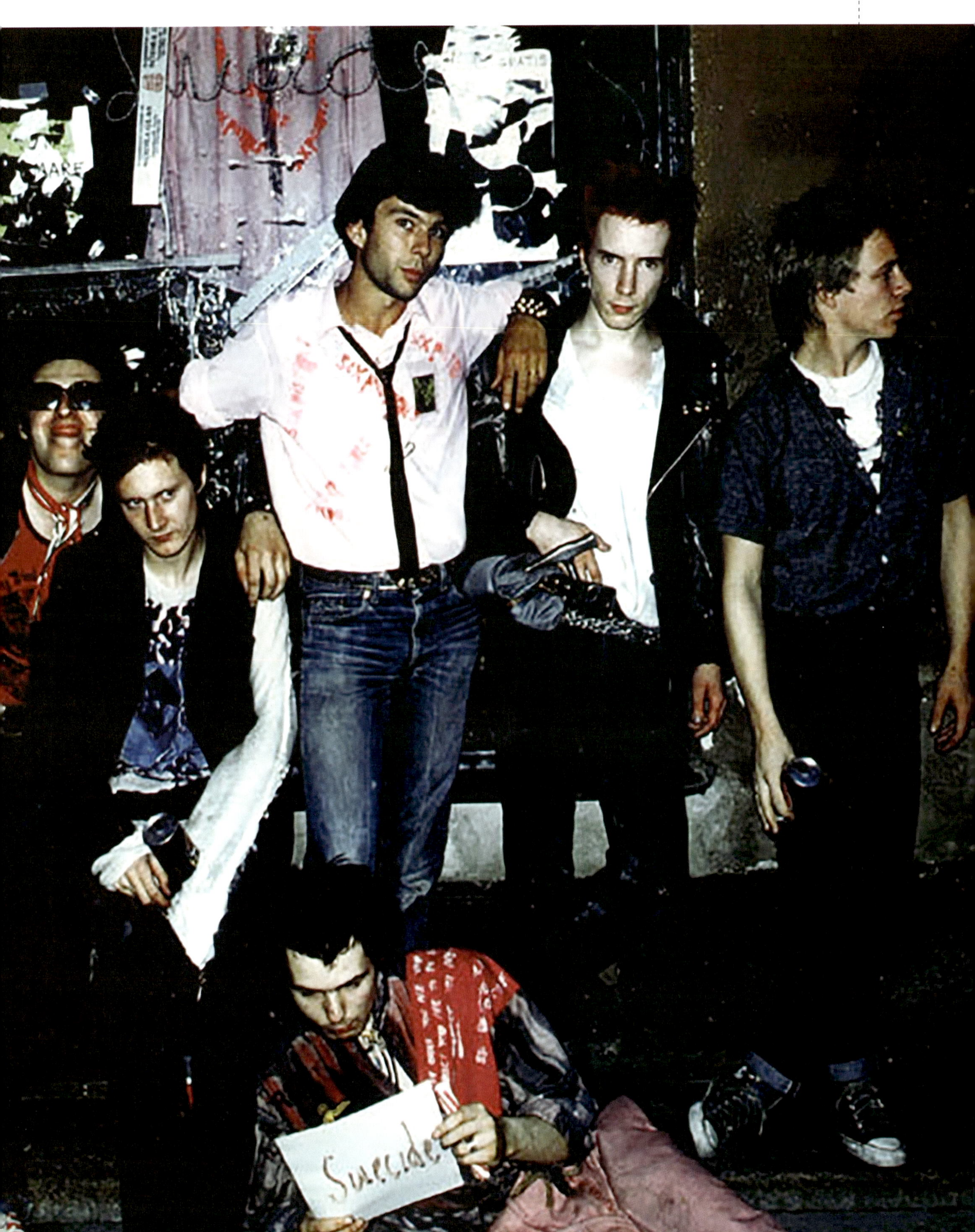
Suicide

NEW YORK VS LONDON

The debate over the true birthplace of punk has long fuelled transatlantic rivalries, with New York and London each laying claim to the origins of the movement. Those who argue that the movement originated in America cite garage bands from the late 60's, with performers from the iconic New York music venue CBGB's as the original proto-punks. In the gritty, decaying streets of 1970s New York, punk emerged as a response to a city grappling with financial ruin and rampant crime. New York punk was heavily influenced by the avant-garde art and underground scene. Bands and performers like Richard Hell, the New York Dolls, and Patti Smith, melded rock and roll with experimental sounds and poetic lyricism. The music was raw and minimalist, often characterised by simple, fast-paced chords and stripped-down arrangements.

Across the Atlantic, London's punk scene erupted as a reaction to economic austerity, rising unemployment, and a sense of political and social disenfranchisement. It was about tearing down the old structures and creating something new, something that represented the disaffected youth. The movement coalesced around iconic venues like The Roxy and the incendiary fashion statements coming out of SEX.

English writer Jon Savage commented on punk in England, saying "it was a class mix. You could come from a tower block or be the middle-classed person who went to Cambridge… the whole point of punk is that it was a group of outcasts from whatever background, and that was the common bond", "it was to do with having an attitude and being human, not just part of a system". Punk wasn't just a sound, but rather a political statement.

Vivienne and McLaren understood this instinctively. They weren't just observers of the scene; they were its architects. The dynamic duo crafted the aesthetic and attitude that made punk a global phenomenon.

In truth, punk was less about a specific geography and more about a shared sense of rebellion—two cities, two scenes, one revolutionary spirit.

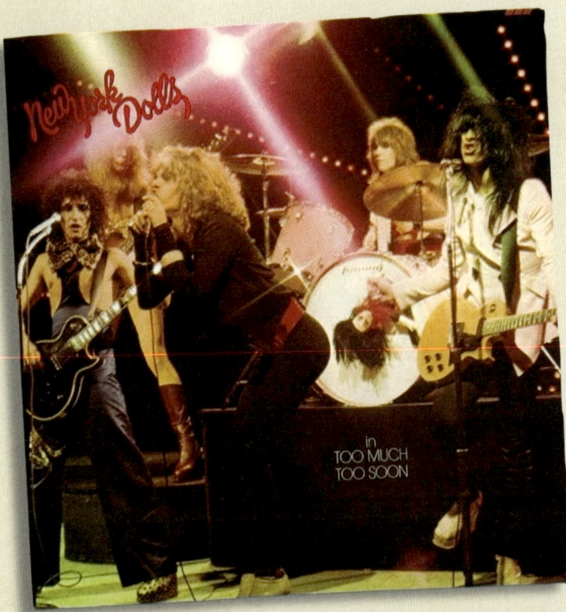

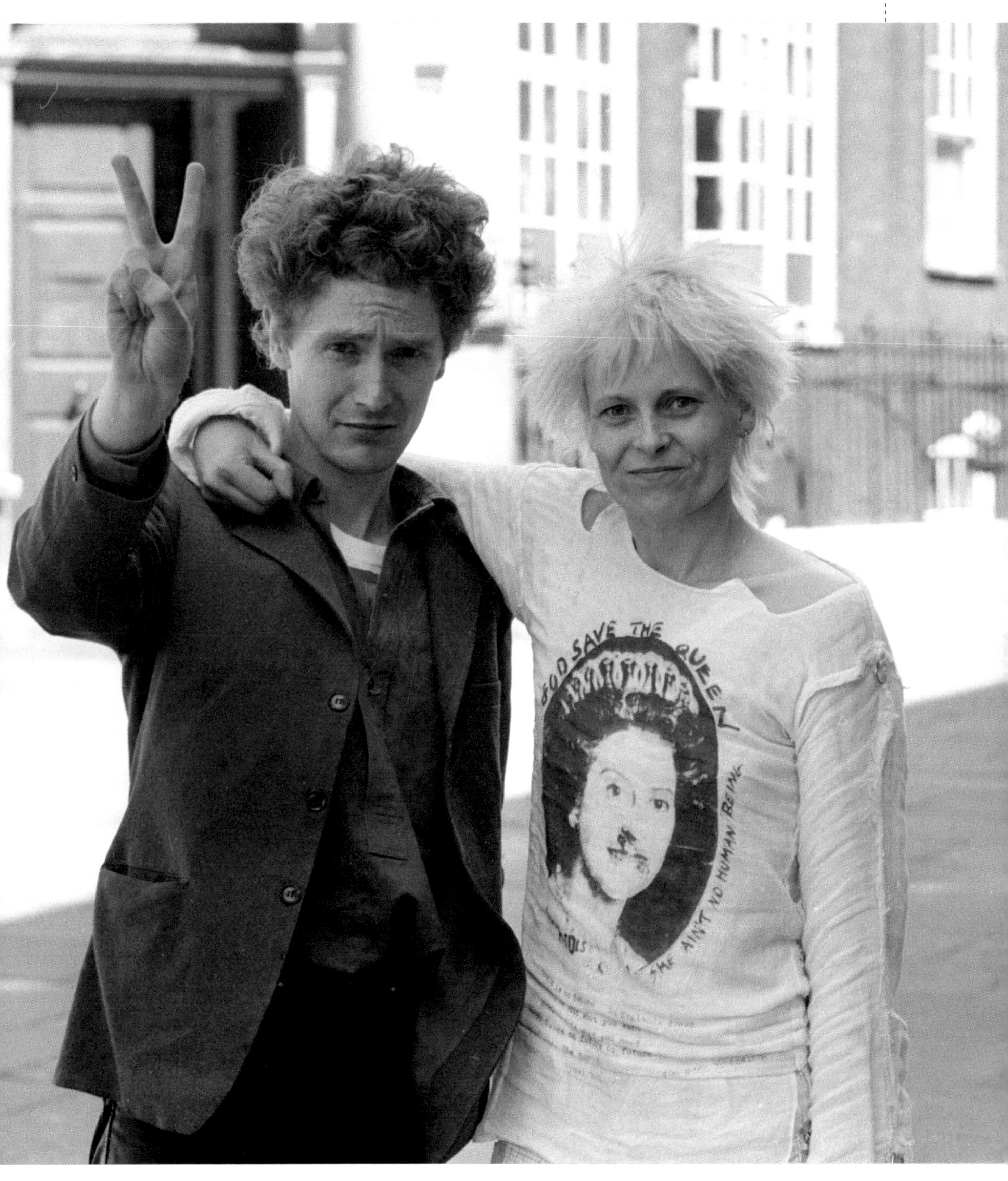

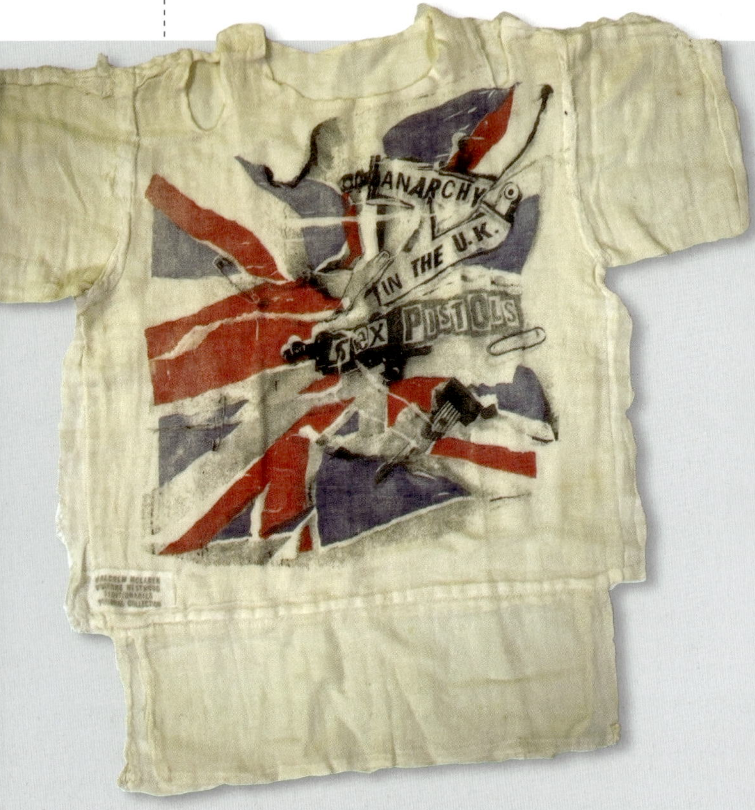

Vivienne Westwood was already a name on the fringes of London's underground scene by 1975. Vivienne and Malcolm's designs were subversive, deliberately ugly, and often offensive. The now-iconic 'God Save the Queen' T-shirt, featuring the Queen's face defaced with safety pins, was a direct challenge to the establishment. Vivienne took traditional symbols of British authority and turned them on their heads, exposing the hypocrisy and repression that she believed lay beneath the surface.

Her punk designs were not just about shock value, though. They were deeply rooted in her understanding of history, art, and politics. She drew on everything from Dadaism and Situationism to the anti-authoritarianism of the French Revolution. Her clothes were designed to provoke thought as much as to provoke a reaction. They were a call to arms, a visual manifesto for a generation that felt betrayed by the promise of post-war prosperity.

As they were growing their clothing brand, Vivienne and McLaren were simultaneously building a band that would become the musical voice of the punk movement.

Malcolm McLaren's foray into the New York music scene in early 1975 was a pivotal moment in his career, and in the evolution of punk. Managing the New York Dolls, McLaren brought his flair for provocation and theatricality to the already flamboyant band, dressing them in red leather and draping them in communist imagery, which only served to heighten their notoriety. Despite his efforts, McLaren's prankster personality started to cause issues and the Dolls' popularity waned, until eventually the band broke up. McLaren returned to England disillusioned but inspired. Determined to use what was happening in New York and turn it into a British phenomenon, McLaren set out to find a band that could embody the rebellious spirit of punk.

This quest led him to form the Sex Pistols, a group that would soon become the face of the punk movement for the UK, but also for the rest of the world. McLaren's experience with the New York Dolls had shown him the power of image and controversy in rock music, lessons he would apply to devastating effect in his next venture.

ABOVE: Anarchy in the U.K. T-shirt, designed by Vivienne
OPP PAGE: Glen Matlock & Steve Jones of the Sex Pistols performing on 21 October, 1976

THE SEX PISTOLS

The Sex Pistols started in the same way as any other band: friends getting together to make music just like their idols. Steve Jones, the guitarist, was a young man with family issues and a nasty penchant for stealing things. He and two of his friends from school, Paul Cook (Pistols drummer) and Wally Nightingale, decided to form a band, playing instruments Steve claimed to have stolen from a David Bowie tour. They called themselves The Strand, occasionally The Swankers, and frequently hung around 430 King's Road, where they quickly befriended owner Malcolm McLaren.

Malcolm saw in this ragtag group the potential to challenge and disrupt the stagnant music scene of the time. He became their manager, infusing the band with his own blend of Situationist theory and anti-establishment fervour. Under his guidance, the face of punk rock was born, and the Sex Pistols were gearing up to take the UK and the rest of the world by storm.

When Malcolm became professionally entangled with Steve and his bandmates, he made some big changes to their setup. First, he demoted Steve from lead vocalist to guitarist and fired Wally Nightingale altogether. He then added Glen Matlock, an employee at SEX, to be the band's bassist. The only thing missing for Malcolm to complete his vision for the Sex Pistols was a charismatic lead vocalist, and so the hunt began.

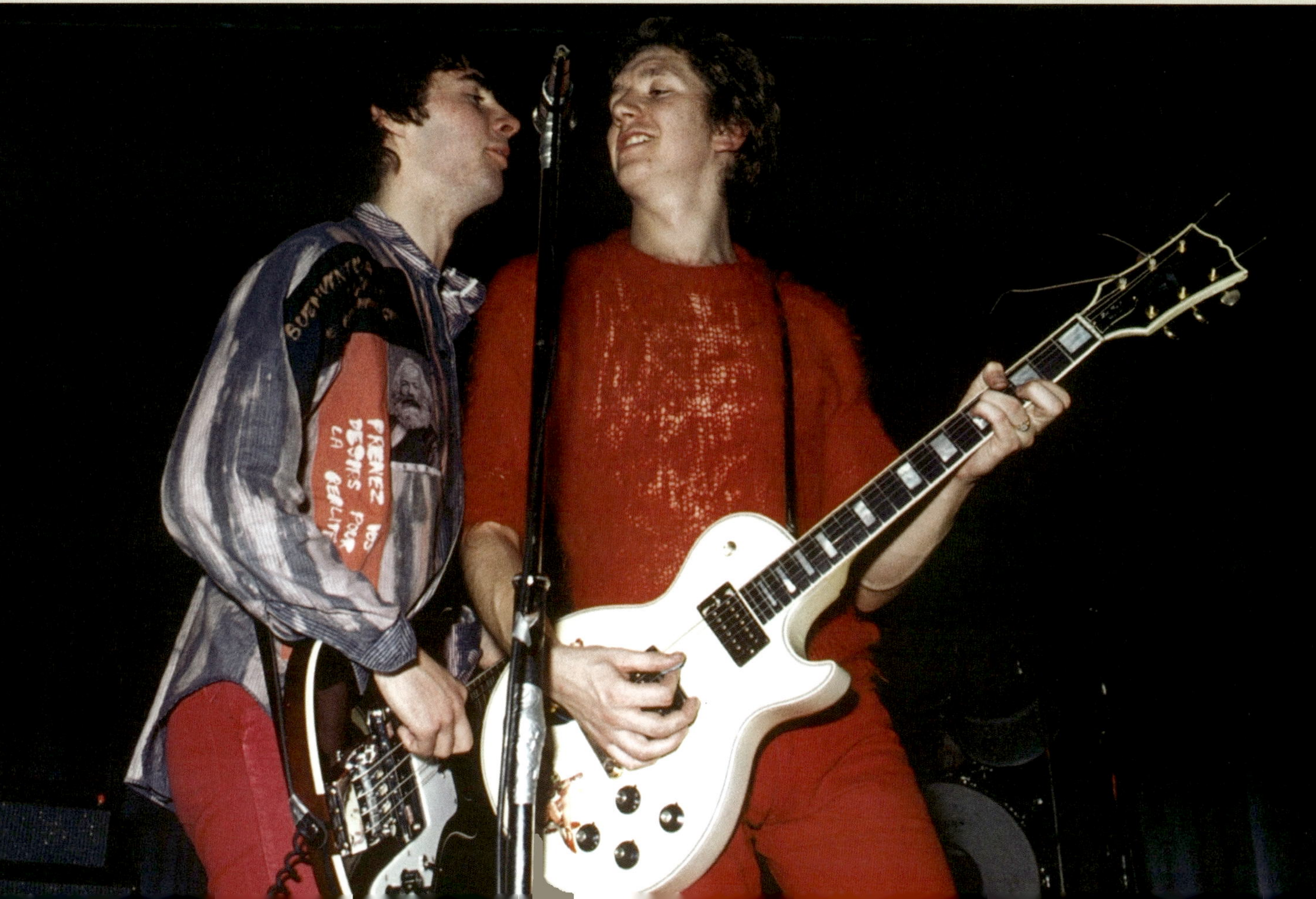

One random day, a young John Lyndon, walked into the SEX shop with his green hair and his 'I Hate Pink Floyd' T-shirt. He improvised to Alice Cooper's 'I'm Eighteen', and though the young man couldn't sing, his look and his attitude convinced Malcolm he was the perfect addition to the band. Lyndon would be renamed by Steve as 'Johnny Rotten' because of his particularly bad teeth.

Now that the band was assembled, it was time to make music. There was only one rule: no Beatles chords.

The band's early performances were notorious for their intensity and unpredictability. Johnny Rotten's snarling delivery of lyrics that spat in the face of British institutions, combined with the band's aggressive sound, quickly caught the attention of the press and punks alike. Their 1976 single 'Anarchy in the U.K.' was a rallying cry for a generation, and the Sex Pistols were their unwitting spokespeople.

However, it was their expletive-laden appearance on the *Today* show with Bill Grundy in December 1976 that truly catapulted them into the national spotlight. The British press was horrified, but the youth were electrified. Punk was no longer just a subculture; it was a full-blown movement, and McLaren and Vivienne were at its centre.

Vivienne's influence on the band's image was unmistakable. She dressed them in her designs, creating a look that was as confrontational as their music. The ripped T-shirts, leather jackets, and bondage trousers became the uniform of punk. Vivienne and Malcolm even renamed their shop on 430 King's Road to 'Seditionaries', the non-official shop for the punk look.

The Sex Pistols' rise to fame—and infamy—was swift. As quickly as they had risen, the Sex Pistols' story began to unravel, torn apart by internal tensions, the pressures of fame, and the destructive nature of the very chaos they had unleashed. They disbanded in early 1978, but their brief, incendiary time in the spotlight left an indelible mark on the world, ensuring that the Sex Pistols would be remembered not just as a band, but as the catalysts for a cultural revolution.

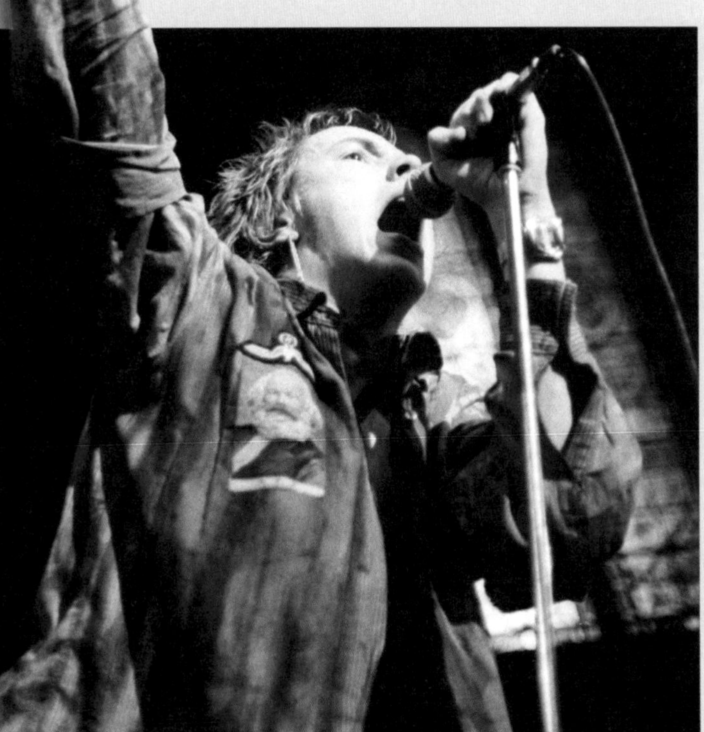

ABOVE: Johnny Rotten, 6 January 1977
OPP PAGE: Sex Pistols 'God Save The Queen' T-shirts from the Seditionaries boutique modelled by Pamela Rooke, aka Jordan, and Simon Barker, aka Six, 18 May 1977

But as the punk movement grew, it also began to change. What had started as a raw, underground scene began to be co-opted by the mainstream. By the late 1970s, punk fashion was being sold in high street shops, and the once radical designs of Westwood were being imitated by mass-market retailers. Vivienne herself began to move away from the punk aesthetic, feeling that it had lost its edge and its meaning.

However, the impact of her work during the punk years cannot be overstated. She had not only created a new fashion movement, she had helped to define a cultural moment.

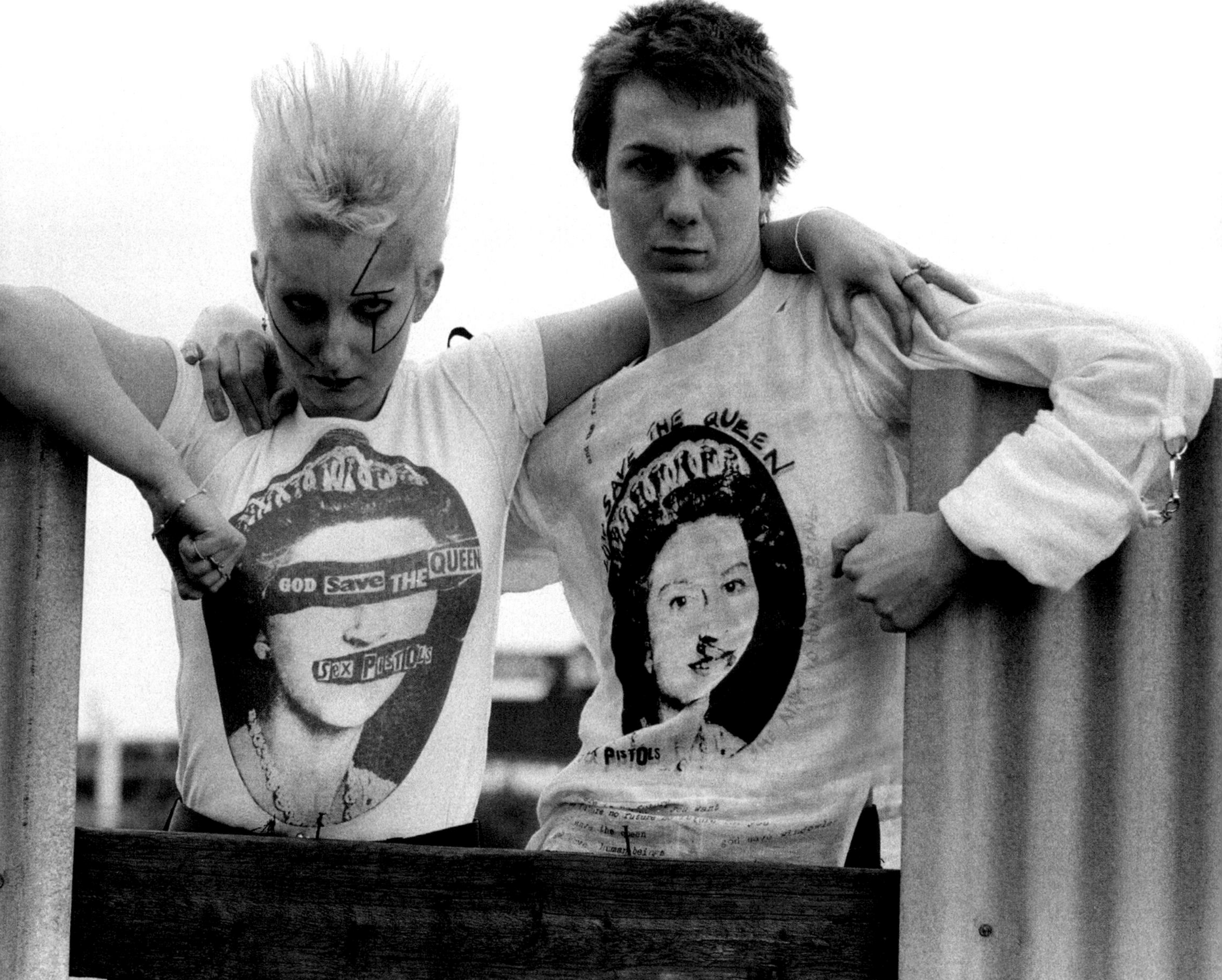

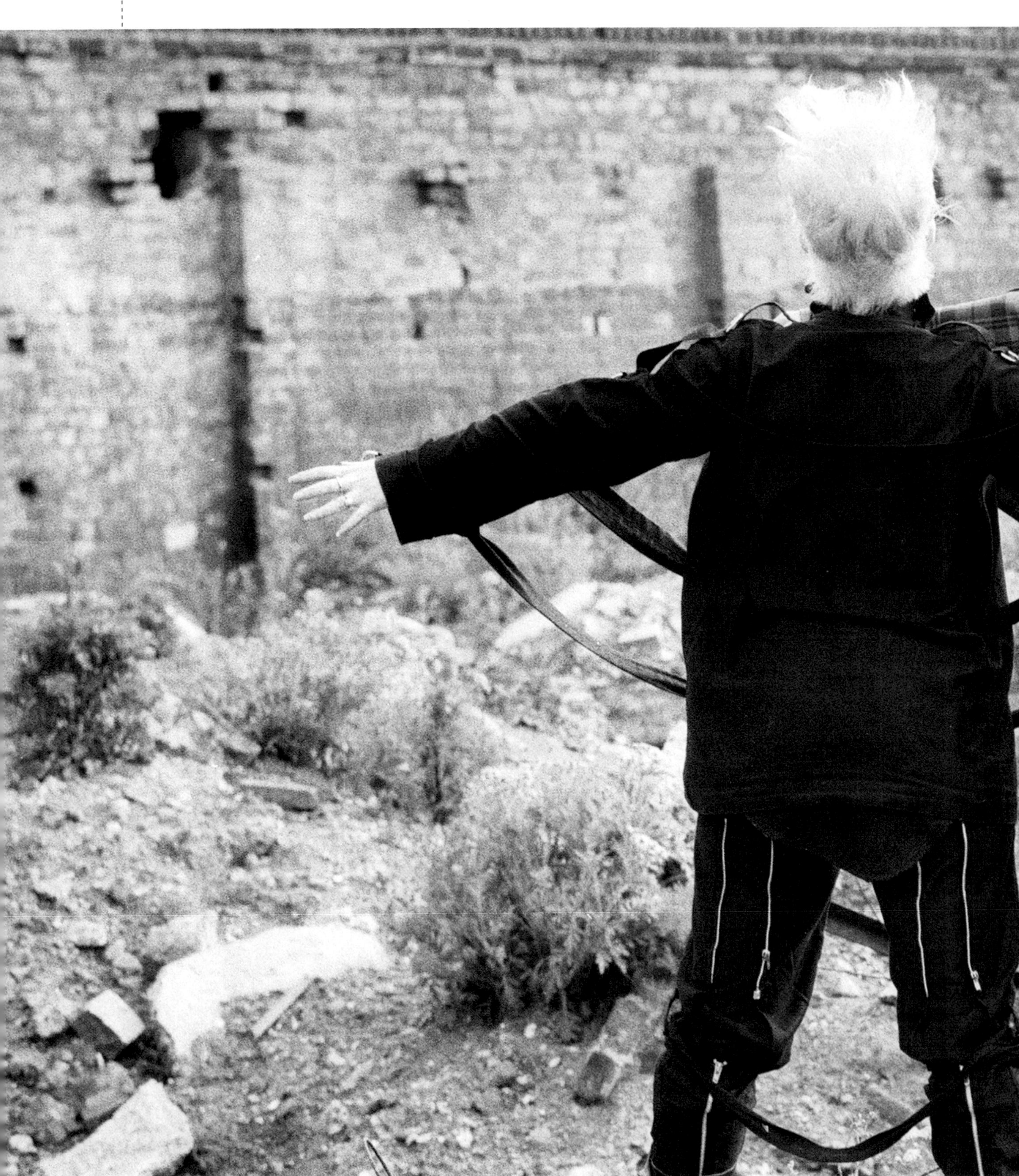

ABOVE: Pamela Rooke and Simon Barker modelling
bondage gear from the Seditionaries boutique on
King's Road, London, 18 May 1977

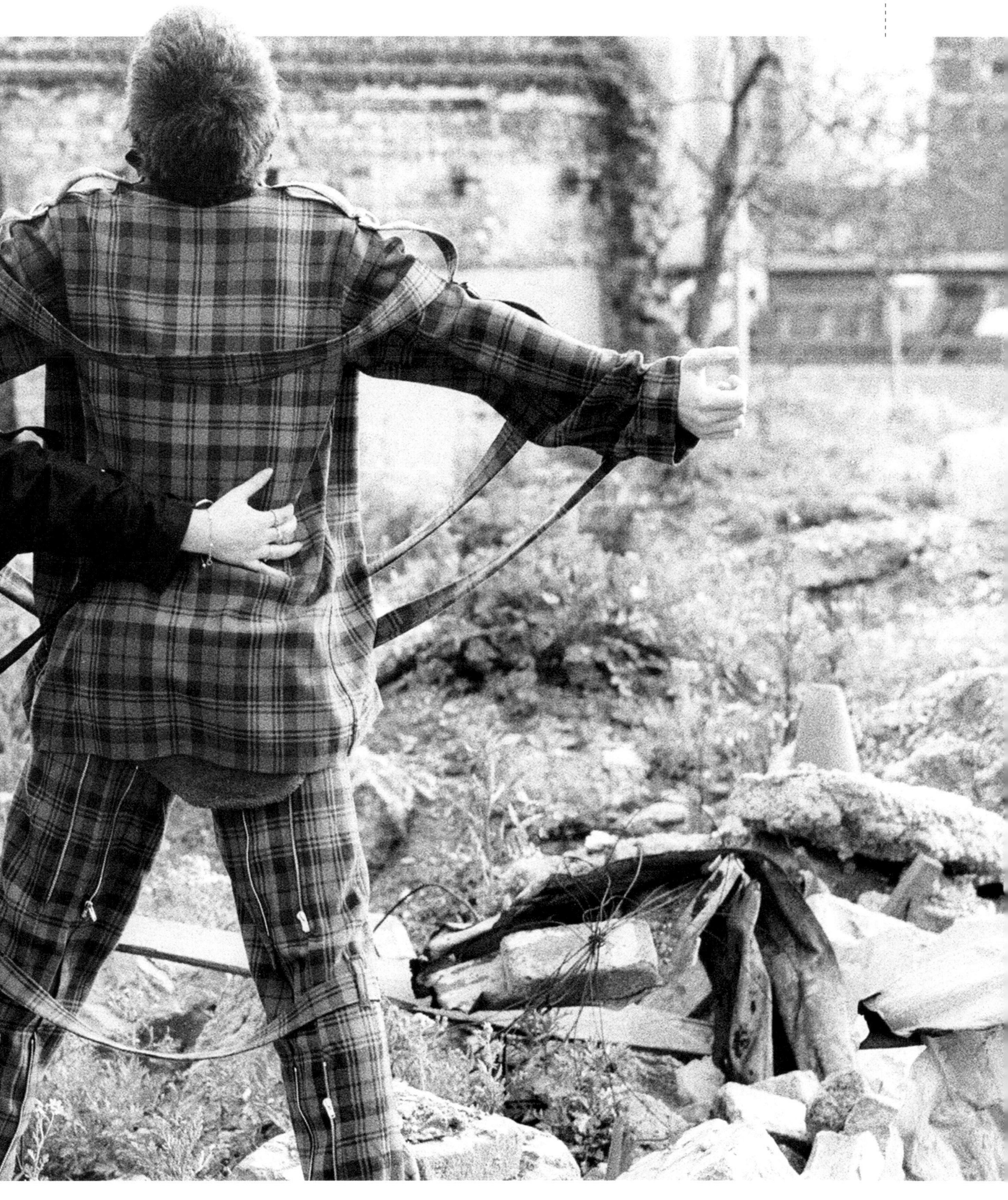

"VIVE LA REVOLUTION!"

1979-1980

"The French revolution taught us the rights of man."

Thomas Sankara

In 1979, Vivienne found herself alone once again. Her two boys were away at boarding school and McLaren was living in Paris. Unencumbered by children and an eccentric partner, Vivienne retreated to Nightingale Lane for some much-needed respite after the whirlwind of the punk years. However, her period of rest and relaxation was short-lived, as Vivienne was eager to get back to work on creating a new look for her label. She wanted to stray away from the post-war youth movements she had previously drawn inspiration from and instead found her muse in a book on 18th and 19th century fashion. The designer became captivated by the clothes worn by 'Les Incroyables' and their female counterparts, 'Les Merveilleuses', from post-revolution France. These elegant garbs became the jumping-off point for Vivienne's next collection.

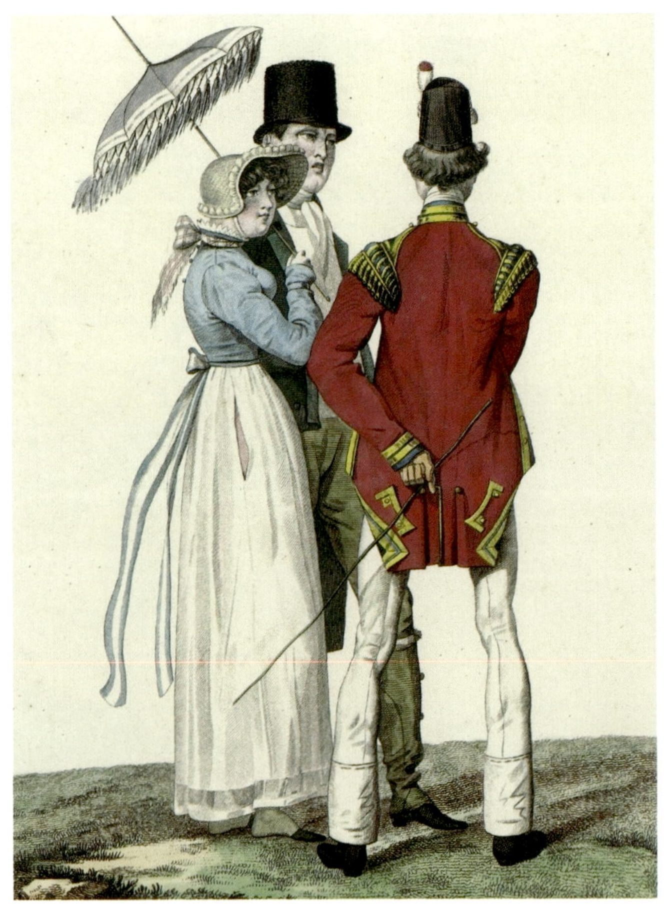

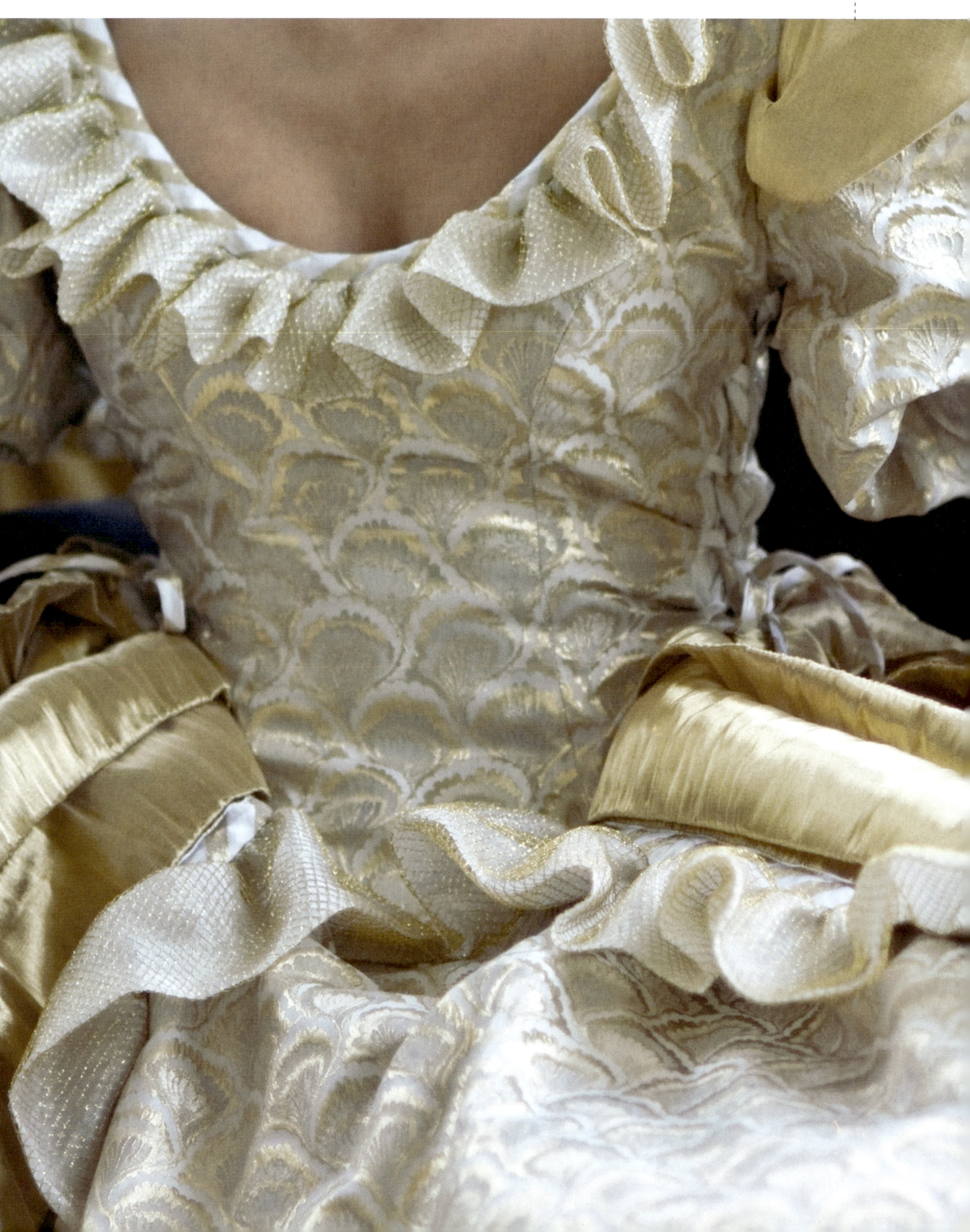

PRESENTING 'LES INCROYABLES' ET 'LES MERVEILLEUSES'

The late 18th century in France was a period of radical change, when the French Revolution brought an end to centuries of monarchical rule and ushered in a new era of social, political, and cultural transformation. Amidst the upheaval, a subculture emerged that would challenge traditional norms and leave a lasting mark on the fashion world.

'Les Incroyables' (The Incredibles) and 'Les Merveilleuses' (The Marvelous Ones), emerged during the French Directory period (1795–1799) and were often the offspring of wealthy bourgeois families or nobility that had managed to survive the Terror. In reaction to the austerity and violence of the previous years, they embraced a lifestyle of luxury, excess, and flamboyance, using fashion as their primary vehicle of expression.

The fashion of 'Les Incroyables' was characterised by an exaggerated, almost caricatural style that was both a parody of the old aristocracy and a departure from the sombre clothing associated with the Revolution. Their outfits were notorious for their oversized proportions—extraordinarily large lapels, high cravats that wrapped around the neck multiple times, and coats with voluminous tails.

On the other hand, 'Les Merveilleuses' embraced a different kind of excess, one that drew inspiration from classical antiquity. Their fashion was defined by sheer, flowing dresses made from fine muslins, often inspired by the classical drapery of ancient Greece and Rome. These dresses were cut close to the body, creating a revealing silhouette that was in stark contrast to the heavily structured and layered garments of the previous century. Their look was completed with dramatic accessories like long shawls, elaborate hats adorned with feathers, and sandals that laced up the calf.

Fast forward nearly two centuries, and the influence of fashion from the French Directory found a new incarnation in the designs of British fashion designer Vivienne Westwood.

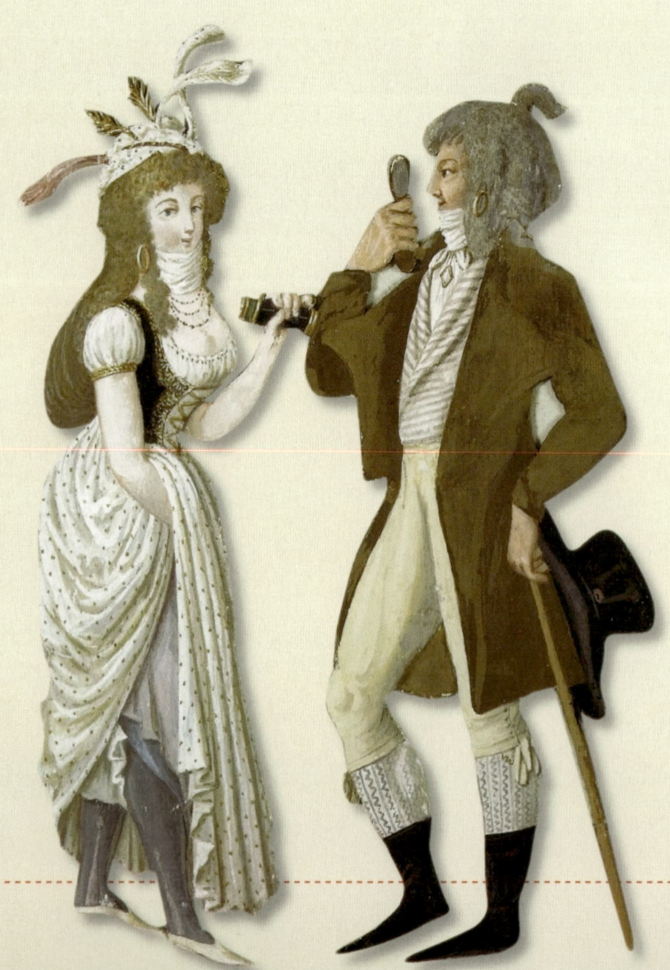

RIGHT: Les Incroyables and Les Merveilleuses
OPP PAGE: Malcolm left Paris and returned to London just as Vivienne was dreaming up a French inspired collection

Upon Malcolm's return to London after a year spent in Paris, Vivienne eagerly presented him with her sketches for their up-and-coming clothing line. Malcolm, the ideas man of the dynamic duo, was sceptical at first, commenting that "18-year-olds just aren't going to get it. It isn't rock 'n' roll". He instead suggested to Vivienne that she focus on pirates as an aesthetic, as "pirates are another form of punk".

Malcolm's role in Vivienne's work cannot be understated. He would give focus and topicality to Vivienne's meanderings and had a deep understanding of what would entice the youth. However, this power dynamic within their partnership often led Vivienne to believe her contributions to the brand were lesser, even going as far as saying that she would be nothing without McLaren. Obviously, that statement was far from true.

The new theme for the collection was simple: 'sun, sea, and piracy'. And so, Vivienne Westwood's 'Pirate' collection was created.

The 'Pirate' collection featured garments with exaggerated proportions and intricate detailing. Jackets with oversized lapels, breeches with voluminous cuts, and high, tightly wrapped cravats were all nods to the flamboyant menswear of the French Directory. Vivienne reimagined these historical elements in bold, vivid colours and luxurious fabrics, making them both a tribute to the past and a statement of modernity.

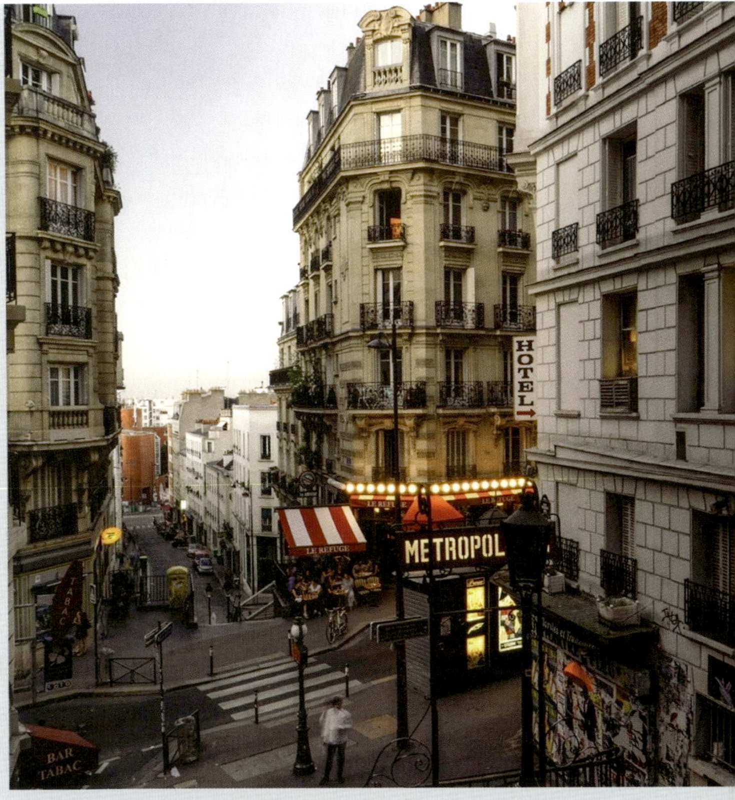

The collection was a departure from the punk styles that had defined her earlier work, introducing a more romantic and whimsical approach that would become a hallmark for her later designs. Despite her shift in style, her clothes remained politically charged. Vivienne's incorporation of historical elements wasn't simply for aesthetic appeal, it was also a form of cultural commentary. Like 'Les Incroyables' and 'Les Merveilleuses', her creations challenged conventional norms and pushed the boundaries of what fashion could be.

Vivienne had previously created the uniform for punks in the 70s, and with her new designs, Vivienne was about to do it all again for the burgeoning movement of the next decade.

YOUNG FOGEY V NEW ROMANTICS

At the beginning of the 80s there were two distinctive aesthetics influencing the culture.

Young Fogeys were a group defined by its members' nostalgic longing for the past and a deep-seated love for tradition. The term 'Young Fogey' was coined by the journalist Alan Watkins in *The Spectator* to describe a new breed of conservative young people who embraced the styles and sensibilities of an earlier time.

Young Fogeys drew their inspiration from the classic English gentleman, and their fashion choices reflected this reverence for the sartorial codes of the past. They favoured tweed jackets, corduroy trousers, brogues, and Oxford shoes—garments typically associated with the British upper class and rural aristocracy.

In an era defined by bold experimentation and the breaking down of old barriers, the Young Fogeys' adherence to tradition stood out as a new form of rebellion.

In stark contrast to the Young Fogeys, the New Romantics represented a completely different approach to fashion and culture in the 1980s. Emerging from the nightclub scene in London, the New Romantics were characterised by their flamboyant, eclectic style, which drew inspiration from a wide range of historical periods, art movements, and pop culture references. If the Young Fogeys looked to the past for guidance, the New Romantics looked to it as a source of endless possibilities for reinvention and fantasy.

The New Romantic movement began in the late 1970s and early 1980s, as a reaction to the austerity and anti-fashion stance of punk. While punk had been about stripping things down to their rawest, most confrontational elements, the New Romantics embraced excess, glamour, and artifice. Their fashion was characterised by dramatic, highly stylised looks that borrowed from a variety of sources: the Victorian era, 18th-century rococo, science fiction, and the world of fantasy.

ABOVE: The Young Fogey Handbook
OPP PAGE: Adam & The Ants performing in the early 80s

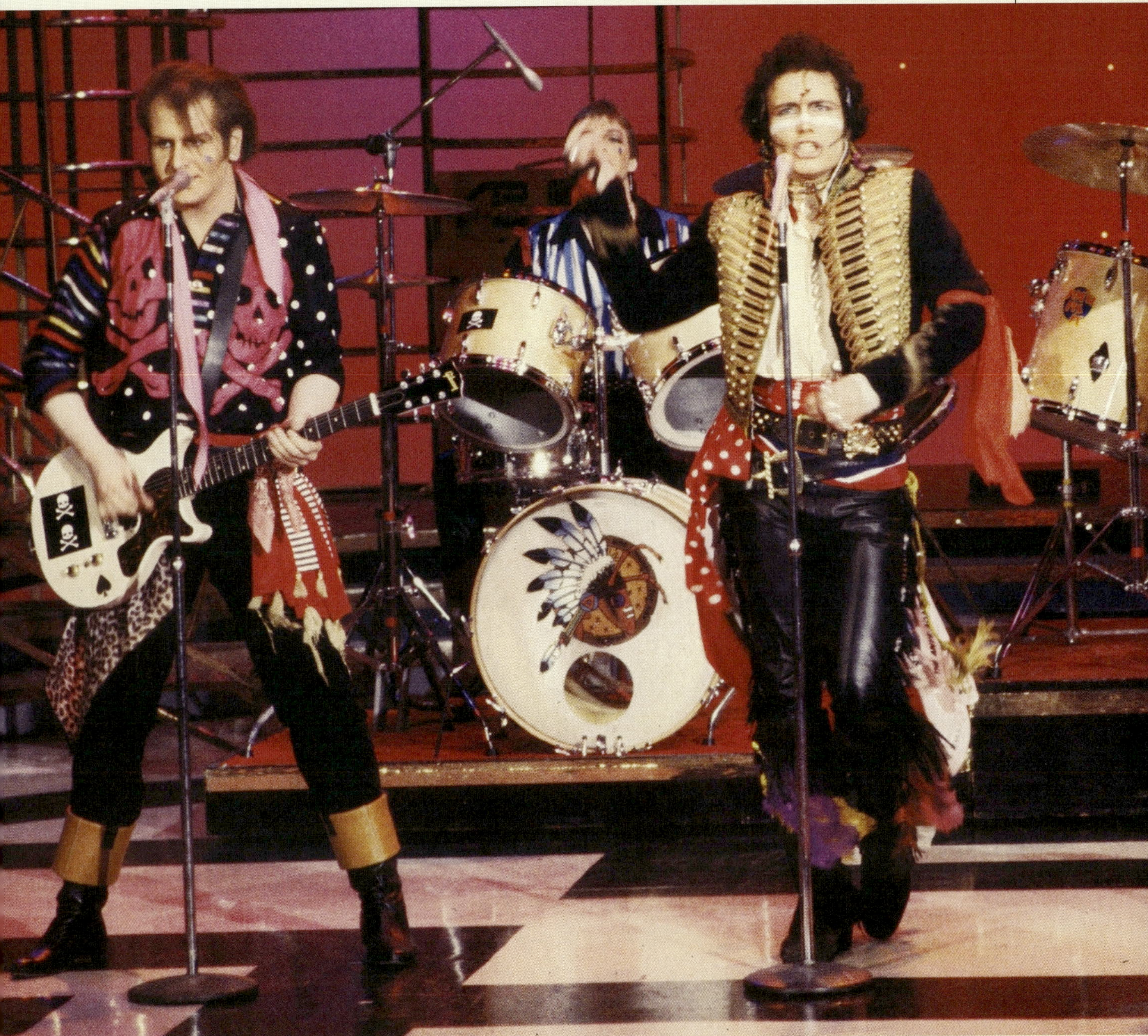

Members of the New Romantic movement, including influential figures like Boy George, Steve Strange, and Adam Ant, were known for their androgynous style, heavy makeup, and elaborate costumes. They played with gender roles and blurred the lines between the masculine and the feminine, the past and the future. Ruffles, velvet, lace, military jackets, and extravagant hats were all part of their sartorial vocabulary, as were the theatrical, almost operatic, levels of self-presentation that defined their look.

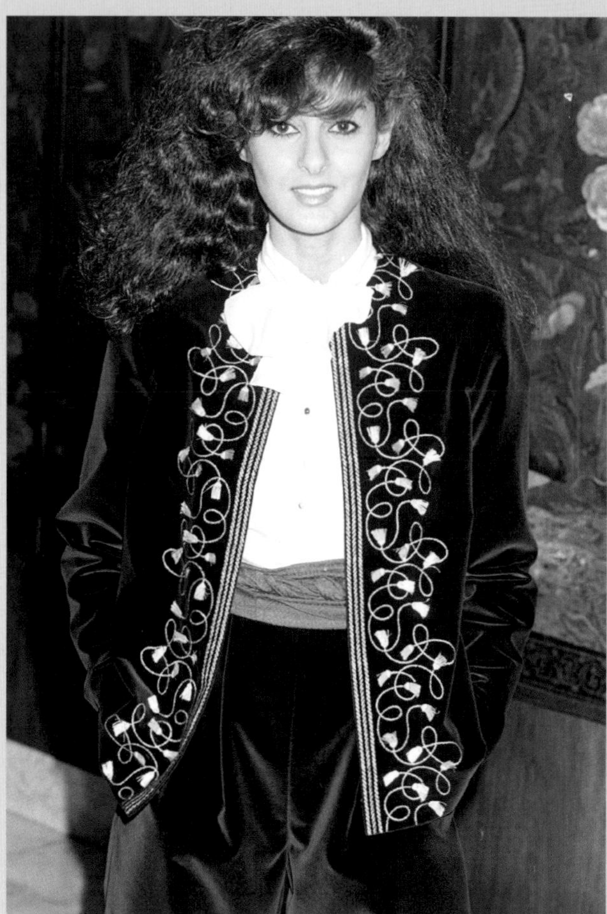

The 'modern pirate' look was first donned by Adam Ant, formerly the lead singer of Bazooka Joe. Adam was a regular customer at 430 King's Road and friend to Malcolm. During one of his visits to the store, Adam shared his desire to find a new image for his band Adam and the Ants, and Vivienne and Malcolm were the perfect people for the job.

McLaren eventually ended up taking over management of the band, and by January of 1980, he had managed to convince all the original band members, except for Adam, to come join his new band Bow Wow Wow.

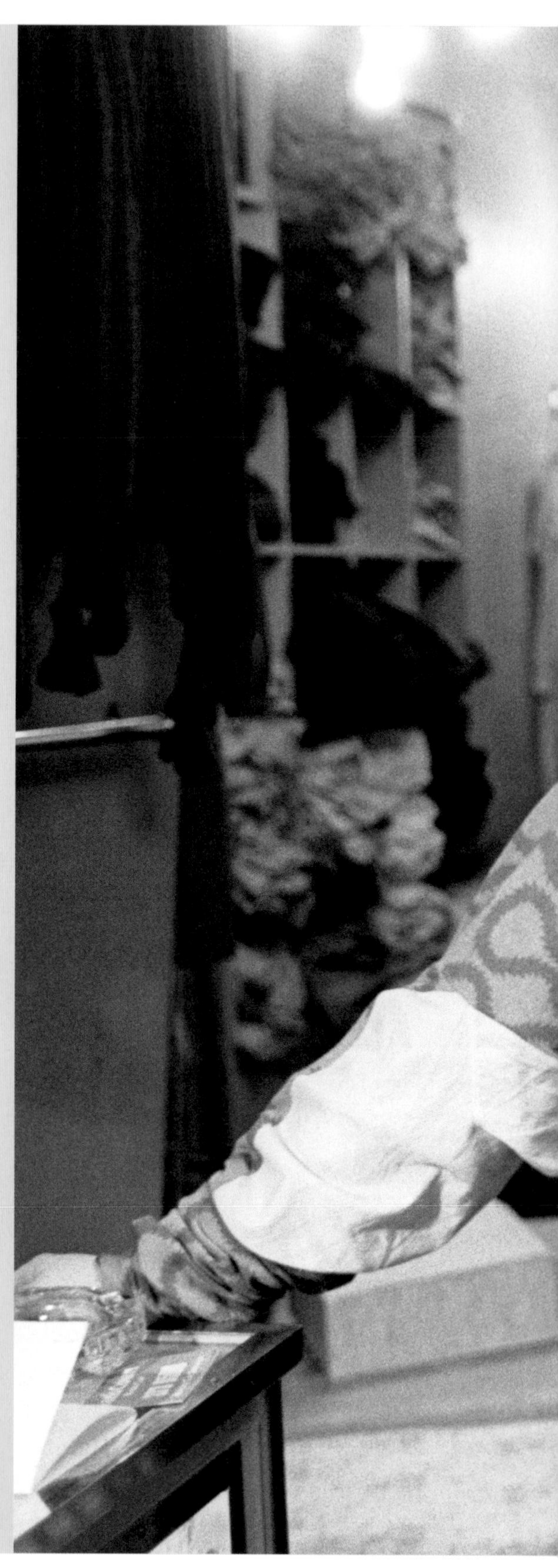

ABOVE: Vivienne Westwood 'Pirate' Collection
OPP PAGE: Jordan (Pamela Rooke) and Steve Severin in Malcolm McLaren and Vivienne Westwood's World's End shop, Kings Road, London, 24 February, 1981

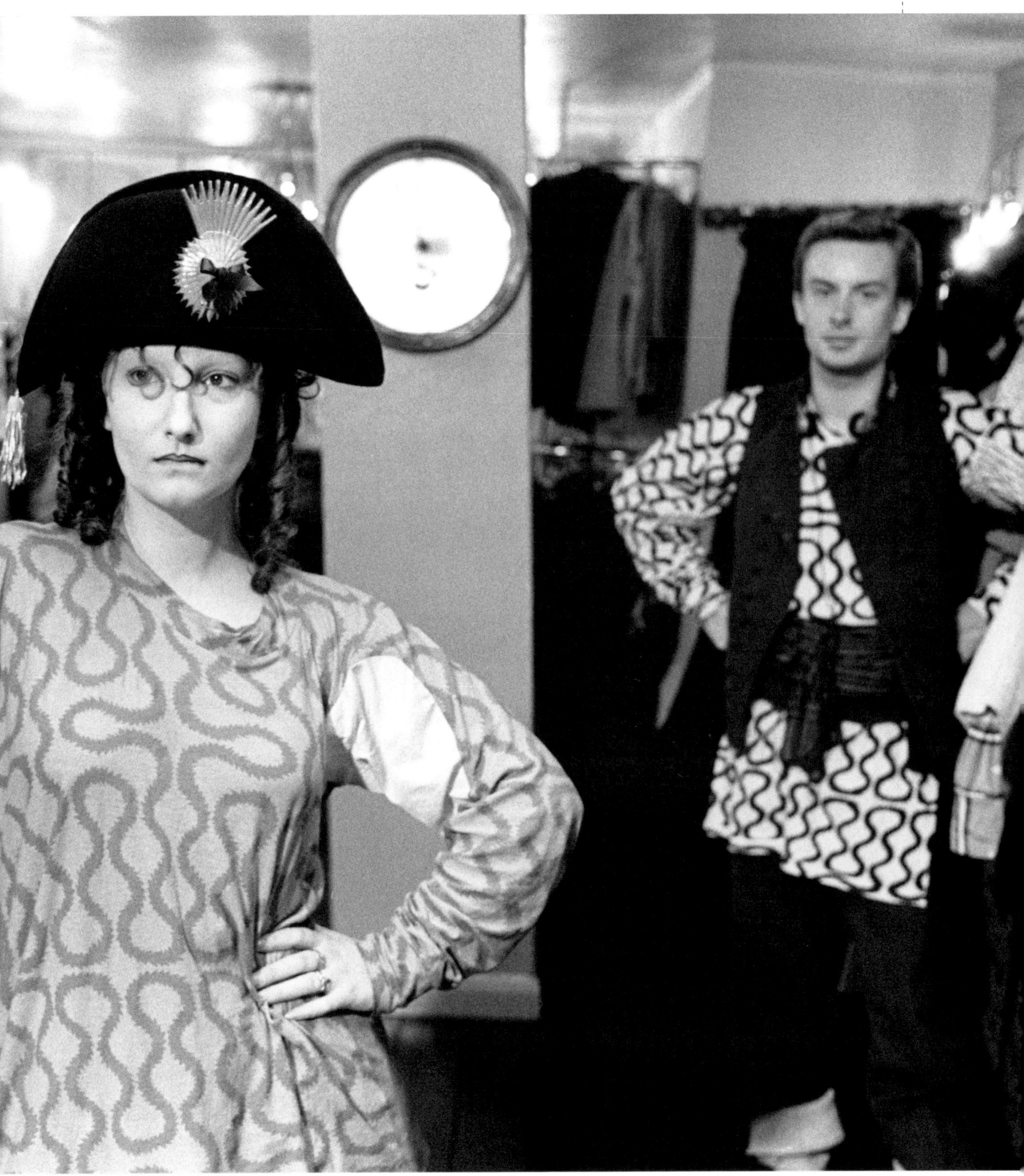

BOW WOW WOW

Bow Wow Wow were an English new wave band, created by former Sex Pistols manager Malcolm McLaren in 1980. Malcolm persuaded musician David Barbarossa (also known as Dave Barbe), guitarist Matthew Ashman, and bassist Leigh Gorman to leave Adam Ant's band and form a new group under McLaren's management. The band embarked on a six-month audition process for a lead singer until talent scout, Dave Fishel, heard 13-year-old Annabella Lwin singing along to the radio at a West Hampstead dry cleaner where she worked, and pushed Malcolm to allow the young girl to audition for the band. Shortly after Lwin joined the group, McLaren added a second lead singer, George Alan O'Dowd, dubbed 'Lieutenant Lush', though his stay was short-lived. O'Dowd soon formed a new band called Culture Club and went on to stardom under the name 'Boy George'.

Bow Wow Wow released their debut EP *Your Cassette Pet* in 1980 and had their first UK top 10 hit with 'Go Wild in the Country' in 1982. The band's music was characterised by a danceable new wave sound that drew on a Burundi beat provided by Dave Barbarossa on drums, as well as the subversive, suggestive, and sometimes exuberant lyrics sung and chanted by their teenage lead vocalist.

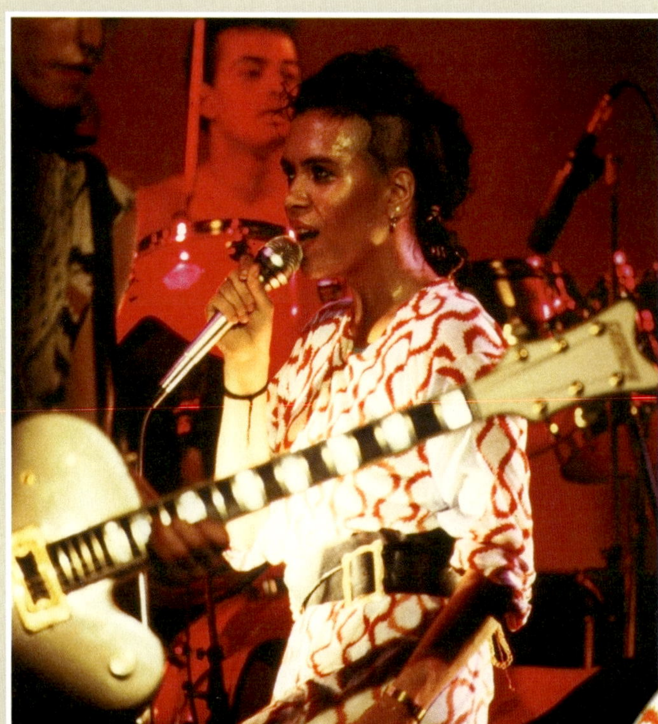

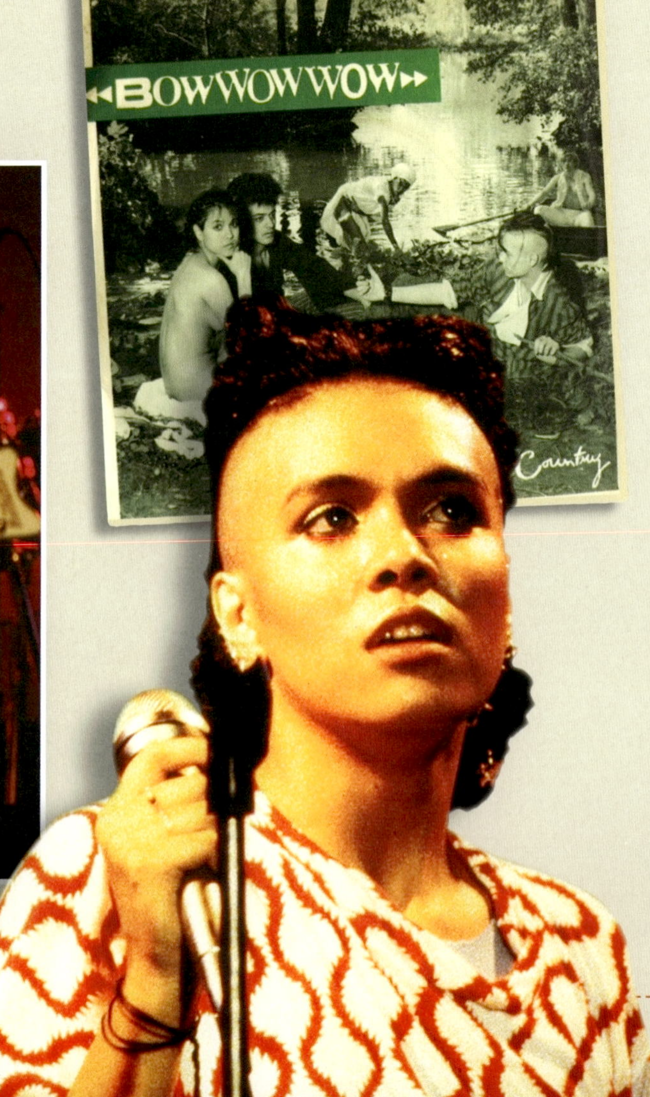

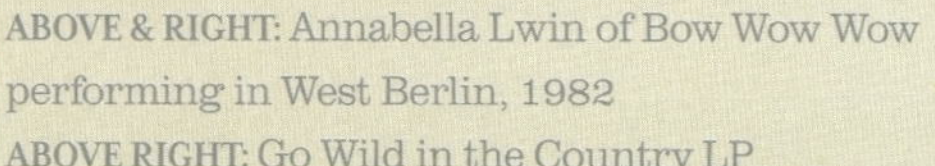

ABOVE & RIGHT: Annabella Lwin of Bow Wow Wow performing in West Berlin, 1982
ABOVE RIGHT: Go Wild in the Country LP

Just as the Sex Pistols dressed in Seditionaries clothes promoting the punk fashion, Bow Wow Wow promoted the 'Pirate' look, an amalgamation of pirate costumes throughout history and decorative details borrowed from the Apache Indians. The colours of the clothes were a vivid palette of African Gold Coast colours including saffron, chrome yellow, orange, vermilion, and lapis lazuli. The pirate look showcased one of the most distinctive aspects of Vivienne's designs, which is the extensive research she does before starting a project. Vivienne's obsession with the past made her the first modern day designer to adopt the exact construction and cut of historical dress and turn them into her own contemporary patterns.

The link between music and clothing remained an intrinsic part of Vivienne and Malcolm's brand DNA.

McLaren, the opportunist, decided to further capitalise on the theme of his fashion label to promote his own music whilst simultaneously undermining the domination of the recording industry giants. He did so by using pirate radios.

Since the invention of Sony's Walkman in 1979, Malcolm was quick to grasp the potential of the product. He formulated a plan to defy copyright laws by encouraging young people to record his hits from the radio. In July 1980, Bow Wow Wow released their single 'C30 C60 C90, Go!' in which the lyrics promoted home taping. Even the title of the song referred to the amount of recording time on blank cassettes. This clever marketing strategy created a way of life to go with Vivienne's designs, making their 'Pirate' collection one of the most identifiable fashion lines to date.

Although Vivienne and Malcolm's professional relationship would continue to flourish for another few years, it was around this time where their romantic entanglement started to falter. In response to her relationship breakdown, Vivienne adopted a new, softer look. She traded in her bleached blonde pixie cut for bright ginger plaits and sported a fresh, makeup-free face.

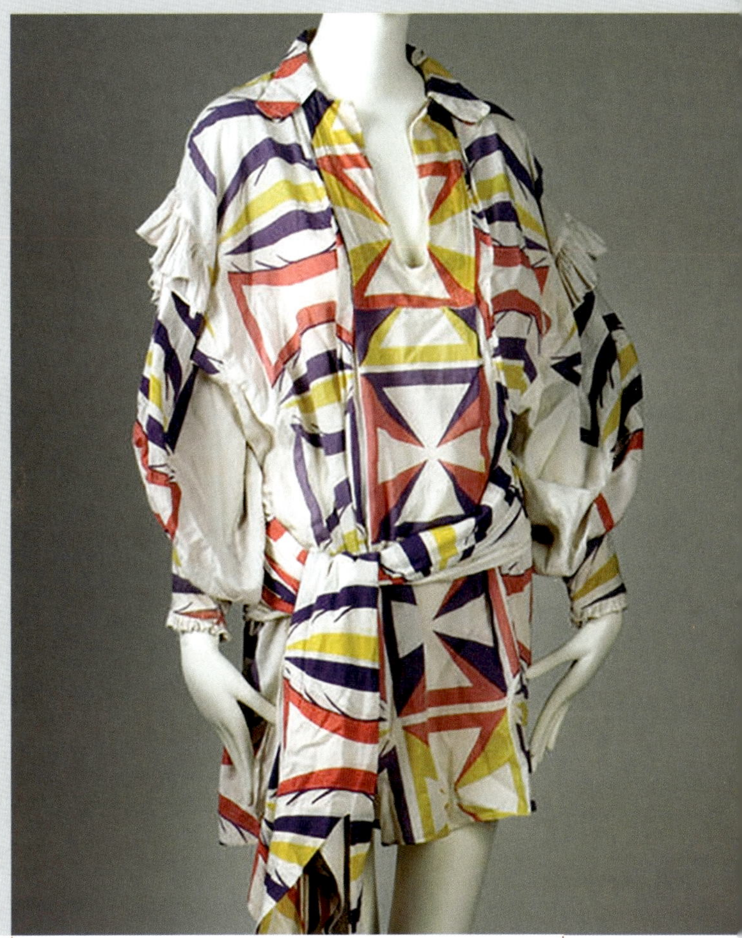

ABOVE: 1981 Vivienne Westwood and Malcolm McLaren dress and sash from the 'Pirate' collection

PIRATES AND SAVAGES

1981-1982

"In history, people dressed much better than we do today."
Vivienne Westwood

The groundbreaking 'Pirate' collection was both a critical and commercial success, cementing Vivienne's spot as one of Britain's up-and-coming designers. What should have been a period of joy and elation in the Westwood-McLaren household, was instead a time marred by fighting and deep-seated pain. Malcolm finally left Vivienne and Nightingale Street, moving in with his new girlfriend, a young, emerging German designer named Andrea Linz. It was their differences in ideologies that ultimately broke the couple apart. Vivienne and Malcolm would continue to work together for another few years as business partners, but this would be the last time the pair would ever live together again.

In the midst of this emotionally intense change, Vivienne immediately got back to work, pouring all of her energy into her creations. Up until then, Vivienne had only released her collections in two or three-year

RIGHT: Vivienne Westwood at her shop on the King's Road, London, 1981

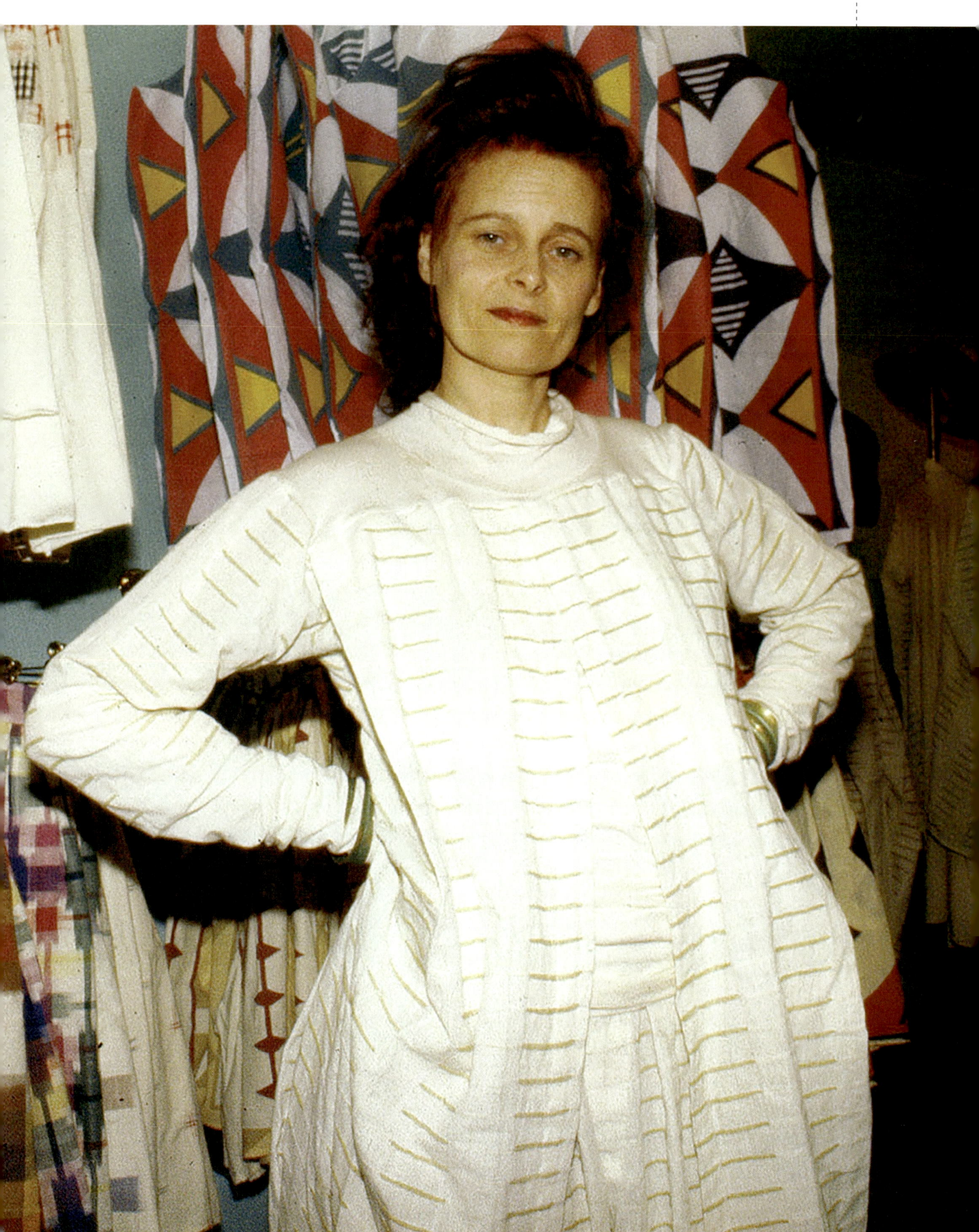

cycles, but now, she was committed to releasing her designs every six months. Over the next year and a half, Vivienne would release three fashion collections including 'Savage', 'Buffalo', and 'Punkature'.

THE 'SAVAGE' COLLECTION (SPRING/SUMMER 1982)

Following the success of the 'Pirate' collection, Vivienne continued to explore new themes and cultural references to incorporate in her designs. The 'Savage' collection for Spring/Summer 1982, shown for the first time at Olympia in 1981, was a bold statement characterised by its eclectic mix of references, from indigenous cultures to historical garments and modern street style.

Vivienne's designs, as she describes them, represented 'primitive' fashion and featured a range of different materials and textures, from animal prints and faux fur to shredded fabrics and rough-hewn edges. The silhouettes were deliberately asymmetrical, with garments often appearing deconstructed or unfinished, giving the clothes a raw and wild feeling. These designs were a far cry from the polished, tailored looks that dominated mainstream fashion at the time and instead embraced an aesthetic of controlled chaos.

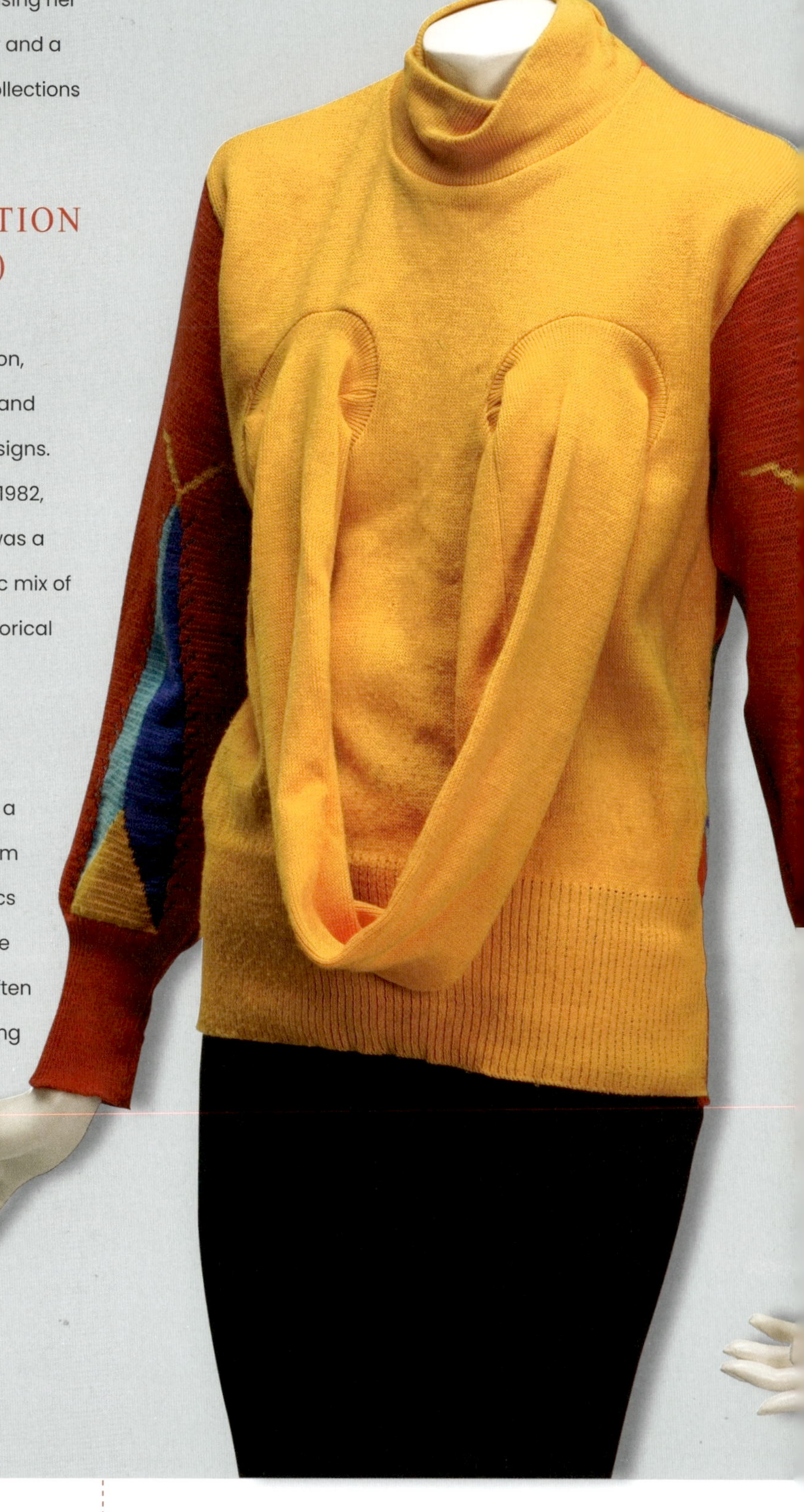

One of the key elements of the 'Savage' collection was the use of unconventional accessories, such as oversized belts, tribal-inspired jewellery, and headpieces that evoked a sense of nomadic or warrior-like identity. The colour palette was earthy and muted, with browns, beiges, and dark greens dominating the collection, further highlighting the connection to nature and the 'primitive'.

Malcolm added his own touch to the collection with the addition of three neon 'go faster' stripes, inspired by the fashionable sportswear brand, Adidas. He also infused his love of art into the designs. During the fashion show, a few of the models set off down the catwalk wearing togas which they opened to reveal copies of Matisse's cut-outs, Picasso's 'Guernica', and Andy Warhol's 'Campbell Soup Can', all of which were McLaren's favourite paintings.

Vivienne's use of tribal and indigenous motifs raised questions about the ethics of borrowing from non-Western cultures, but it also pushed the boundaries of what fashion could be, encouraging designers and consumers alike to rethink their relationship with clothing and identity.

THE 'BUFFALO' COLLECTION (AUTUMN/ WINTER 1982–83)

Vivienne Westwood's Autumn/Winter 1982–83 collection, often referred to as the 'Buffalo Girls'

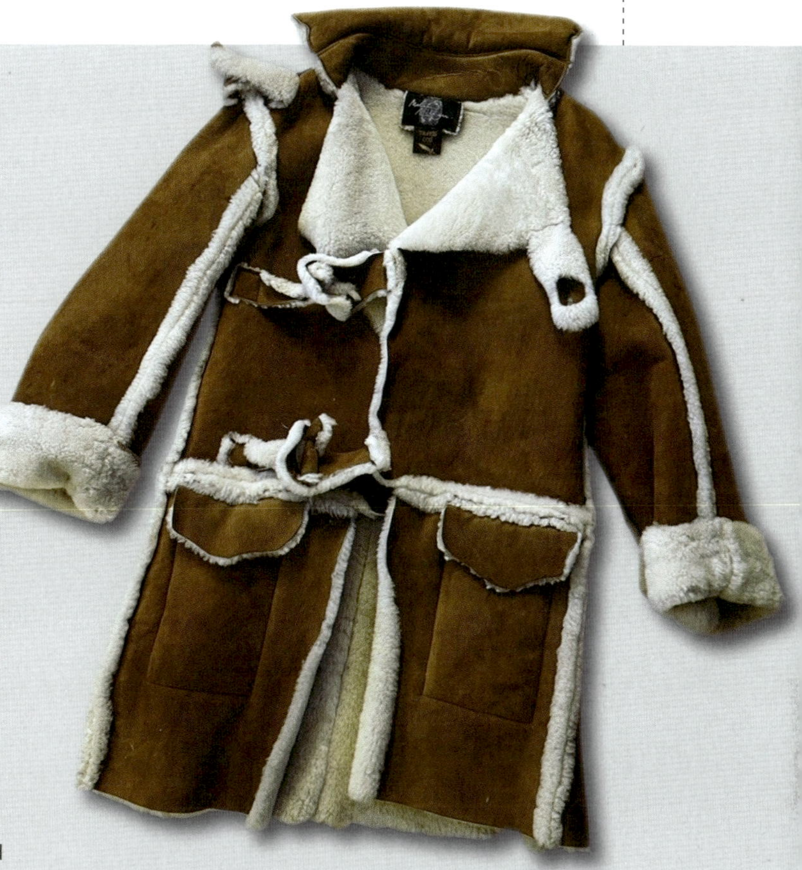

collection, builds upon the themes of 'Savage' and draws inspiration from a variety of different sources. This collection seamlessly integrates elements of American Western wear, hip-hop culture, and traditional British working-class attire. Continuing in the tradition of Vivienne and Malcolm's business model, the designs from the 'Buffalo' collection were directly inspired by the music scene, in particular, Malcolm's latest musical release 'Buffalo Gals'.

The release of 'Buffalo Gals' played a significant role in shaping the aesthetic and cultural identity of Vivienne's designs. The fusion of hip-hop culture and avant-garde fashion in the 'Buffalo' collection is a perfect example of how music and fashion can shape one another, creating a look and sound that are inseparable.

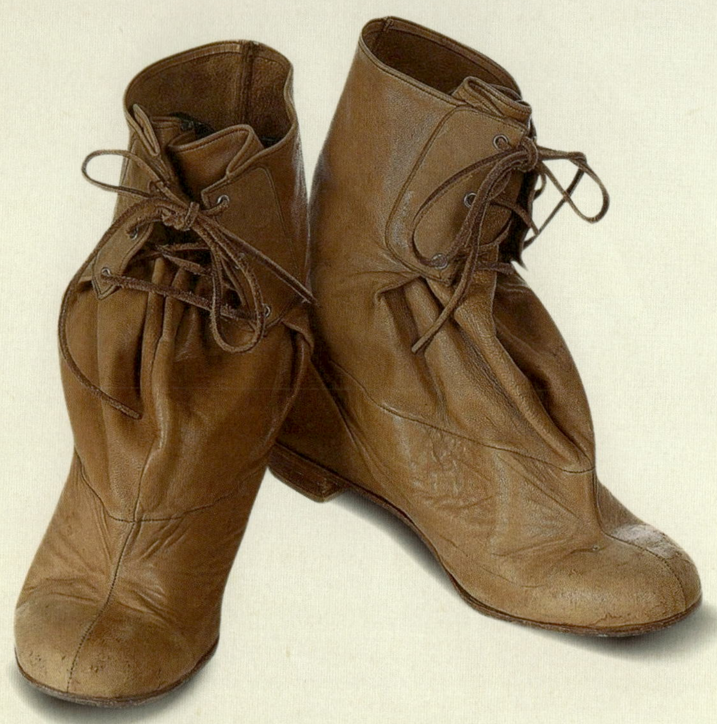

BUFFALO GALS

Released in 1982, 'Buffalo Gals' was McLaren's bold foray into the world of hip-hop, a music genre that was still in its infancy in the UK, but rapidly growing in the United States.

The title 'Buffalo Gals' refers to an old American frontier song of the same name, published in 1844 by the minstrel John Hodges. The song was widely popular throughout the United States and was frequently altered to suit local audiences: 'New York Gals' in New York City, 'Boston Gals' in Boston, or 'Alabama Girls' in Alabama.

Malcolm's track creatively mixes elements of traditional square dancing, with the beats and the scratching techniques of hip-hop DJs, creating an interesting and provocative sound.

Twenty years later, rapper Eminem would sample the chorus from Malcolm's 'Buffalo Gals' in his hit song 'Without Me'.

The music video for 'Buffalo Gals' introduced UK audiences to hip-hop culture, featuring breakdancers, DJs, and graffiti artists—subcultures that were central to the burgeoning New York street scene. McLaren, always keen on subversive and experimental art, saw hip-hop as a new form of rebellion, much like punk had been just a few years earlier. He saw the potential for crossover between music, fashion, and street culture, which perfectly aligned with the ethos that he and Vivienne had built their careers on.

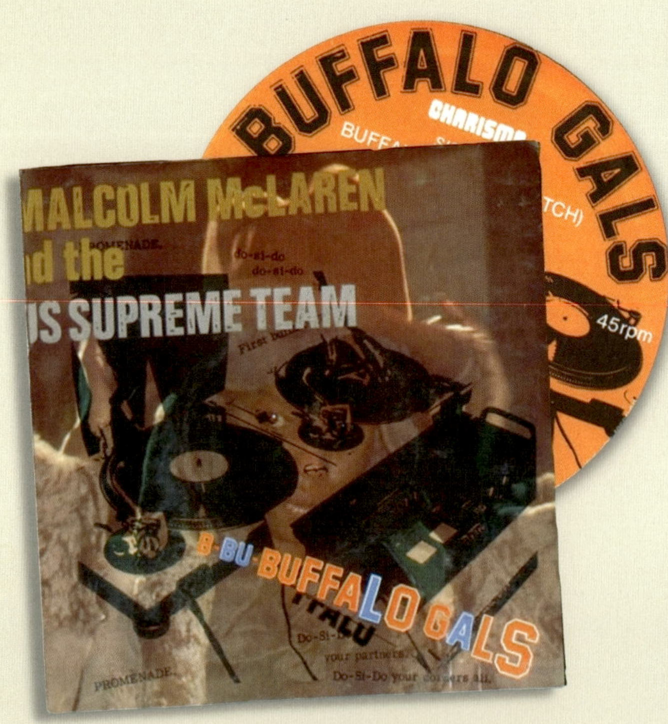

The 'Buffalo' collection was defined by its exaggerated silhouettes and its use of heavy, durable fabrics such as wool, denim, and leather. Nothing was rigid or fitted in this collection. All the clothes were deliberately cut to be oversized, forcing the wearer to shrug the garments up their shoulders or pull them in at the waist, giving the illusion of clothes falling off a body. The casualness of the designs gave the collection an air of wild abandon, something Vivienne found very provocative and deeply seductive. In contrast to the vibrant colours used in the infamous 'Pirate' collection, Vivienne instead opted for a more sombre colour palette for her pieces in 'Buffalo', choosing to dye her clothes in dark earthy tones. She wanted to make life shine through the dullness of her creations.

A revolutionary aspect of the collection was its embrace of androgyny and gender fluidity. Many of the pieces in 'Buffalo' were designed to be worn by either men or women, allowing the wearer to play with how they presented themselves. The clothes were designed to be lived in, moved in, and interacted with, rather than simply displayed, echoing a breakdancer's ability to flow and dance freely in their garments. This rejection of high-fashion standards paralleled McLaren's rejection of mainstream musical structures.

The fluidity of the collection even extended to the way the clothes were styled. Garments were often layered in unconventional ways—dresses worn over trousers, coats slung over multiple layers of shirts, and accessories that mixed masculine and feminine elements.

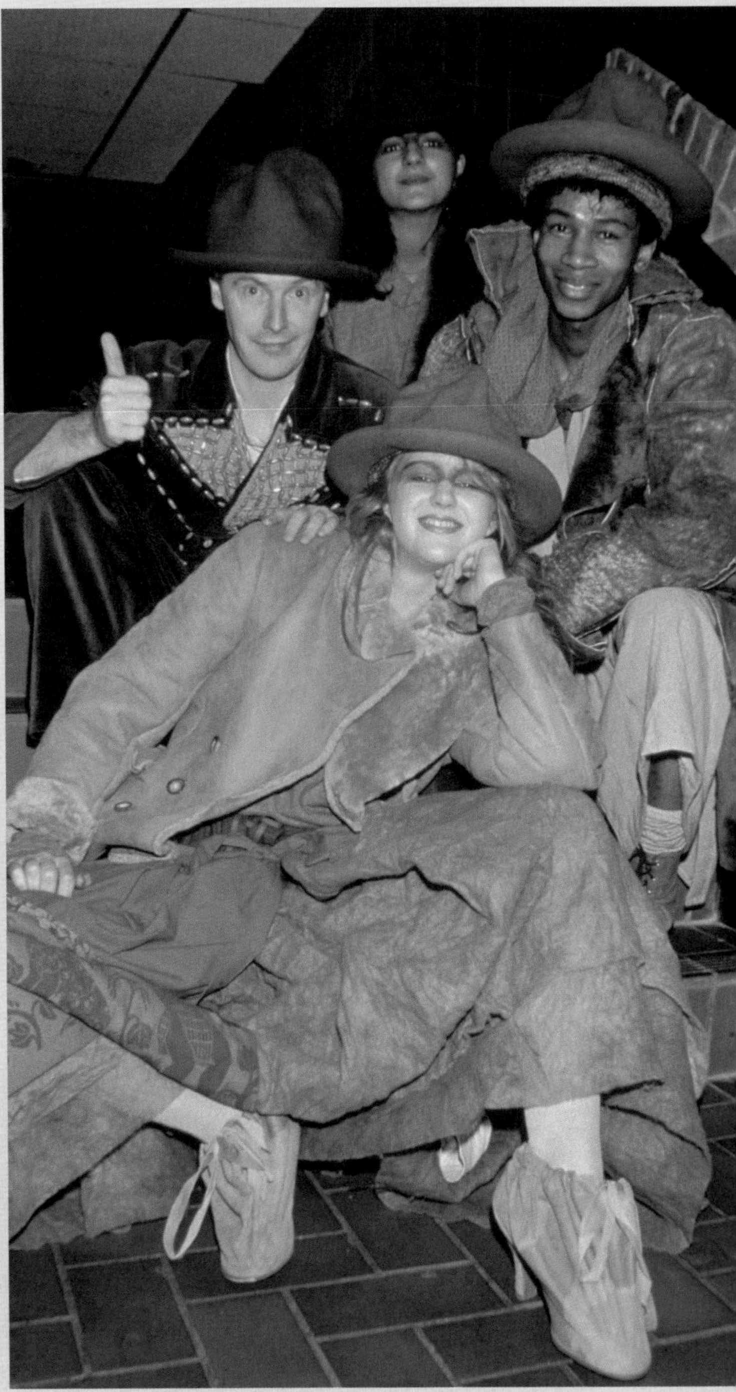

ABOVE: Malcolm McLaren (left), Herbie Mensah (right), and models wearing outfits from Vivienne Westwood's 'Buffalo' collection, 1983

ICONS OF THE COLLECTION

One of the most memorable pieces from the fashion collection was undoubtedly a satin 1950s bra styled on top of a tunic. This unconventional way of wearing a bra, or lingerie in general, made waves in the fashion world. McLaren came up with an array of promotional catchphrases, including the iconic 'underwear as outerwear' to market the garment to mass audiences. Designers like Jean-Paul Gaultier would use this staple of 'Buffalo' to inspire their own fashion collections.

The bra would even go down in pop culture history, when it was worn by Madonna on her 1989 *Blonde Ambition* tour.

Another key piece from Vivienne's line was a large, floppy, wide-brimmed hat, known as the Buffalo hat, which became a signature of the collection. The hat was inspired by American frontier wear and rural traditions, but also took on an urban hip-hop sensibility when paired with the slouchy, oversized pieces in the collection. McLaren is seen sporting the Buffalo hat in the music video for his song 'Buffalo Gals'. Over 30 years later, singer/ songwriter and record producer, Pharrell Williams, was pictured at the 2014 Grammy's wearing an original Vivienne Westwood Buffalo hat he had bought in her 'Worlds End' shop in 2009.

RIGHT: Recording artist Pharrell Williams wearing his Vivienne Westwood Buffalo hat while attending the 56th Grammy Awards in 2014

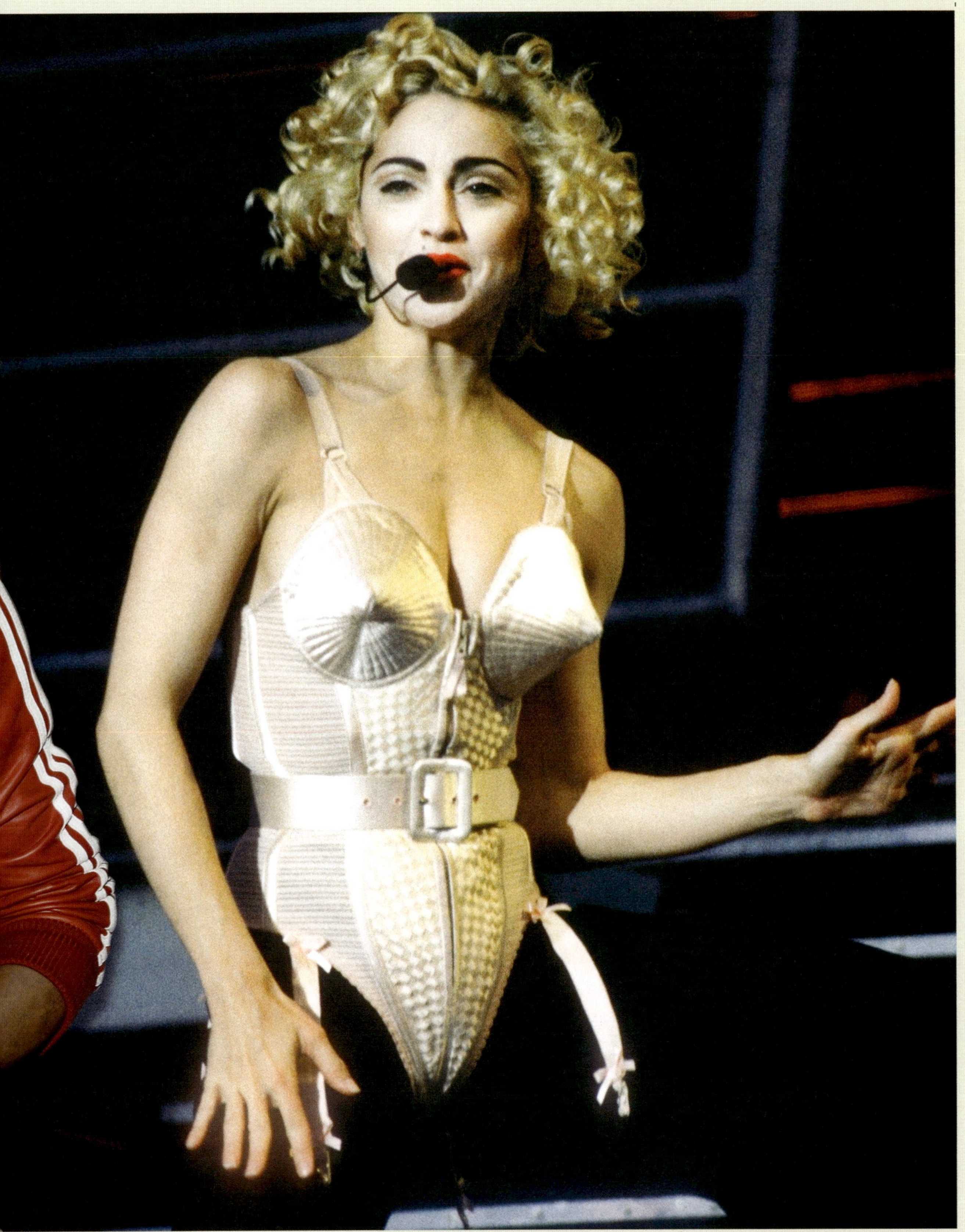

ABOVE: The 'underwear as outerwear' look inspired many designers like Jean Paul Gaultier. Madonna famously wore his iconic conical bra corset on tour in 1990

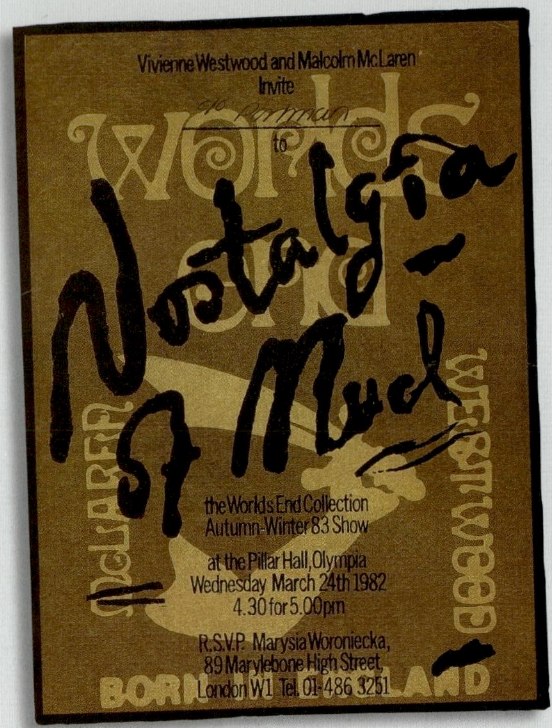

opened with the name 'Nostalgia of Mud', translating literally from the French expression *nostalgie de la boue*.

As Vivienne's designs began to inspire Paris-based designers, McLaren was convinced by designer and friend Jean-Charles de Castelbajac, to show their clothes in Paris. 'Buffalo' was presented in a tearoom in Paris. Despite having to work on a shoestring budget, Vivienne and Malcom's work was received with great excitement by other avant-garde artists, particularly Japanese designer, Issey Miyake. 'Buffalo' also became a high-street success, with many brands coming out with their own recreations of Vivienne's unique designs.

McLaren has conceded, since the release of 'Buffalo', that "Vivienne was contributing to at least 75 percent" of the final collection. By then, Vivienne was desperate to distance herself from her partner in crime and instead stand as a designer in her own right. The success of 'Buffalo' was palpable, and its impact on culture was even greater.

Vivienne and Malcolm's work reached a much wider audience than ever before, and McLaren capitalised on the extra attention to pursue his new interest: Hollywood.

The new 'Buffalo' look required a new Buffalo shop, and in the spring of 1982, McLaren and Vivienne undertook the renovations of their store on St Christopher's Place, off Oxford Street. They brought in a group of Californian architects and gave the vague brief of mud, Peruvian women, and scratch music. The design of the store was so odd that even on its opening day, passersby thought the building was still under construction. In the summer of 1982, the shop

Upon their return to London, Vivienne moved her workshop out of her flat and into an art studio in the heart of Soho. Despite the success of the 'Buffalo' collection, Vivienne struggled financially. Malcolm was spending an increasing amount of time abroad, furthering his music career and dipping his toe in the movie industry. The physical separation between the two only intensified Vivienne's desire to work on her collections alone. During this time, the business partners' relationship turned sour. It all came to a head when, on one occasion, after Vivienne hung

ABOVE: Invitation to the Autumn/Winter 1982 Nostalgia of Mud Show
OPP PAGE: Vivienne moved her workshop to Soho

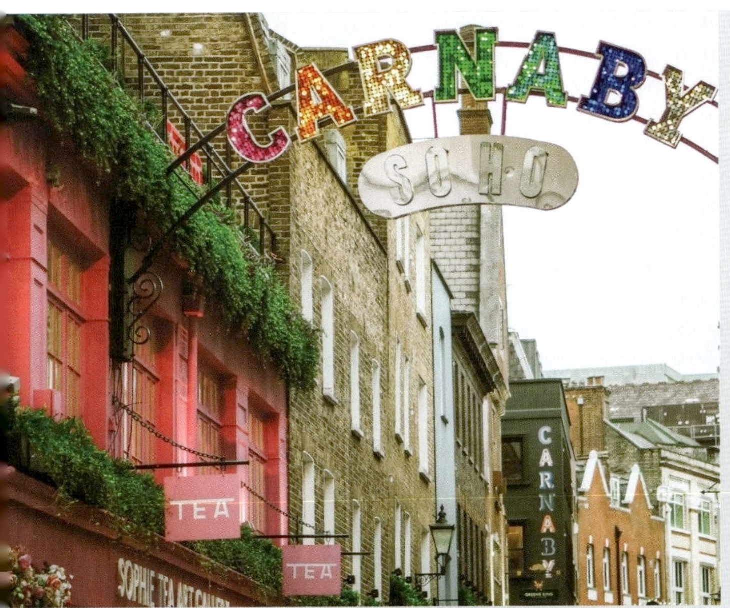

up the phone to Malcolm, she made her way to Malcolm's flat that he shared with his girlfriend and allegedly threw a brick through the window of the young couple's living room.

Vivienne was in a bad way both emotionally and financially, but she needed to get herself together as she prepared for her next clothing collection.

THE 'PUNKATURE' COLLECTION (SPRING/ SUMMER 1983)

As the name suggests, 'Punkature' was a fusion of punk aesthetics and haute couture—Vivienne's radical attempt to blur the lines between anti-establishment street style and the structured world of high fashion. The collection reflected Vivienne's ongoing desire to redefine the boundaries of fashion, while also presenting herself as a 'serious' designer.

'Punkature' was deeply rooted in Vivienne's early work with the punk movement, and adopted the concept of bricolage, a technique borrowed from art and anthropology where disparate elements are combined to create something new. Similarly to the punk ethos of DIY fashion, the designs from 'Punkature' were intentionally rough around the edges, with visible stitching, frayed hems, and mismatched fabrics giving the garments a raw, unfinished quality. The British designer took this idea further by incorporating vintage fabrics and repurposing old materials, which not only made a statement about sustainability but also played into the punk rejection of mass-produced, pristine fashion.

Upon its release, the collection received mixed reviews. On the one hand, critics regarded 'Punkature' as Vivienne's departure from subcultural fashion to becoming a serious player in the fashion world. But on the other hand, many people from the fashion world saw the roughness and disjointedness of her designs as too unrefined for haute couture. The critiques of the clothes intensified when some of Vivienne's models for the fashion show in Paris were rumoured to have collapsed on the runway.

Despite the polarising reviews, Vivienne and McLaren acquired a few wholesale customers, including boutiques in New York, Italy, and Japan. This marked a definite change for the 'World's End' brand, propelling it onto the international stage.

LAST DANCE WITH MALCOLM

1983

"There's a wonderful Chinese proverb. If a horse is yours, he will always come home."
Vivienne Westwood

Since the beginning of their partnership, McLaren had always been the one in charge of handling the business and commercial side of things, but as he was spending more and more time abroad, it was up to Vivienne to manage the admin. Vivienne never shared her partner's shrewd business acumen and so stocktaking procedures and accounting were foreign concepts to her. To make matters worse, Michael Collins, the manager of the World's End shop was completely ravaged by his heroin addiction and would frequently steal clothes and money from the store. By 1983, finances were so stretched that Vivienne struggled to pay for the materials she needed to complete her orders. Despite this lack of money and her evidently turbulent relationship with McLaren, Vivienne's determination never seemed to falter. Indeed, there was no time for Vivienne to sit around, as she was getting ready to release her next clothing line.

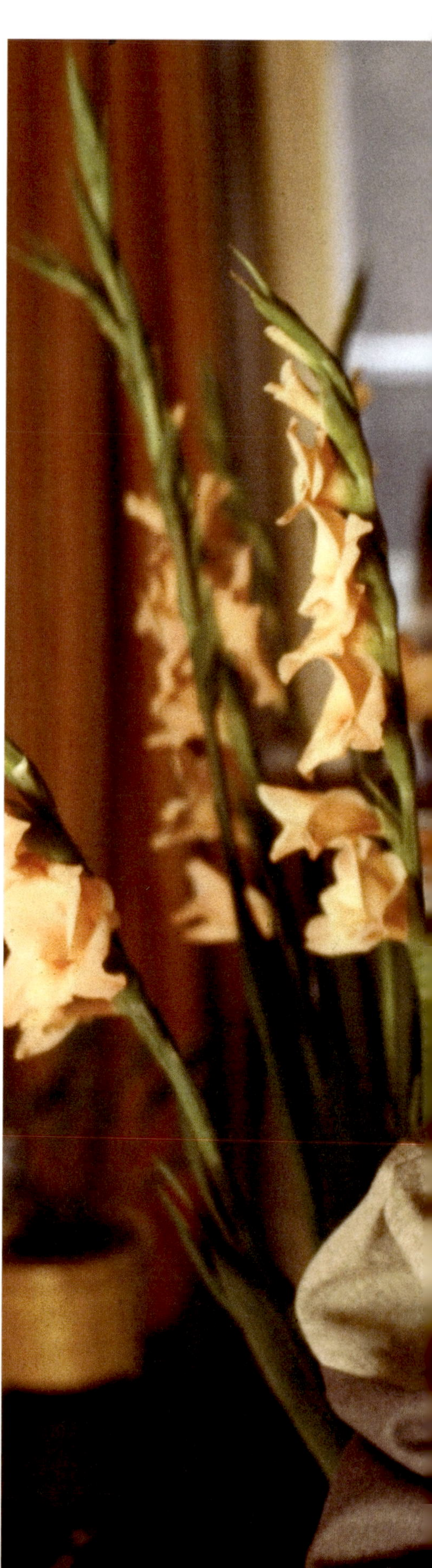

RIGHT: Malcolm McLaren, at home in London, 1983

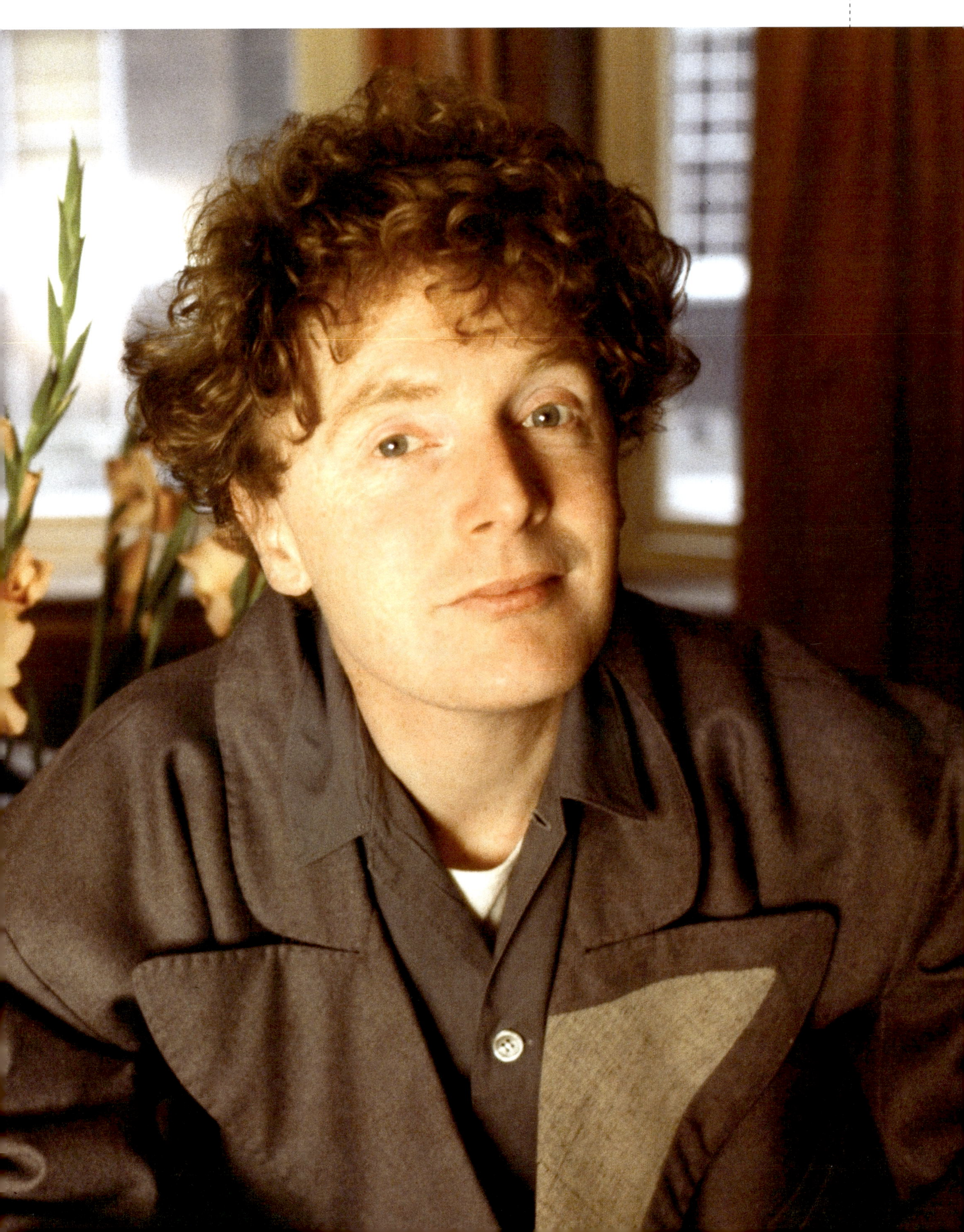

THE 'WITCHES' COLLECTION (AUTUMN/ WINTER 1983–84)

The 'Witches' collection, unveiled for the Autumn/Winter 1983–84 season, stands out as one of Vivienne's most eclectic and artistic collections to date, as well as marking her embrace of graphic art in fashion. This collection also marks Vivienne and Malcolm's last official collaboration for their label World's End, known henceforth as Vivienne's eponymous brand Vivienne Westwood.

Through this collection, Vivienne ventured into the world of mysticism, urban subcultures, and artistic expression, creating a distinctive visual narrative that merged fashion with street art. The influences for 'Witches' were wide, spanning from Haitian voodoo to contemporary pop art, most notably the distinctive, graffiti-inspired work of American artist Keith Haring.

Keith Haring, a rising star in the New York City art scene at the time, provided a major source of inspiration. Haring's bold, cartoon-like drawings and radiating lines were visually striking, easily recognisable, and full of social commentary. His graffiti art deeply resonated with Vivienne's own punk philosophy of challenging the mainstream and giving a voice to the marginalised.

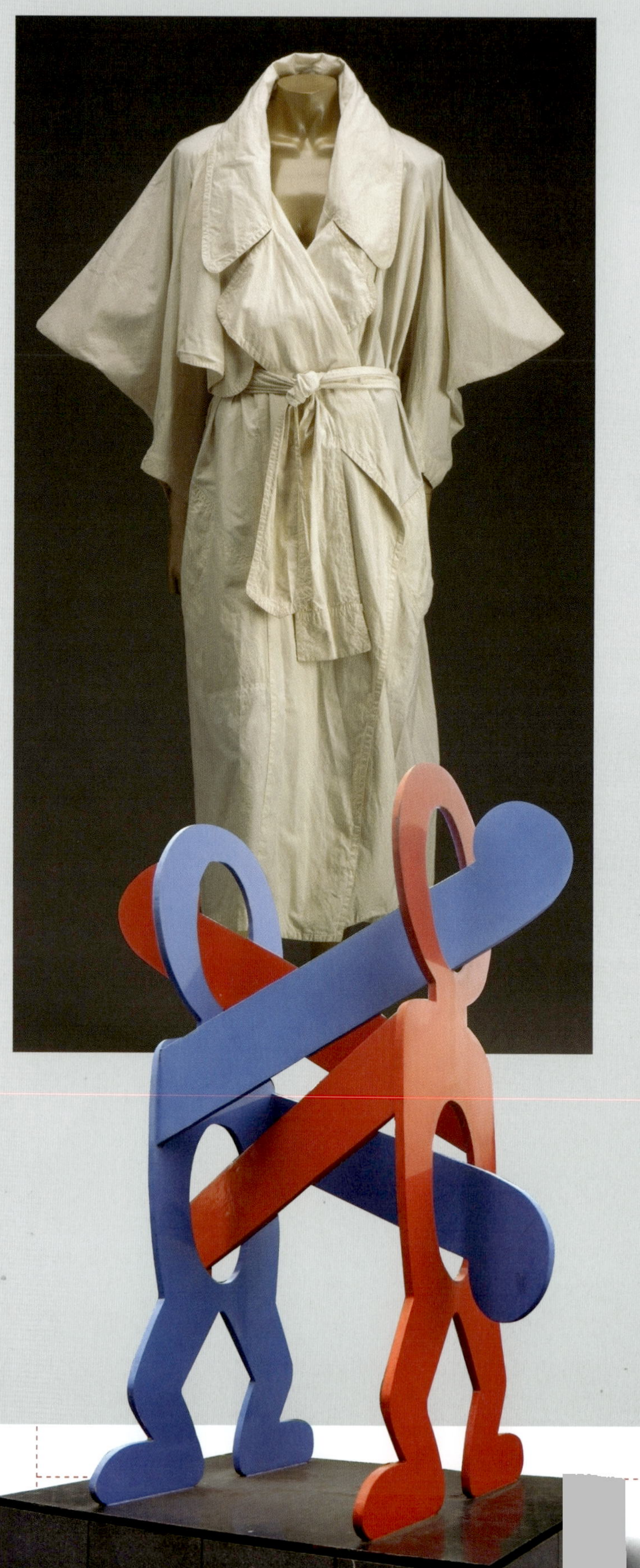

ABOVE: Coat from the Witches collection 1983-84
RIGHT: Haring's The Boxers (1987) sculpture in Berlin, Germany

KEITH HARING

Keith Haring (1958–1990) was an American artist and social activist renowned for his vibrant, graffiti-inspired artwork that combined cartoon-like figures with bold lines and bright colours. Born in Reading, Pennsylvania, and raised in nearby Kutztown, Haring showed an early interest in drawing, heavily influenced by popular culture, especially comic books and cartoons.

In 1978, Haring moved to New York City to attend the School of Visual Arts (SVA), where he was quickly immersed in the city's underground art scene. He began using chalk to create his iconic line drawings on empty advertising panels in subway stations. His graffiti art—featuring recurring motifs such as dancing figures, radiant babies, barking dogs, and UFOs—soon gained widespread attention.

Haring's work was highly accessible and often carried social messages, addressing issues such as AIDS, apartheid, and nuclear disarmament. He created public murals in cities worldwide, including his famed 'Crack Is Wack' mural in Harlem. A committed activist, Haring used his art to advocate for LGBTQ+ rights and AIDS awareness, founding the Keith Haring Foundation in 1989 to support organisations fighting AIDS, and children's programs.

Keith Haring died of complications related to AIDS in 1990 at the age of 31, but his art continues to inspire and influence popular culture and social activism today.

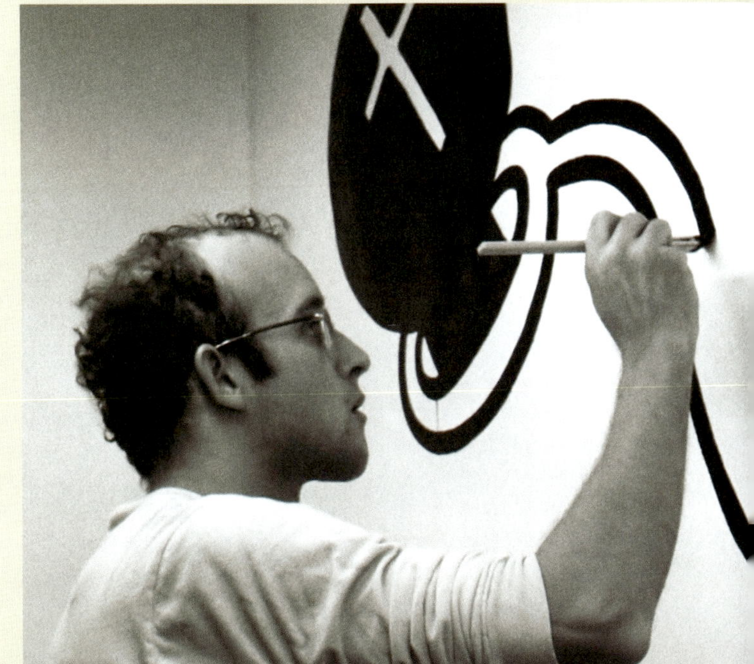

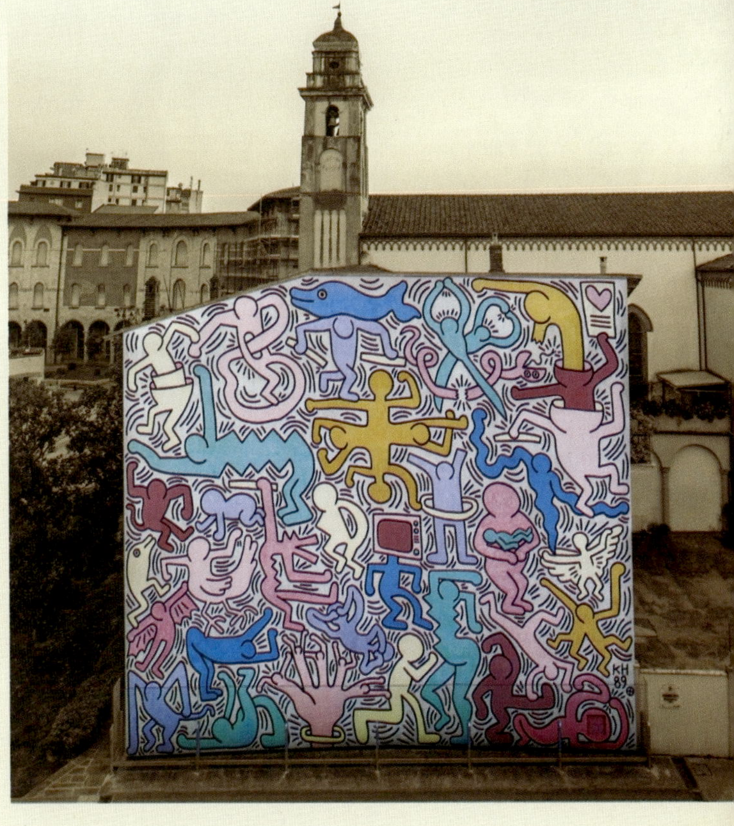

TOP: Haring painting a mural in 1986
ABOVE: Haring's 1989 Tuttomondo mural at the church of Sant' Antonio Abate in Pisa, Italy

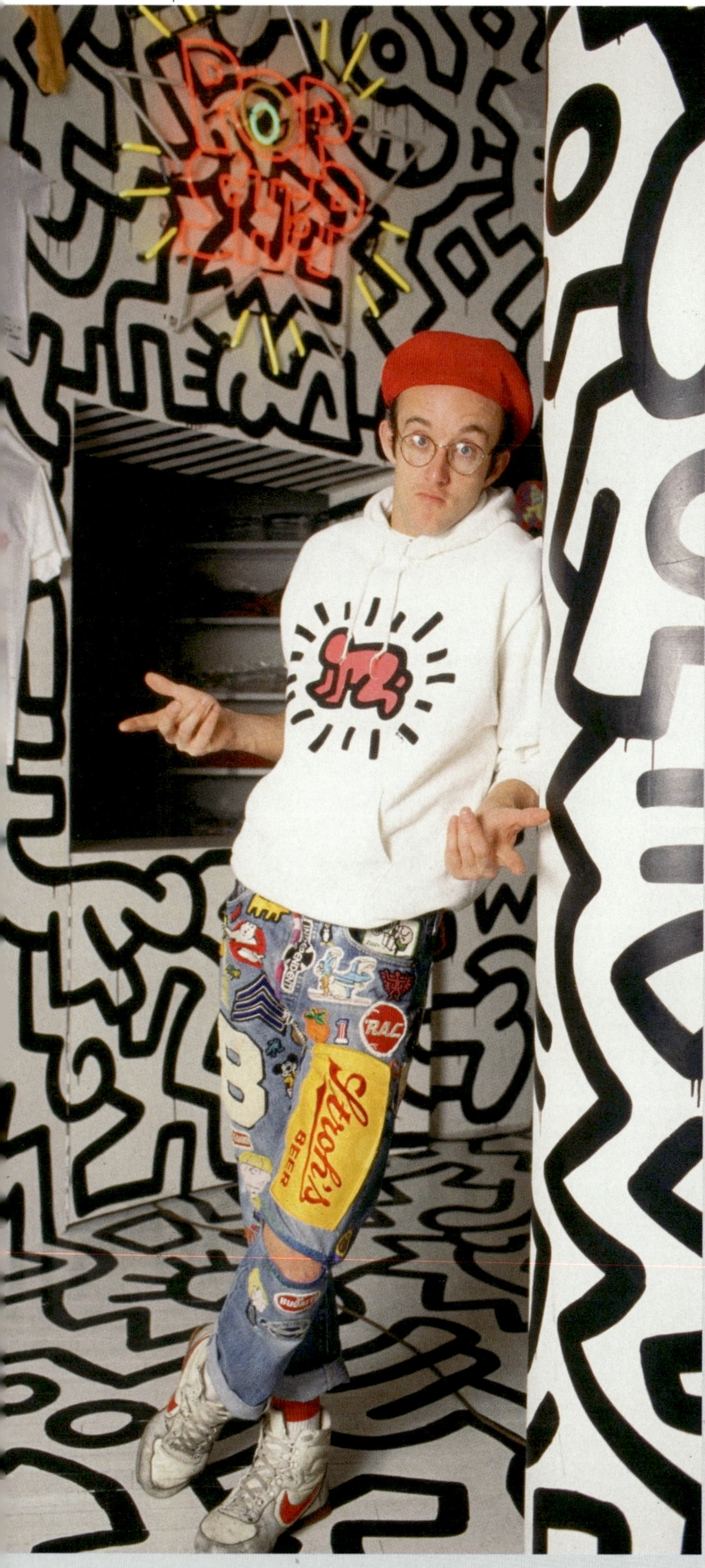

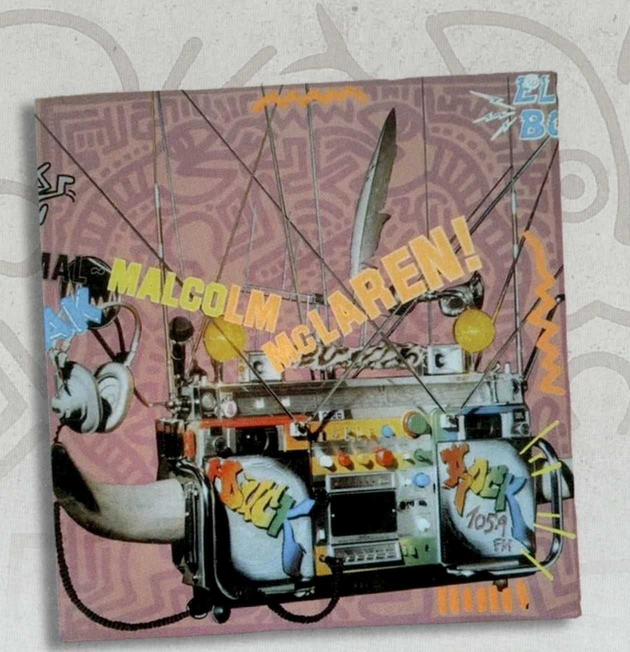

The urban, anarchic energy of Haring's drawings and their playful, almost primitive style fit perfectly into the rebellious and experimental aesthetic Vivienne wanted to capture in 'Witches'.

This wasn't the first time Haring had lent his work to the masterminds behind the World's End label. A few months before the release of 'Witches', Malcolm used Haring's hieroglyphic designs as the backdrop for his newest album cover, titled 'Duck Rock'. Continually inspired by the hip-hop scene happening in the United States, McLaren combined the hip-hop sound with beats from Africa, South America, and the Caribbean to create an unforgettable record.

McLaren's 'Duck Rock' soundtrack accompanied the 'Witches' collection on the catwalk, and was

ABOVE: Keith Haring poses at opening of Pop Shop
ABOVE RIGHT: Album cover for Duck Rock, showcasing Haring's work
OPP PAGE: Vivienne Westwood X Keith Haring knitwear

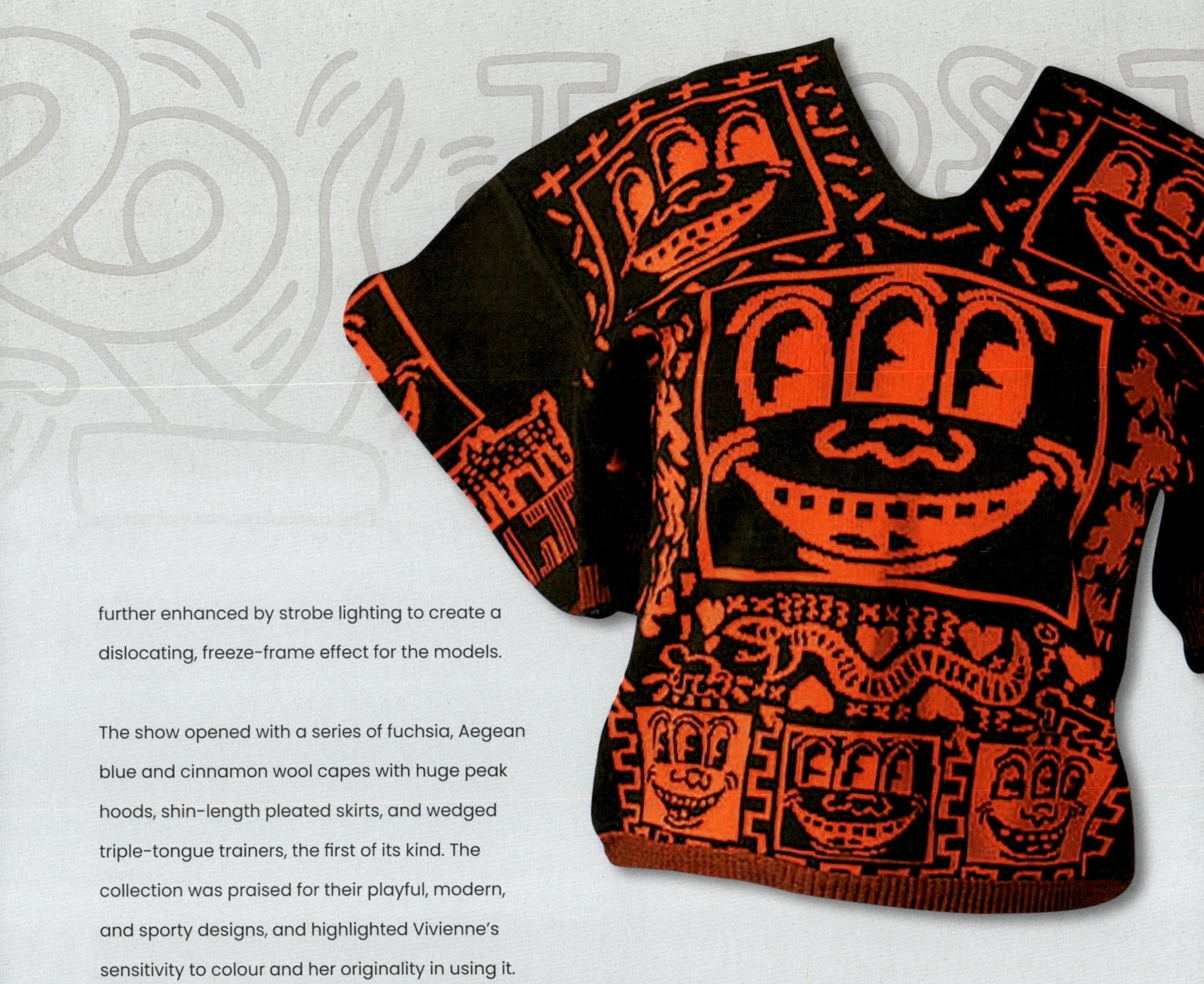

further enhanced by strobe lighting to create a dislocating, freeze-frame effect for the models.

The show opened with a series of fuchsia, Aegean blue and cinnamon wool capes with huge peak hoods, shin-length pleated skirts, and wedged triple-tongue trainers, the first of its kind. The collection was praised for their playful, modern, and sporty designs, and highlighted Vivienne's sensitivity to colour and her originality in using it. The 'Witches' garments captured the attention of big publishers in the fashion world, including *Vogue* magazine. A writer from the famous magazine wrote, "You had to miss Givenchy to see Westwood, but it was worth it".

'Witches' was not only a commercial success, but more importantly, it was a personal success for Vivienne. The collection was almost entirely conceptualised by Vivienne, allowing her to step into her new career as a solo designer.

The void created by Malcolm's departure was initially difficult to fill, but not long after the dissolution of their business partnership, two new men stepped into Vivienne's life.

CARLO D'AMARIO

Following the 'Witches' fashion show in Paris, Vivienne met Carlo D'Amario, a stocky Italian man, five years her junior, and crucially, about to become a future partner in the Vivienne Westwood empire. Despite being a well-known figure in the fashion industry today, his career could've easily taken a different path.

As a teenager, D'Amario was picked by the Italian Communist Party to go to Lumumba University in Moscow, the former Soviet Union's international training centre for party cadres. His family's financial problems cut short his revolutionary career, and on his mother's orders, he returned to Italy after six months with instructions to find a job. He then landed one with Fiorucci. After seven years at the brand, D'Amario set out on his own and earned a living travelling along the hippie trail to Afghanistan, dealing in fabrics and other commodities.

When he first met Vivienne, he was running his own public relations company, Casanova.

Through her partnership with D'Amario, Vivienne was able to transform her annual turnover from a few hundred thousand pounds, into a multimillion-pound luxury brand.

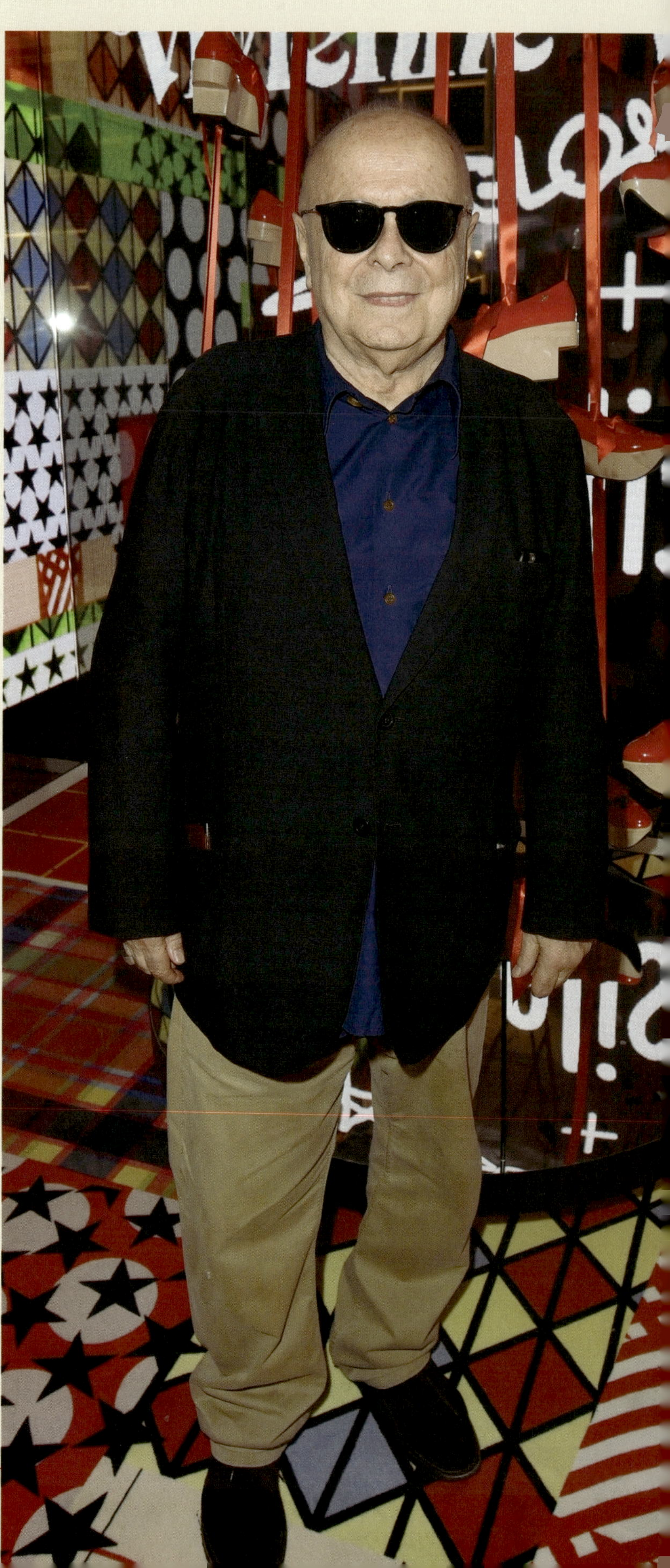

GARY NESS

Gary Ness was a Canadian academic, art historian, and teacher whose intellectual contributions, particularly in the realm of classical history and aesthetics, had a notable impact on Vivienne's evolution as a designer.

His influence on Vivienne's designs was particularly well-documented in the 80s, when historical references and theoretical ideas started to be incorporated into her work. Rather than simply creating clothes for shock value, Vivienne began to embed narrative and meaning into her collections, elevating fashion to a form of cultural commentary.

Following the absence of McLaren, Vivienne needed to find herself somebody to take on that role. Gary offered just that; he would take her to art galleries, show her books, and introduce her to high culture. Vivienne had found her mentor, saying "he took me back from punk to culture".

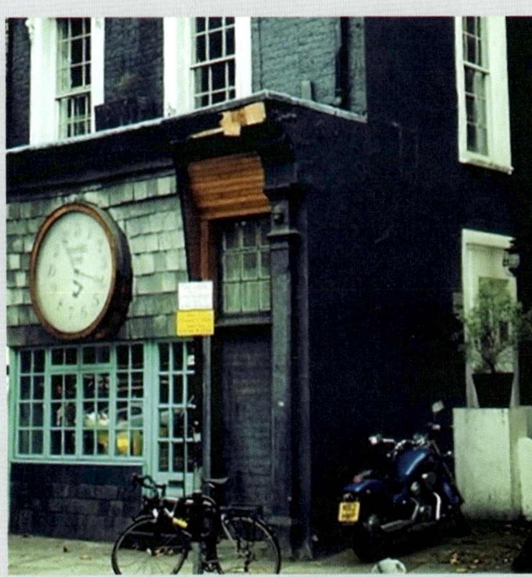

Despite the lasting impact of the World's End label on fashion history, this moment marked the end of nearly two decades of partnership between two of the greatest trendsetters of the 20th century.

D'Amario saw the immense potential in Vivienne and persuaded her that Malcolm's anti-establishment attitude held her back a great deal. Vivienne quickly became enchanted by the Italian, and it wasn't long until the two formed a professional and romantic relationship.

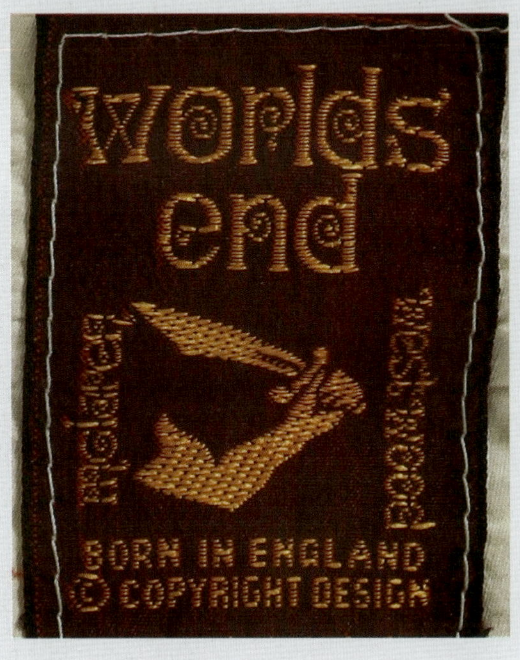

OPP PAGE: Carlo D'Amario attends Melissa X Vivienne Westwood Anglomania: Ride The Rocking Horse in 2016
ABOVE LEFT: World's End, 430 King's Road, London
ABOVE: The World's End label. Still in demand today

"I MAY BE A REBEL, BUT I'M NOT AN OUTSIDER"

1984-1986

"Shoes must have very high heels and platforms to put women's beauty on a pedestal."

Vivienne Westwood

Vivienne's rise from a rebellious outsider in London's underground fashion scene to a globally renowned designer with a multimillion-dollar empire is a story that involves a critical turning point in the 1980s: her partnership with Italy. This relationship helped transform her brand from an avant-garde, niche label into a high-fashion powerhouse.

Italy's post-war economic boom owed much of its success to the country's deep-rooted tradition of luxury craftsmanship and rich artisanal practice. There was an entire generation of designers who deeply believed that well-designed products would outshine the competition.

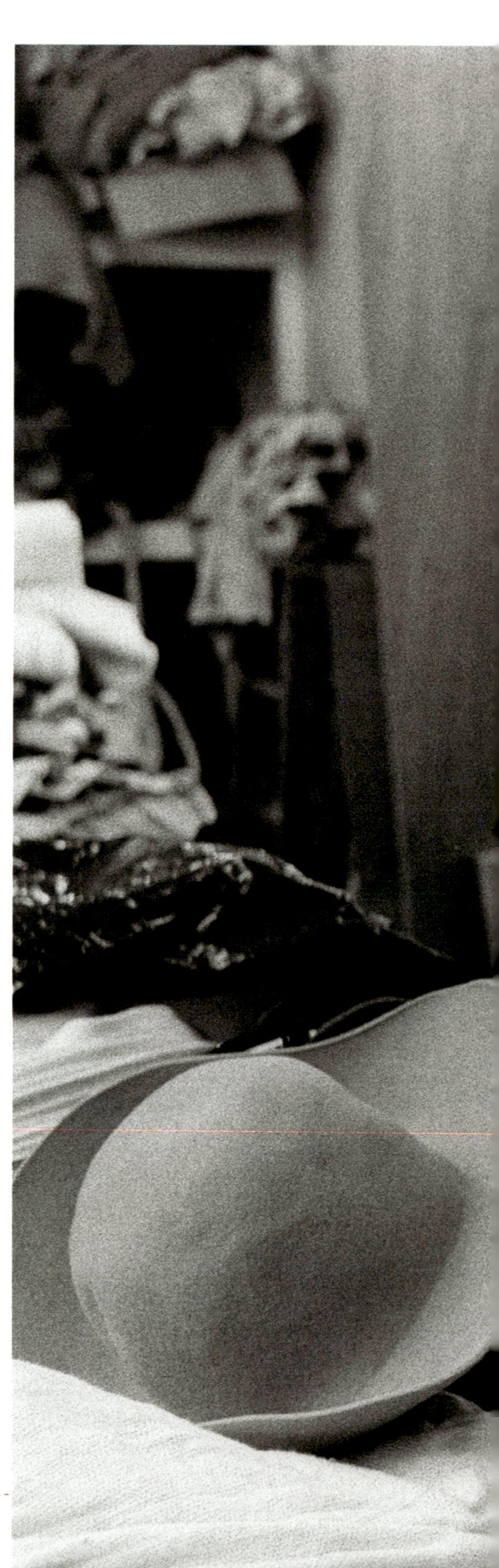

RIGHT: Vivienne Westwood, 1983

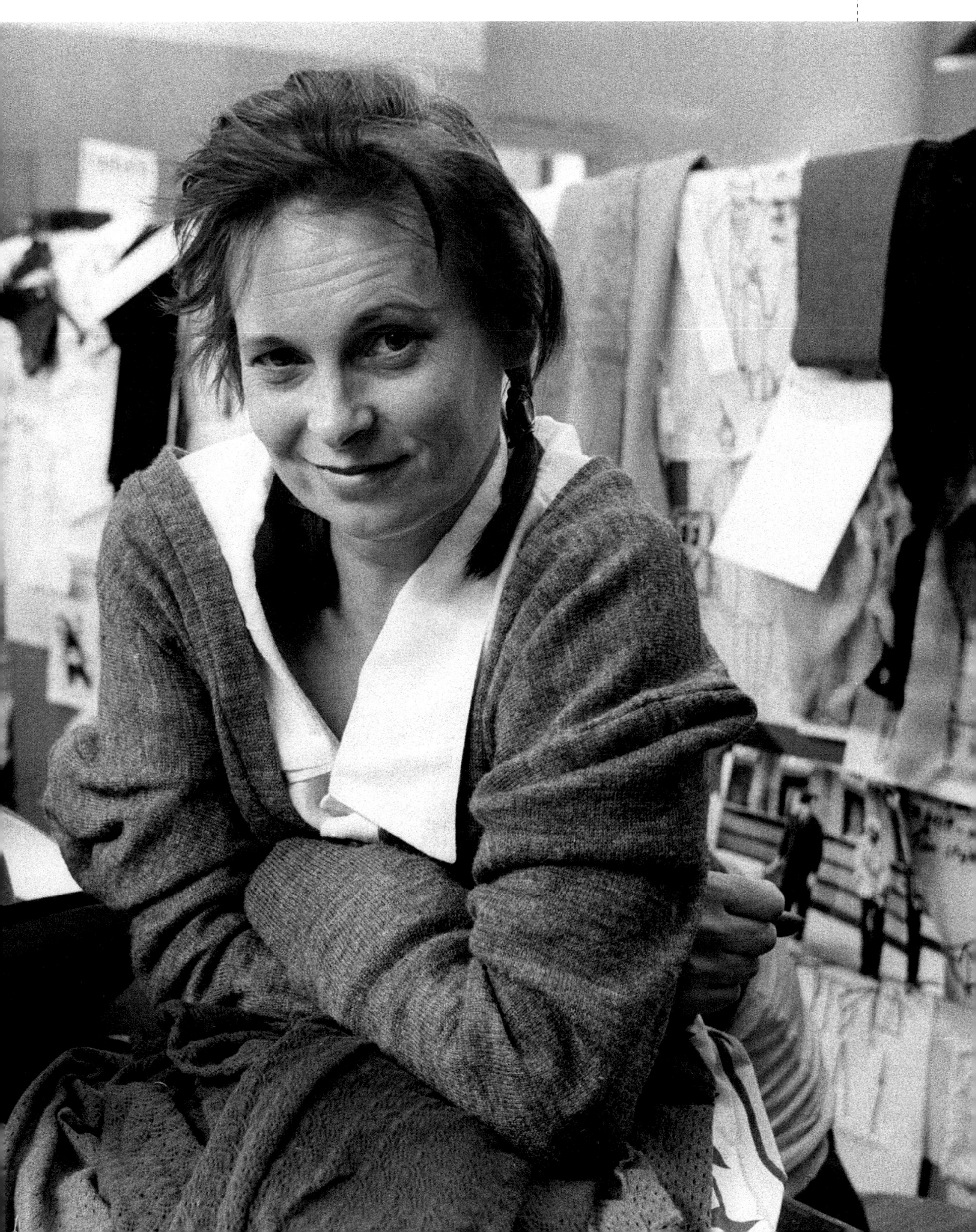

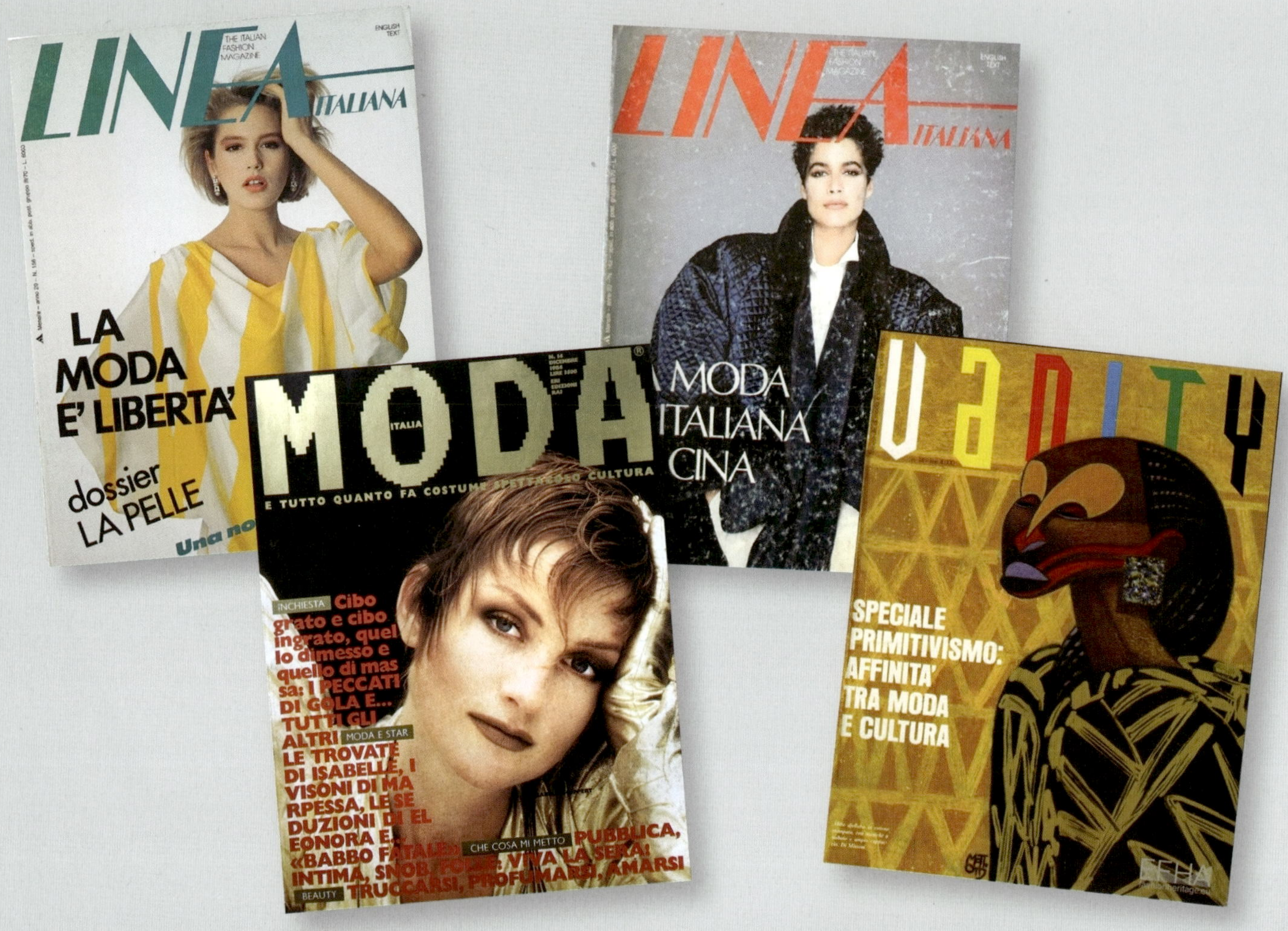

The Italians were now at the forefront of industrial design, a field that had long been dominated by the United States. They became known for their 'sophisticated use of form, detail, and colour', differentiating them from many of their competitors.

D'Amario was instrumental in connecting Vivienne with Italy's fashion industry and helped her navigate the world of international business. Under his guidance, Westwood formed relationships with Italian manufacturers, who began producing Vivienne's designs, bringing a level of precision and luxury to her work. Vivienne would find not only critical acclaim in Italy but, more importantly, financial backing.

Prior to her relocation to Italy, Vivienne and McLaren were designing the most inventive clothes on the market, yet no one in fashion really took any notice. Vivienne no longer wished to be a bystander to fashion, saying "I may be a rebel, but I'm not an outsider". The avant-garde designer needed to bridge the gap between subculture and couture in order to build a sustainable business.

ABOVE: Italian magazine covers from the 1980s
OPP PAGE TOP: Bronze Head of the Greek god Hypnos
OPP PAGE BOTTOM: Hypnos' jacket

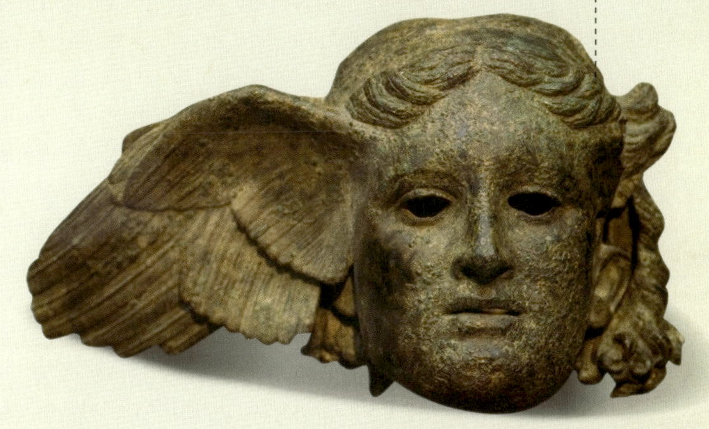

THE 'HYPNOS' COLLECTION (SPRING/SUMMER, 1984)

Vivienne's next collection 'Hypnos', released for the Spring/Summer 1984 season, was her first fashion line designed and produced in Italy. The collection drew its name from Hypnos, the Greek god of sleep, signalling Vivienne's growing fascination with classical mythology and her interest in exploring themes related to ancient cultures.

'Hypnos' was a continuation of her journey into classicism, an interest sparked by her intellectual collaborator, Gary Ness.

Vivienne's newfound love for ancient Greece and Rome is evident in the silhouettes and designs of the collection. She drew inspiration from the draped garments of antiquity, such as the Greek chiton and Roman toga, and translated those historical styles into modern-day fashion. However, her designs were never simple recreations of the past, subverting the classical influences with the use of bold prints, fluorescent accents, and unexpected juxtapositions.

She printed clothes with erotic Greek figures including a Medusa-like character, whose head was decorated with penises rather than snakes, as well as a satyr fornicating with a cloven-hooved beast. A magazine publication dubbed the 'Hypnos' collection as the 'Porno Olympics' collection.

The themes of dreams and sleep also permeated throughout her designs with soft, flowing silhouettes and languid, relaxed shapes, evoking a sense of otherworldliness. At the same time, she invoked the symbolism of Hypnos to comment on the notion of 'awakening' on both philosophical and political levels, nodding to the idea of waking up to societal issues and using fashion as a tool for cultural critique.

Big buyers from America, including Macy's and Bloomingdales, showed great interest in the collection and made big orders. 'Hypnos' was a perfect combination of both theatrical and wearable garments.

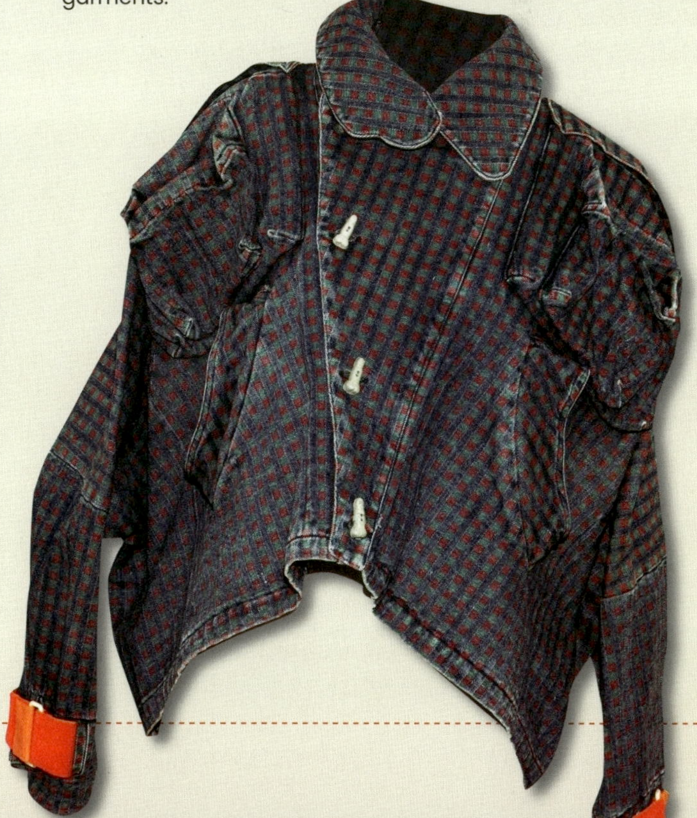

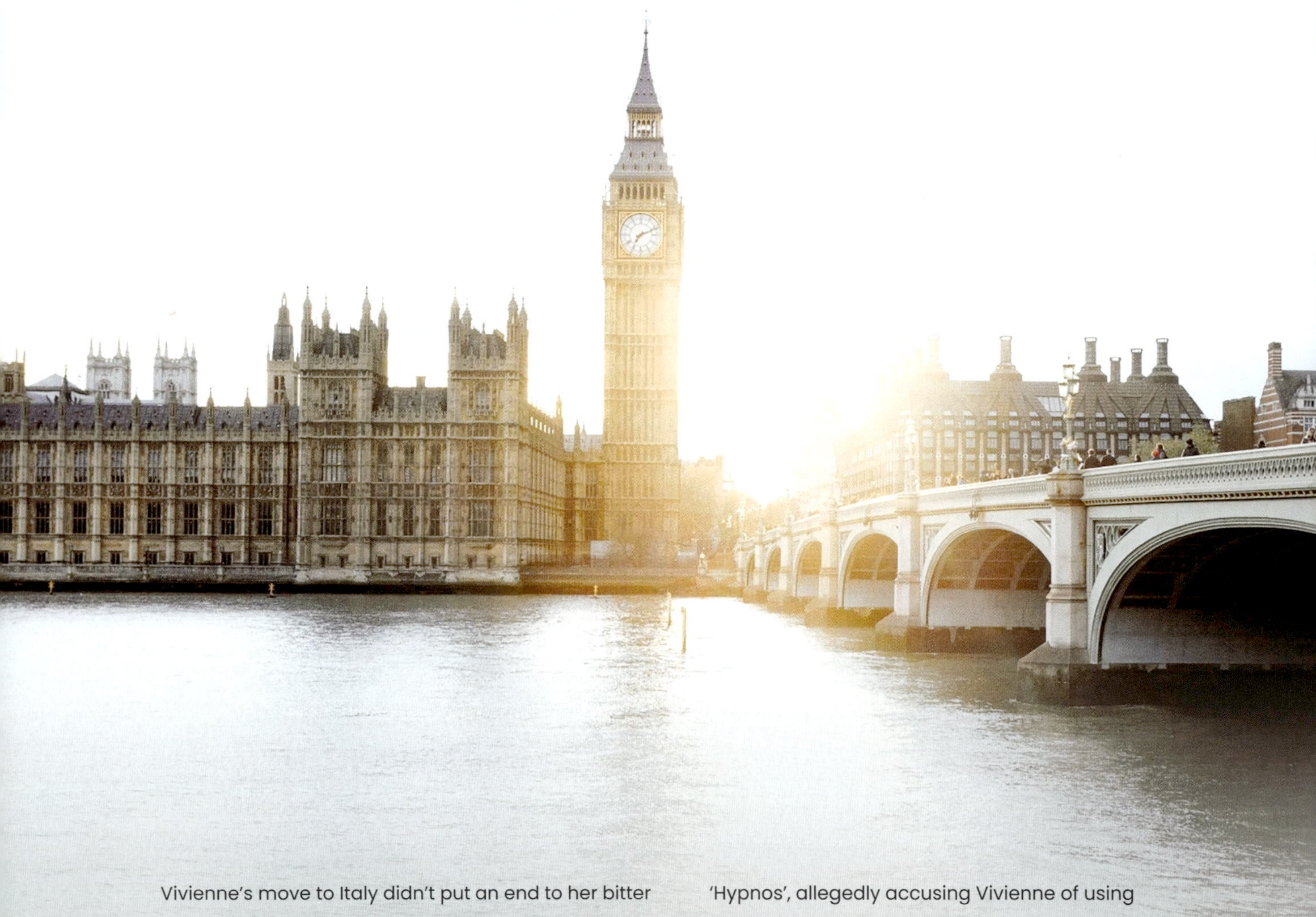

Vivienne's move to Italy didn't put an end to her bitter relationship with McLaren.

Malcolm began to court the press, allegedly continuously putting Vivienne's competency as a designer into question and trying to convince journalists that he was the true originator of the work, while Vivienne was merely the seamstress who executed it.

The influential musician even went as far as contacting the Milanese company producing 'Hypnos', allegedly accusing Vivienne of using patterns from their work room. Back in London, he had new locks put into the art studio they had shared together, forcing Vivienne to buy back some of her early works from auctions and dealers.

Eventually, McLaren began to tire of this behaviour and moved to Hollywood to follow his brief career developing ideas for Twentieth Century FOX.

Finally free from Malcolm's grip, Vivienne continued with her work.

ABOVE: Malcolm moved back to London
OPP PAGE: Bomber jacket from the Clint Eastwood collection

THE 'CLINT EASTWOOD' COLLECTION (AUTUMN/WINTER 1984-1985)

Vivienne Westwood's 'Clint Eastwood' collection, unveiled for Autumn/Winter 1984-1985, was designed as a spoof on spaghetti westerns and demonstrated her ability to infuse fashion with irony. The collection took its name from the legendary American actor Clint Eastwood.

Vivienne was increasingly fascinated by the tension between English and American culture, especially when it came to how masculinity was expressed. She took Clint Eastwood's cowboy persona and tough-guy demeanour, representing the quintessentially American machismo, and contrasted it with traditional English sartorial elegance. The result was a collection that deconstructed notions of masculinity and as a commentary on gender norms, offering a reinterpretation of male fashion that was at once tongue-in-cheek and highly structured.

The 'Clint Eastwood' garments featured fluorescent belted macs and body stockings, nylon and wool jackets, and short bondage trousers covered in Italian company logos such as Fiat and Olivetti. Day-Glo patches inspired by Tokyo's neon signs were also a staple of the collection.

A few weeks before the 'Clint Eastwood' fashion show, Vivienne realised that she hadn't designed any shoes for the collection. Inspired by her triple-tongue trainers for her 'Witches' clothing line, Vivienne came up with a pair of platform shoes raised three inches in the front and four and a half in the back. Initially, she wasn't too pleased with the design, deeming them 'too 70s' looking, but she later revived the shoe in her 1990 'Portrait' collection, where it became one of the house's most iconic pieces of clothing.

Despite the critical acclaim, the 'Clint Eastwood' collection wasn't profitable, further plunging Vivienne into financial uncertainty.

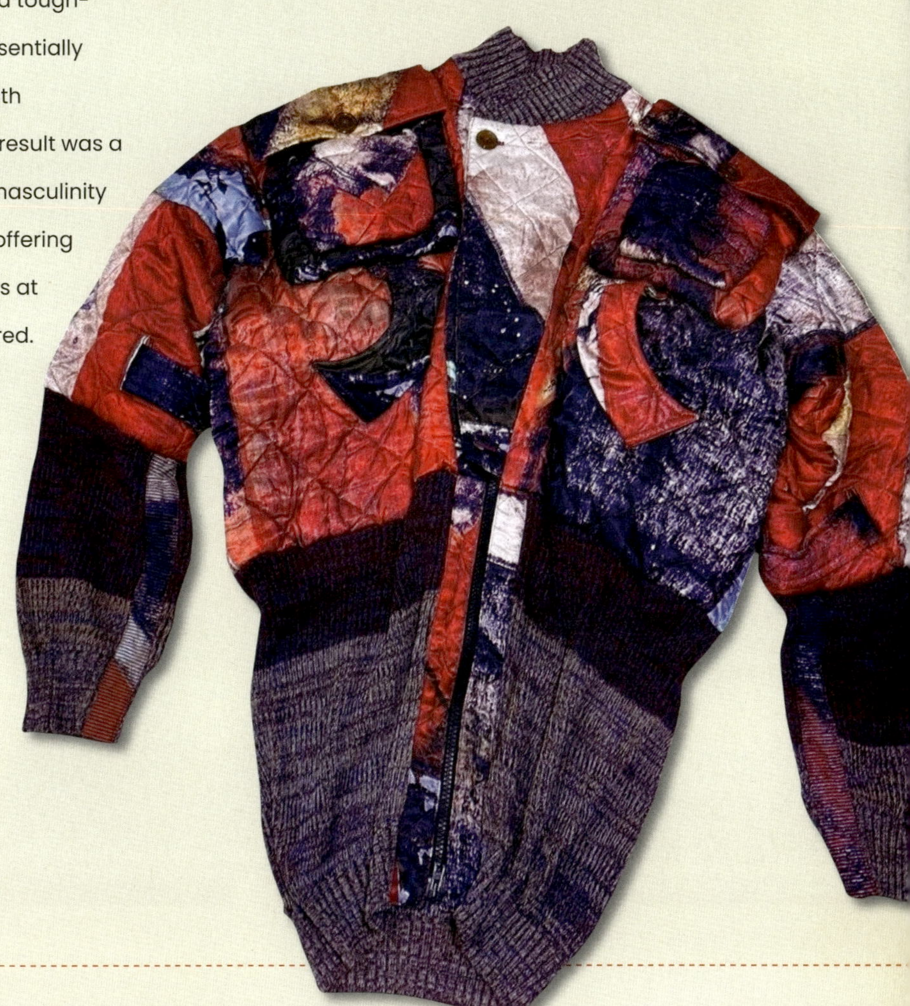

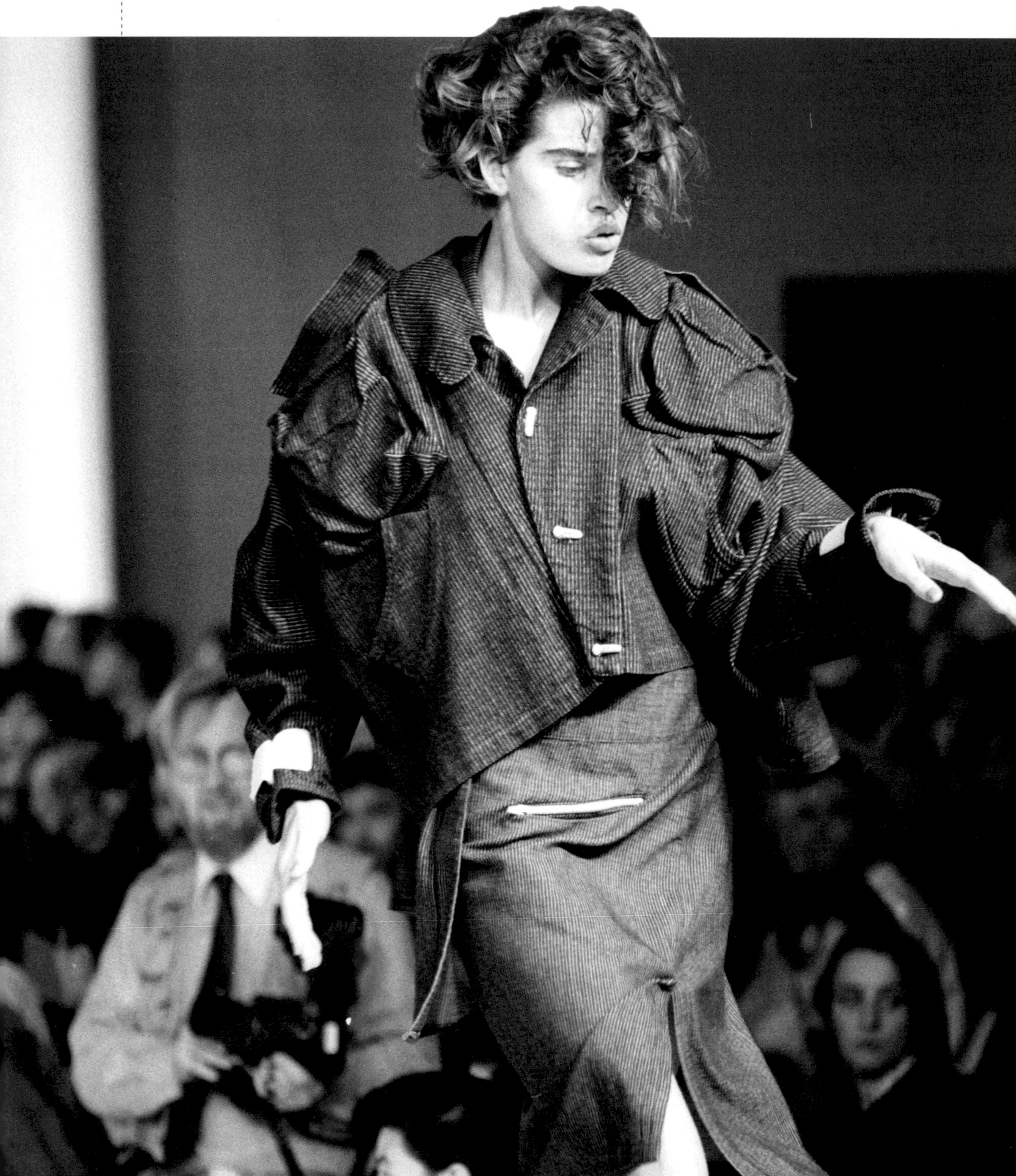

ABOVE: Vivienne Westwood Spring 1984 Sportswear
Collection Runway Show
OPP PAGE: Georgio Armani

In an attempt to assuage their financial issues, Carlo D'Amario held meetings and negotiations with Sergio Galeotti, the business partner of famous Italian designer Giorgio Armani, and came out with a business offer from the Armani house.

The impending Vivienne Westwood-Armani deal was announced in January 1985, and was dubbed as 'one of fashion's stranger couplings' by *Women's Wear Daily*. While Armani's clothes were characterised by their sleek and minimalistic style, worn by modern working woman, Vivienne's work on the other hand was loud, colourful and attention-seeking.

While their design philosophies appeared to be on opposite ends of the fashion spectrum, the commercial success of Armani's brand offered a template that Vivienne could leverage in order to expand her own business. Her partnership with Armani gave her access to resources that helped her scale her business without sacrificing her creative integrity. With access to Armani's Italian manufacturers, she could maintain the high-quality craftsmanship that Italian production was known for, while also increasing the volume of her collections. This finally allowed Vivienne to meet the growing demand for her designs, especially as her reputation began to grow outside the UK and into Europe and the US.

Additionally, Giorgio's already established relationships with major department stores and exclusive retailers around the world enabled the Vivienne Westwood brand to expand its presence in high-end stores and boutiques. Luxury department stores such as Neiman Marcus and Bergdorf Goodman all began to stock Vivienne's designs to cater to their fashion-forward clientele.

It was during this Vivienne Westwood-Armani business collaboration that Vivienne created one of her most famous clothing collections to date.

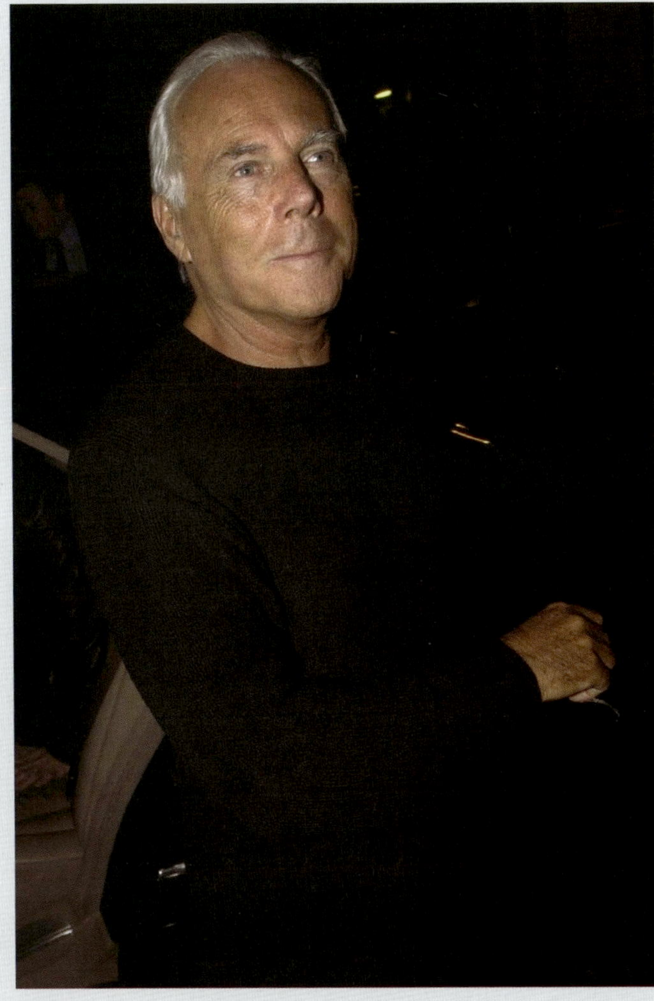

THE 'MINI-CRINI' COLLECTION (SPRING/ SUMMER 1985)

Vivienne Westwood's 'Mini-Crini' collection, presented for Spring/Summer 1985, was described by Vivienne as a "cardinal change" for the label.

The collection marked a departure from the oversized, looser silhouettes seen in her earlier works, and a move towards more fitted and feminine designs.

The 'Mini-Crini' collection was a direct response to Vivienne Westwood's fascination with the Victorian era. She was celebrated for her innovative use of the crinoline, a 19th-century garment designed to create exaggerated, voluminous skirts. She was obsessed with the crinoline's ability to create dramatic shapes and to transform the female body into a symbol of beauty, power, and opulence. She juxtaposed the crinoline with the mini-skirt, the 1960s symbol of sexual liberation and youthful rebellion. In typical Vivienne style, the combination of these elements was both ironic and groundbreaking, representing a dialogue between historic femininity and modern femininity.

Made from materials like tulle, organza, and stiffened cotton, the 'mini-crini' retained the structure and shape of the original 19th-century skirt but was

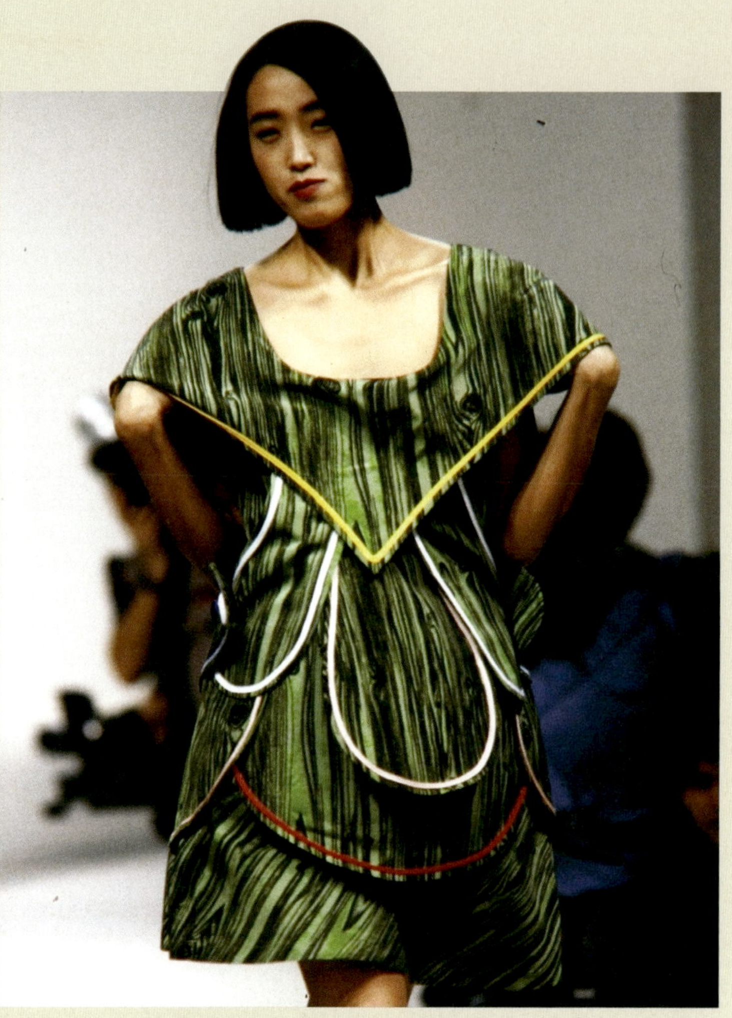

significantly shortened, revealing the legs in a way that was provocative, playful, and daring.

The 'Mini-Crini' collection also featured a handful of other iconic pieces of clothing.

The iconic 'Rocking Horseshoes', first introduced in this collection, became one of the house's signature items and are still considered one of the most distinctive and beloved articles of Vivienne's work. Designed with a high platform and curved sole, the shoe allowed the wearer to appear to glide rather than walk.

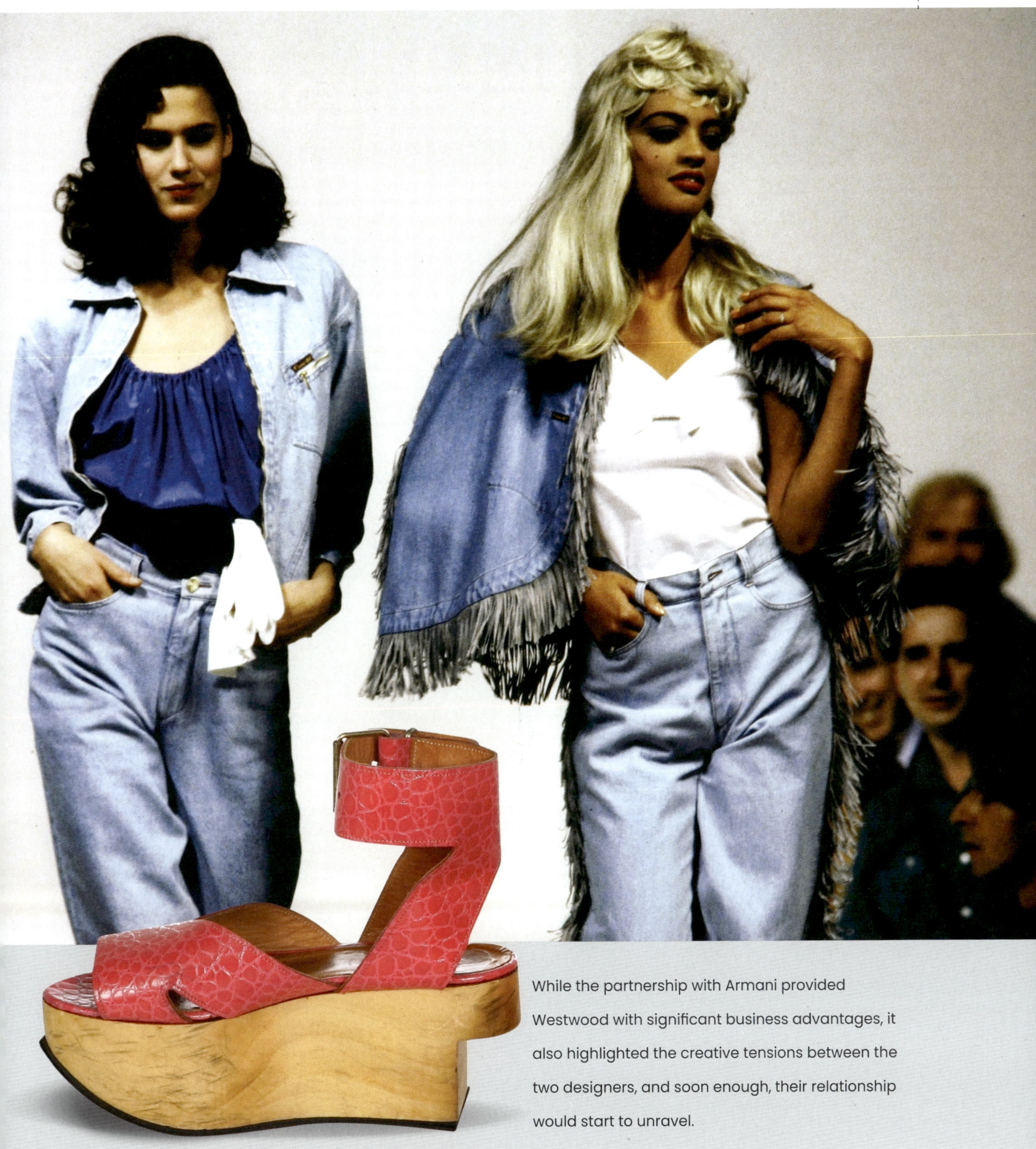

While the partnership with Armani provided Westwood with significant business advantages, it also highlighted the creative tensions between the two designers, and soon enough, their relationship would start to unravel.

OPP PAGE: From the Mini-Crini Collection 1985

ABOVE MAIN: Ready to Wear 1995 Mini-Crini outfits

ABOVE: Rocking Horseshoe sandal, late 1980s-90s

THE BRITISH INVASION

1986-1988

"I'm not really trying to be English — you can't avoid it, it's what you've absorbed."

Vivienne Westwood

At the beginning of 1986, Vivienne found herself, once again, in a precarious situation. The seven-year contract she had signed with the Armani label was abruptly cut short, and her on-and-off relationship with business partner Carlo D'Amario had run its course. She now had very little reason to stay in Italy, and decided to make the move back to her home turf, London. Despite the success she had achieved in Italy, Vivienne found herself back in Britain with very few resources and no McLaren.

Vivienne had always been described by her employees as someone with an unwavering spirit, but her return to London had hurt her morale. She wanted desperately to be the designer she knew she was capable of becoming, and got to work using

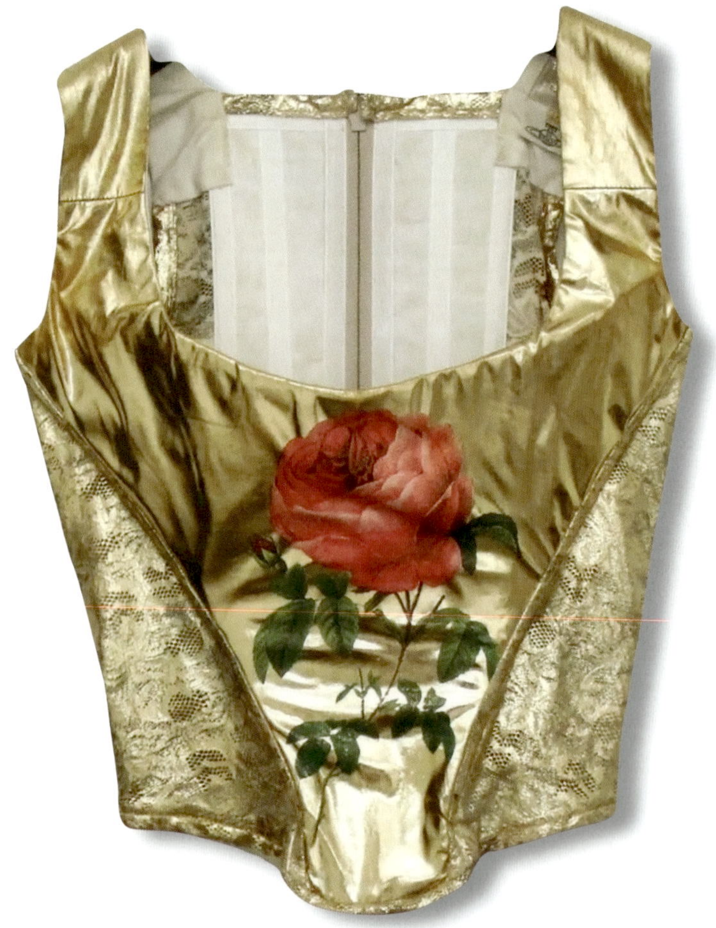

RIGHT: Cafe Society corset
OPP PAGE: Vivienne in her Chelsea shop, modelling an outfit from the 'Harris Tweed' Collection, 1997

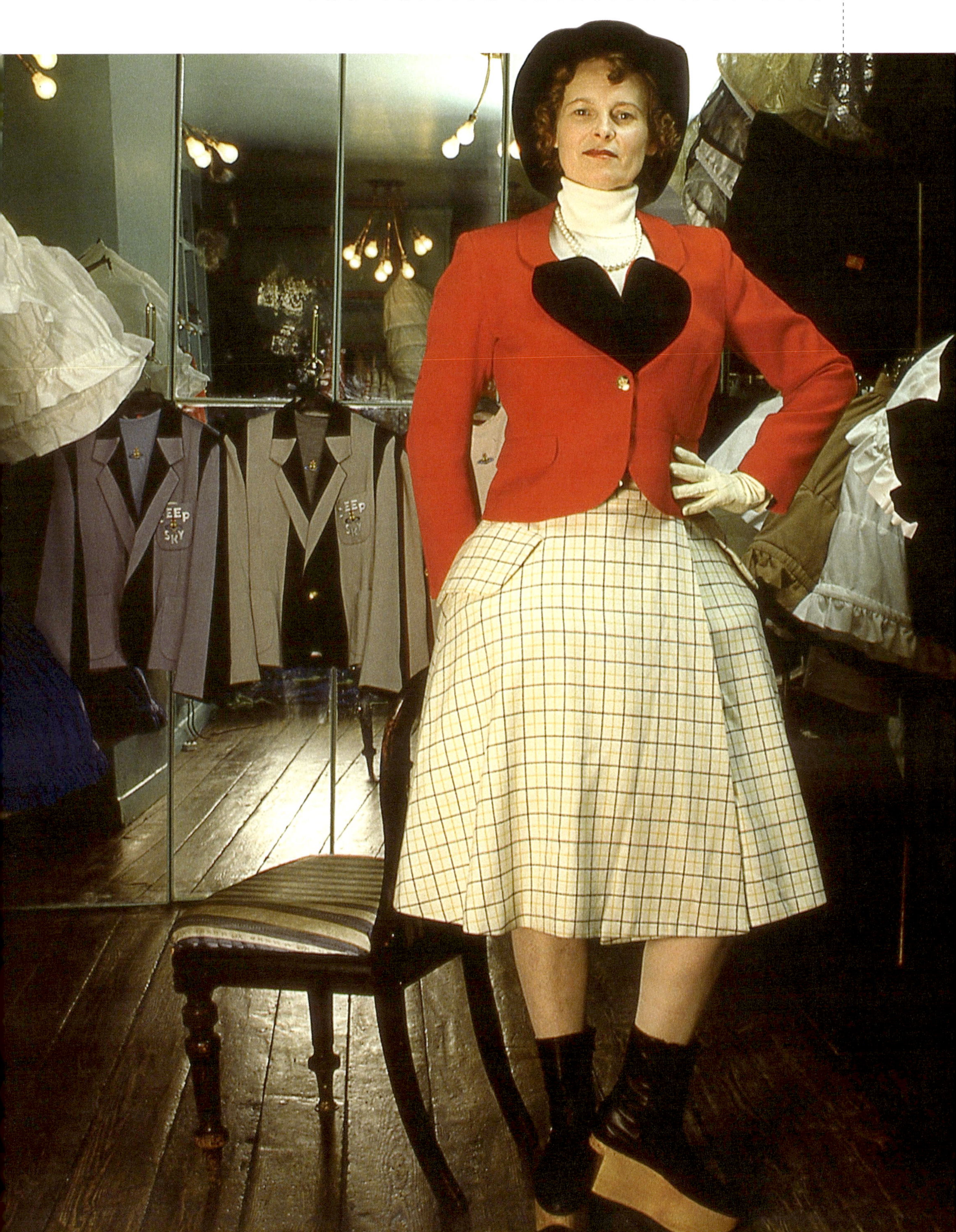

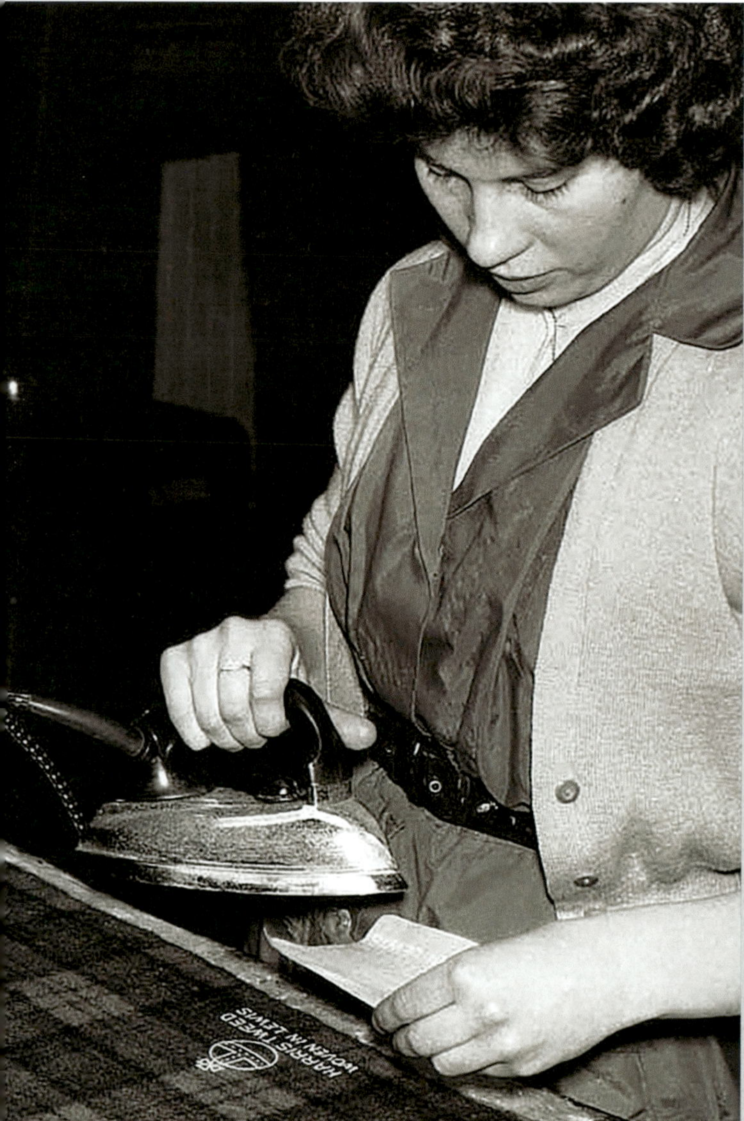

her persuasive powers to elicit loans, advice, and assistance from family and friends.

She reopened her shop on 430 King's Road that had been left empty for over a year. Finances were so tight that she allegedly struggled to pay gas or electricity bills, and on some occasions was forced to welcome customers in a dark store, faintly lit by torch or by candlelight. Now that she had resumed trading

goods, she was set on getting her designs back on the catwalk.

Her friend Jeff Banks, owner of the fashion group Warehouse and future presenter of the BBC's Clothes Show, agreed to loan Vivienne £15,000 – £20,000 on the condition that she create a viable business model.

To uphold her end of the bargain, Vivienne sought

ABOVE: Stamping Harris tweed with the Orb Mark and the Orb stamp on Harris tweed

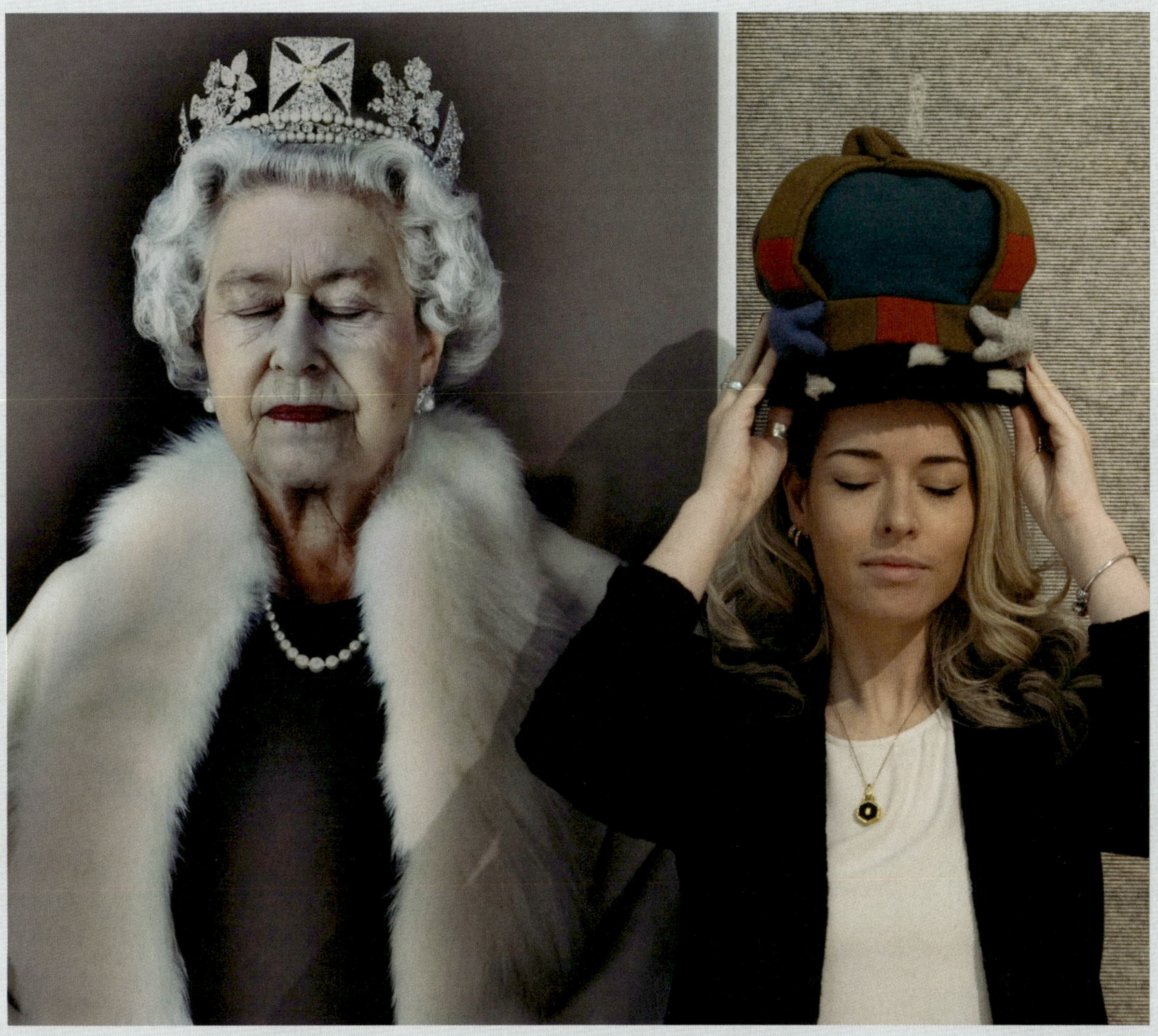

the help of her two boys: Ben, now 24 years old, and Joseph, now 19 years old. The boys helped with the administration of the company and provided emotional support to their mother.

Whenever she faced a challenging time, Vivienne took it as an opportunity to change up her look. When living in Milan, the designer realised the power that came with dressing the part of the person you want to be. She ditched her ragged avant-garde clothes for some prim English tailoring.

During this transformation, Vivienne fell in love with the beautiful garments coming out of the tailoring stores on Savile Row. She appreciated and praised the craftsmanship going into the British tweeds and adored the schoolteacher energy that emitted from the garments.

ABOVE: A staff member holds Vivienne Westwood, 'Harris Tweed' Crown, Autumn/Winter 1987-88 before being auctioned at Bonhams, London, 28 February, 2022

THE 'HARRIS TWEED' COLLECTION (AUTUMN/ WINTER 1987)

The 'Harris Tweed' collection for Autumn/Winter 1987 showcased Vivienne's deep admiration for her UK heritage and traditional craftsmanship, whilst also exploring the quirks of the British upper class.

Vivienne's initial point of inspiration for this collection was a little unexpected. "My whole idea for this collection was stolen from a little girl I saw on the tube one day", she claimed, "She couldn't have been more than 14. She had a little plaited bun, a Harris Tweed jacket and a bag with a pair of ballet shoes in it. She looked so cool and composed standing there".

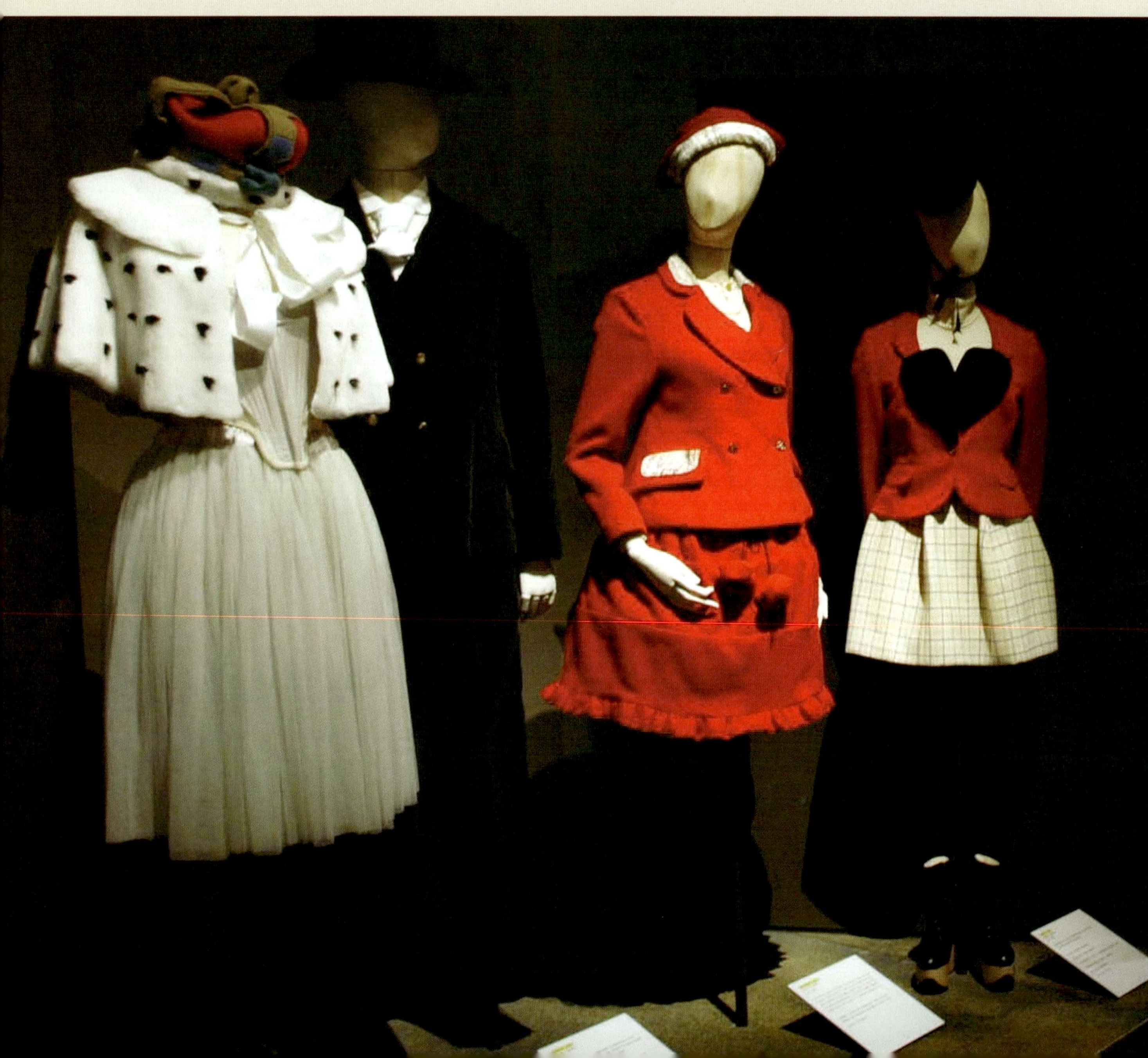

Harris Tweed, a handwoven fabric made in the Outer Hebrides of Scotland, holds a prestigious place in British fashion history. It is known for its durability, warmth, and unique patterns, often featuring herringbone, houndstooth, or tartan designs. The fabric is imbued with a sense of history, representing both the rugged landscapes of Scotland and the refined elegance of British country attire.

Vivienne was drawn to Harris Tweed because of its historical significance and its associations with aristocracy, and their connection to the countryside. Vivienne had long been fascinated by the fashion and rituals of the upper class, particularly how clothing could signify status, power, and tradition. She paid homage to these ideas by using the Harris Tweed fabrics, while also critiquing and deconstructing them.

The collection was dominated by traditional tailored pieces like blazers, coats, and suits with a modern twist through bold proportions, playful embellishments, and unexpected combinations of fabrics and patterns.

The hero piece of the collection was undoubtedly her 'Stature of Liberty' corset that gave the wearer a distinctive, hourglass silhouette. Karl Lagerfeld described her corset as one of the most important fashion ideas of the 20th century. The 'Stature of Liberty' would be endless recreated through Vivienne's career and find itself in the wardrobes of numerous celebrities.

This collection's runway show was Vivienne's first catwalk without McLaren. In an almost rebellious way, she completely went against all the stage production rules she had previously abided by. Instead of the models walking fast, as was common in her shows before, Vivienne now wanted them to slowly stroll down the runway. She also exchanged the high intensity music for some more classical tunes. The backdrop of the fashion show was Harris Tweed's Authority trademark of an orb. Despite the symbol being the brand's logo since 1911, Vivienne adopted it as her own. Today, the orb surrounded by a Saturn ring has become synonymous with the Vivienne Westwood brand.

Vivienne's first collection upon returning to the UK proved to be quite the comeback. Into this line, she poured all the knowledge she had acquired over the years to create a truly masterful oeuvre.

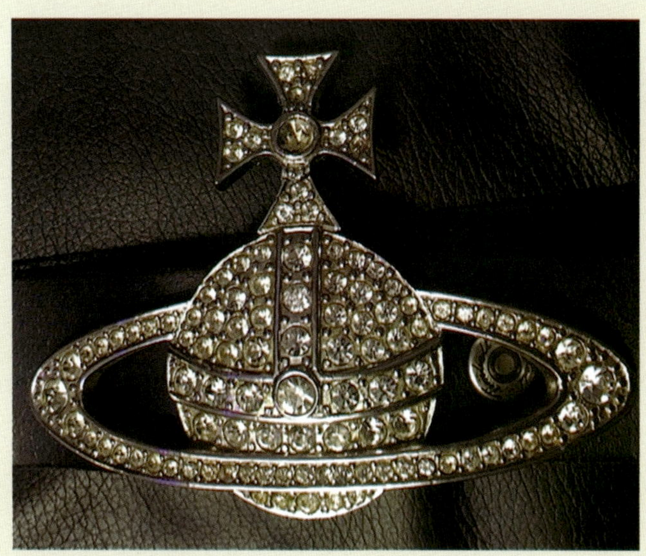

Following the release of 'Harris Tweed', Vivienne was in search for a new studio, and settled on some rooms in a warehouse off Camden high street. Vivienne practically lived in squalor, and the contrast between her workplace and other top designers was stark.

She reminisced about that time saying, "I was very, very poor indeed. I was on my own and even as the press were going mad for what we were doing – right beyond the 'Mini-Crini' collection and Harris Tweed, we had ten very, very hard years".

Vivienne's next five collections were later known as 'Britain Must Go Pagan', in which she explored a diversity of influences, from Sevres porcelain to pornographic Greek scenes. The clothing reflected the inherent contradiction in Westwood's work between respect for tradition and culture and a love of parody and sexual liberty.

Slowly but surely, Vivienne was establishing herself as a profitable businesswoman, and inched closer and closer to becoming an insider of the fashion world.

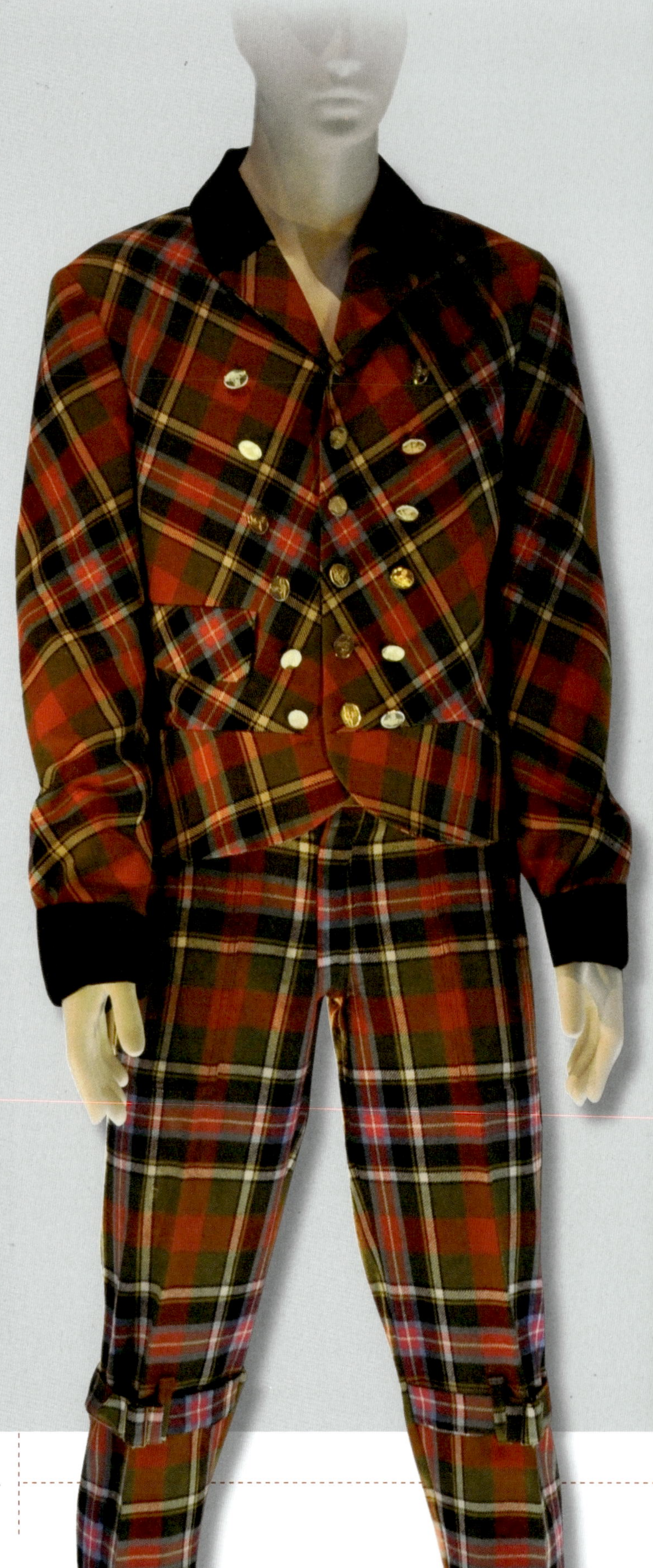

RIGHT: Harris Tweed Suit, by Vivienne Westwood. For her Machine collection Autumn/Winter 1998/99. Part of the permanent collection of the National Museum of Scotland, Edinburgh

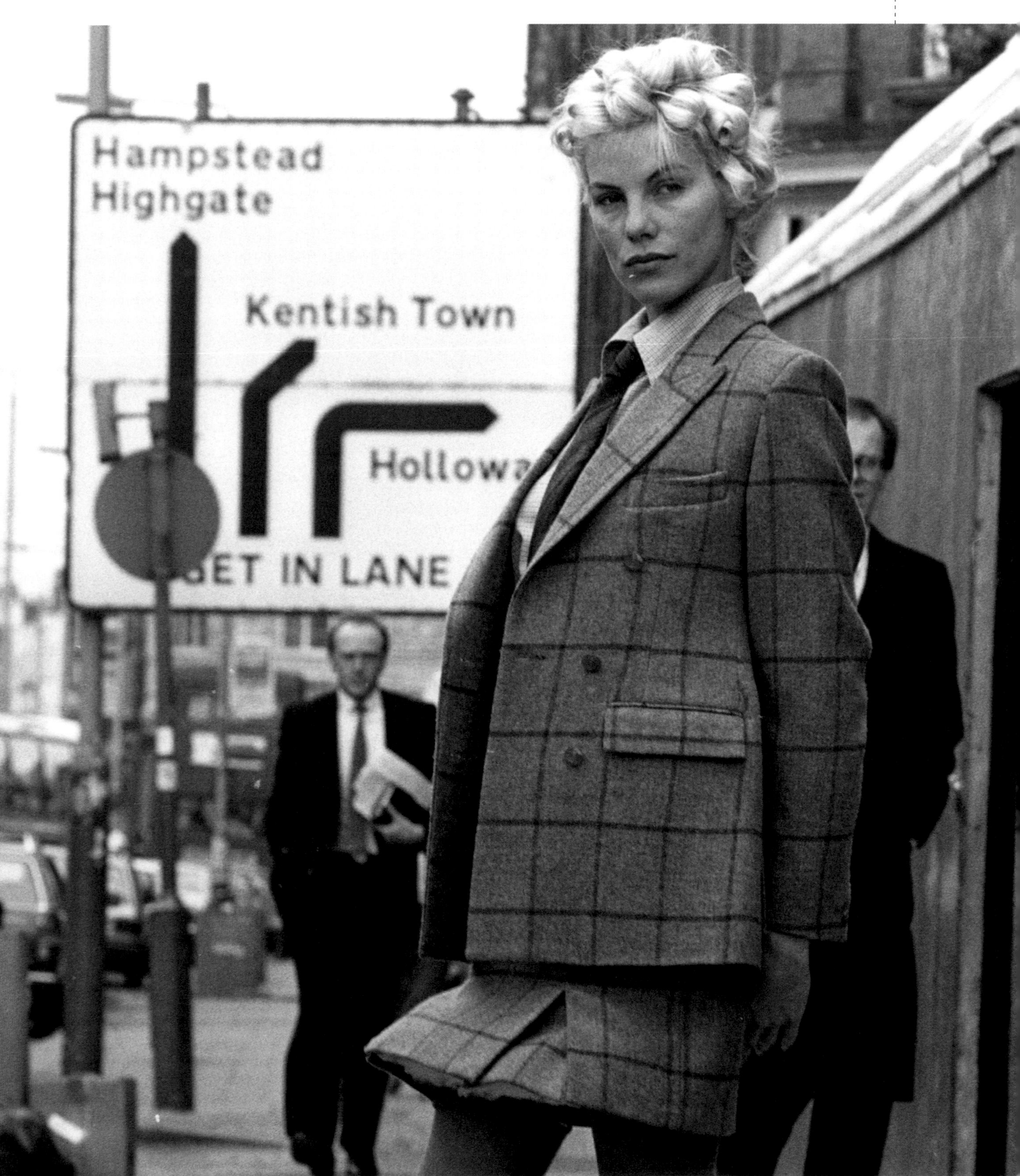

ABOVE: A model wearing Vivienne Westwood Harris Tweed, London, 9 Mar 1988

THE STUDENT BECOMES THE TEACHER

1988-1994

"You can say everything you want to say through tailoring - believe that everything resides in technique. You can't teach creativity and it is from technique that one is able to be creative. This is the terrible mistake of this century - to put creativity first."

Vivienne Westwood

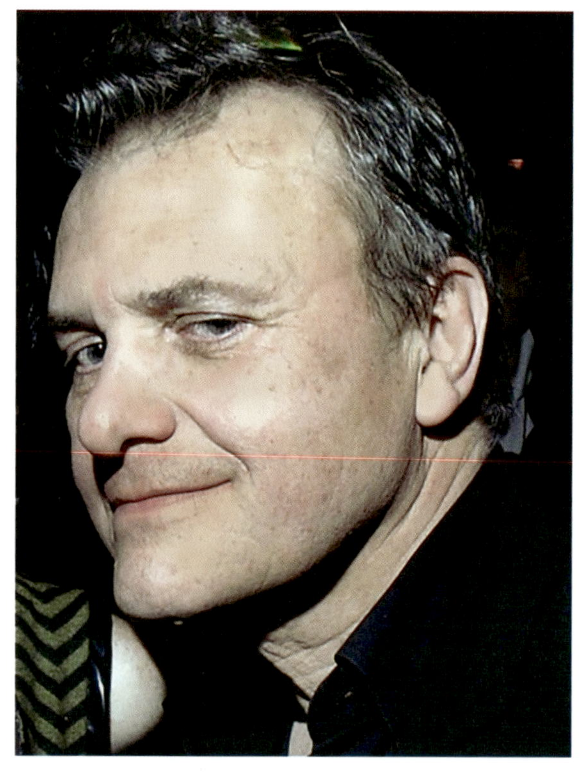

In 1988, Vivienne was convinced by her longtime friend, designer Jean-Charles de Castelbajac, to go back to her teaching roots. Castelbajac, who was a professor at the Vienna Academy of Applied Arts, recommended her to be his successor. She accepted the two-year post, which paid the handsome fee of £4000 per month for three days of work a week, a greatly needed sum of money.

Vivienne had long been a critic of the teachings of art and fashion schools in Britain, particularly the prestigious Central St Martin's. She believed that the school's laissez-faire approach didn't teach students

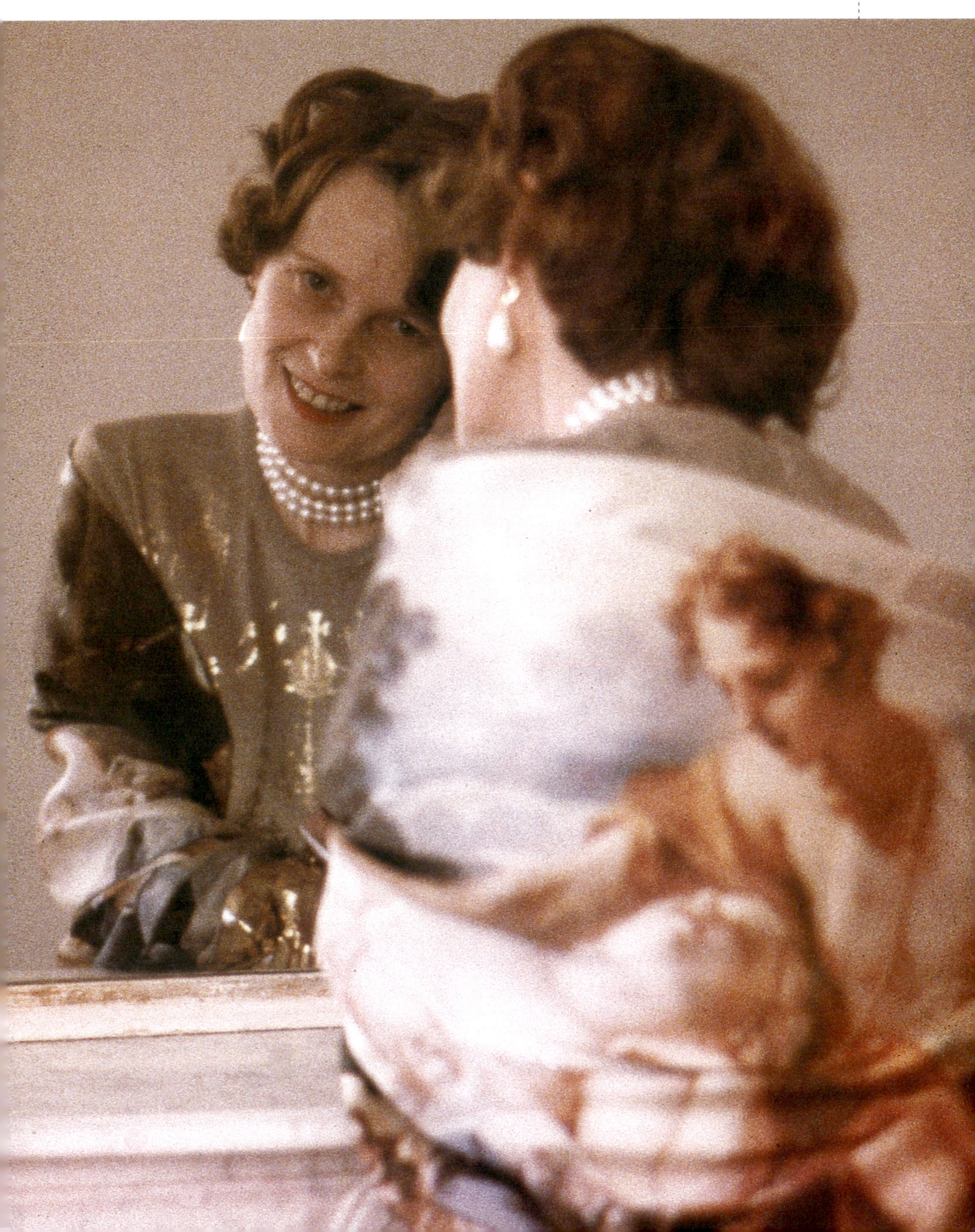

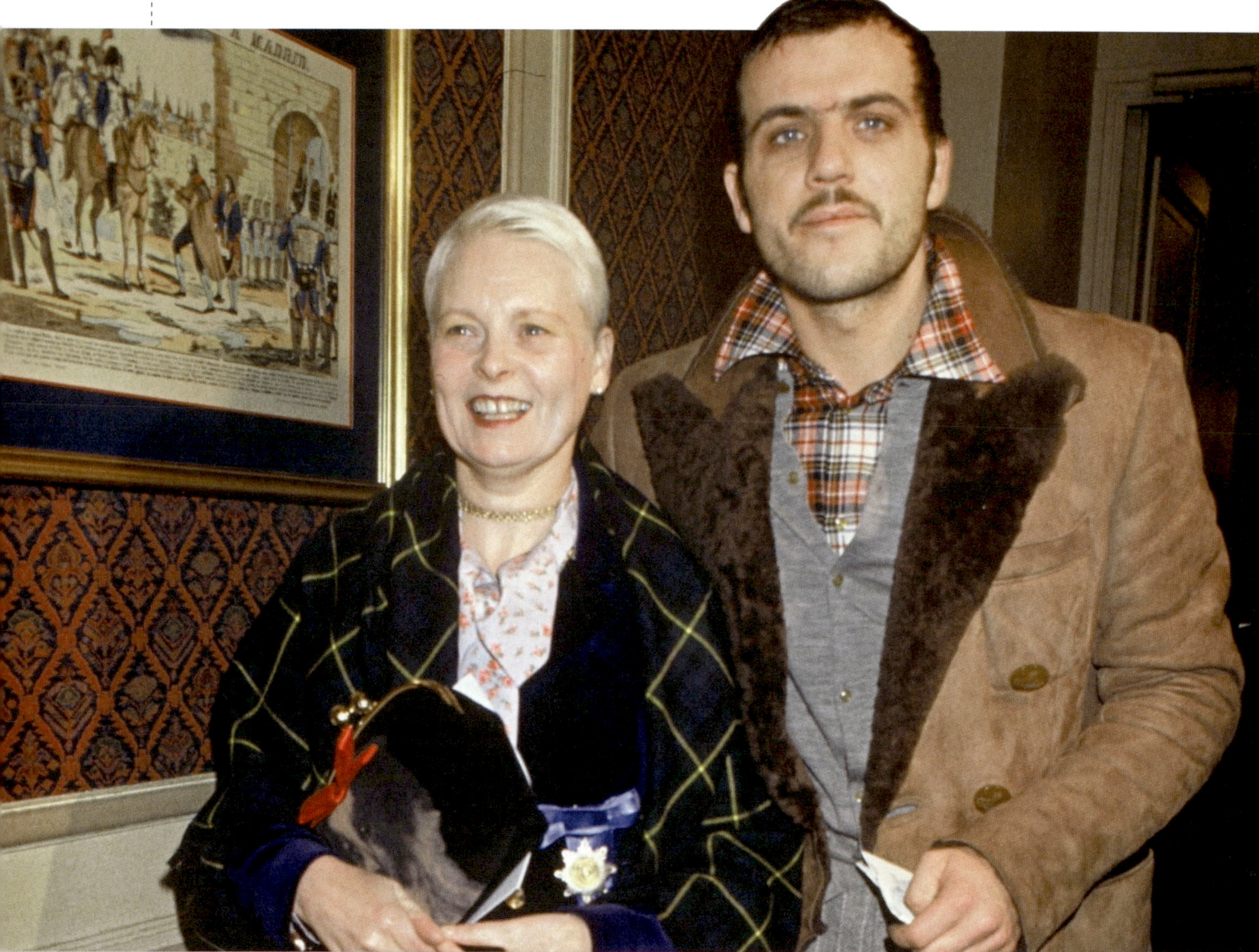

the technical skills needed for dressmaking. She found the freedom overindulgent, and the result of the students' work shoddy. In her opinion, the best way to nurture the next generation of designers was to adopt a more traditional methods such as repeatedly copying well-made garment models. Vivienne also believed in instilling a love of fashion history, to enrich the creativity and originality of their designs.

When she arrived to teach in Vienna, and later Berlin, she made her students replicate various historical pieces of clothing, sometimes spending months on one piece. It seemed paradoxical that Vivienne, a rebellious, self-taught designer, would impose such a conventional technique.

During her tenure at the Vienna art school, Vivienne developed a certain affinity with one of her students, in particular Andreas Kronthaler.

ANDREAS KRONTHALER

Andreas Kronthaler was born in Innsbruck, Austria, in 1966. From a young age, he exhibited a keen interest in creativity and design.

In 1988, while studying fashion at the University of Applied Arts Vienna, Andreas met Vivienne, who was a guest lecturer at the time. This chance meeting would change the trajectory of his life and his career.

Despite their 25-year difference, Kronthaler and Vivienne developed an immediate connection, both artistically and romantically. Their relationship blossomed, and in 1991, he moved to London to work alongside Vivienne in her fashion house. The pair eventually married in 1993, beginning a personal and creative partnership that would last for three decades.

At first, Kronthaler worked behind the scenes, contributing to his partner's collections while learning from her extensive experience. As time went on, he became more involved in the design process, and by the mid-1990s, Andreas had emerged as an influential creative force within the brand.

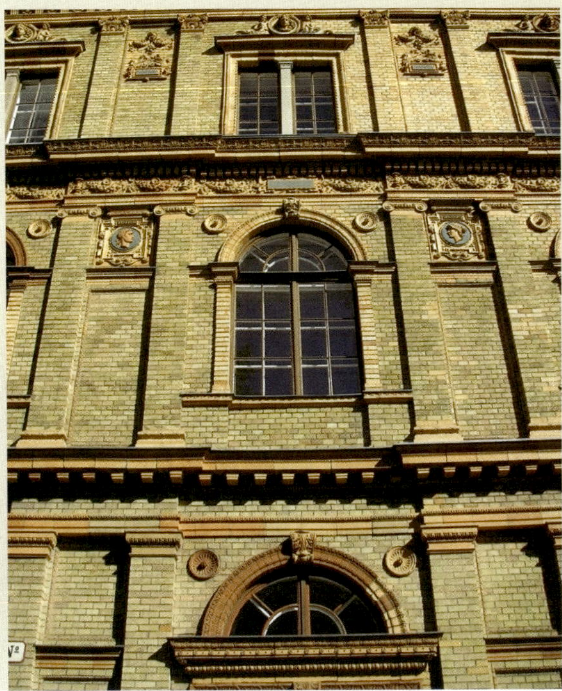

It wasn't until influential figures in fashion acclaimed Vivienne's talent that she was truly appreciated in her home country. Admirers of the British designer included Christian Lacroix, Karl Lagerfeld, Yves Saint Laurent, Jean Paul Gaultier and Azzedine Alaïa.

Vivienne kicked off the 1990s with one of her most influential and revered collections to date, finally cementing her place as a world-class designer.

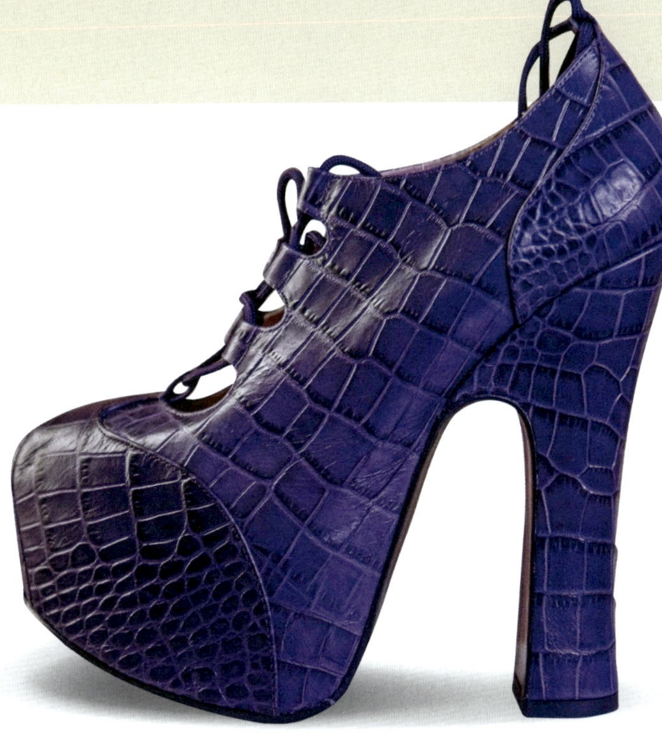

OPP PAGE: Vivienne and her husband Andreas in 1994
ABOVE: University of Applied Arts Vienna
LEFT: Elevated Ghille platforms were first shown in the Spring/Summer 1993 'Anglomania' collection

THE 'PORTRAIT' COLLECTION (AUTUMN/WINTER 1990-1991)

The 'Portrait' collection was critically and commercially described as a 'turning point' for Vivienne. Vivienne had just created one of her richest and most elaborate collections at a time when minimalism was becoming prevalent. Her intention was to suggest that her models had just stepped out of a painting. The collection included her famous corset printed with an Arcadian scene, a stretch velvet dress embellished with gold foil, reminiscent of rococo designs, as well as the return of her platform heels, now referred to as the 'elevated'.

'Portraits' was a big hit amongst the press, and featured extensively in *British Vogue*, driving Vivienne's sales to an all-time high.

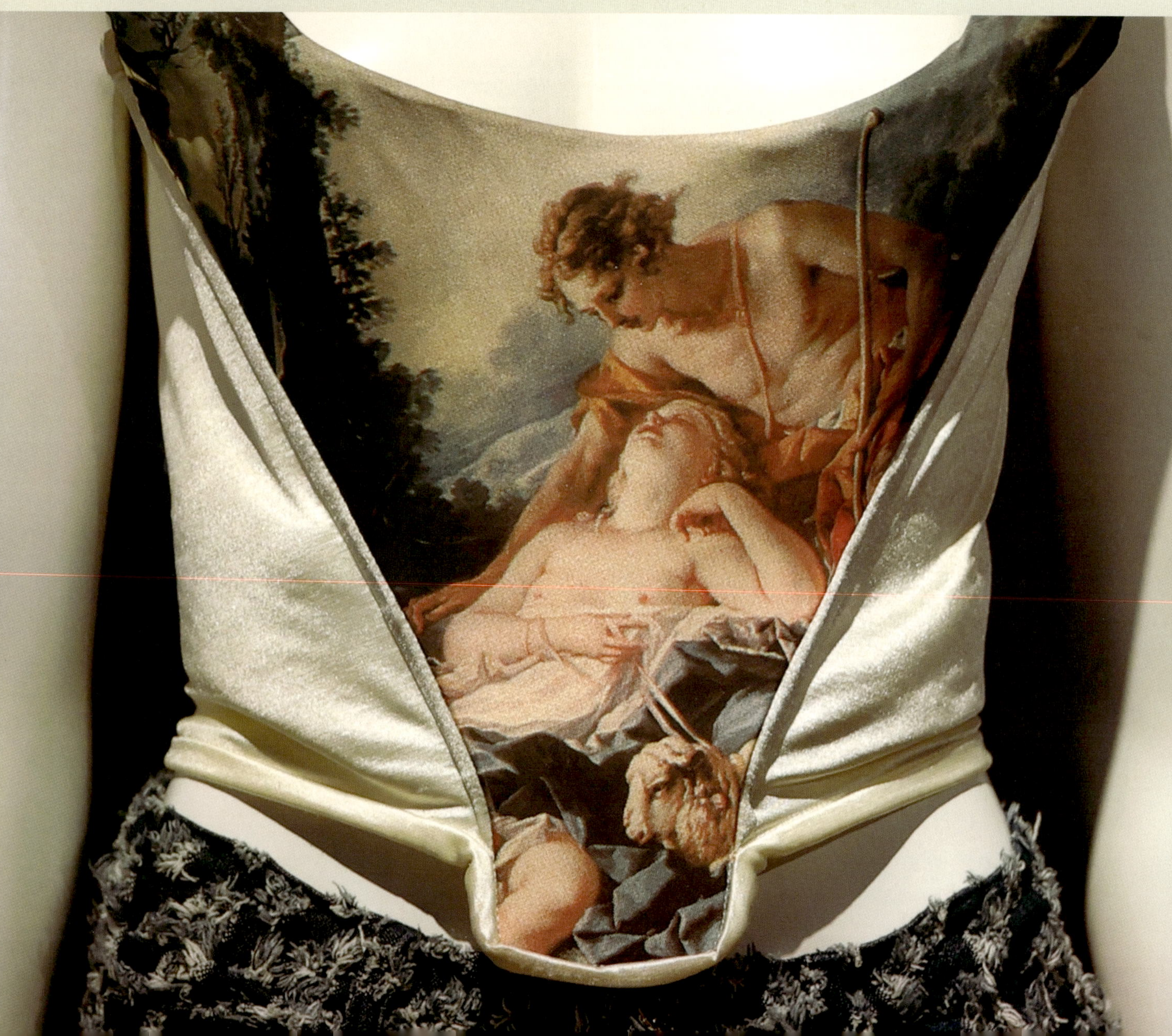

The media became increasingly interested in Vivienne and queued to interview her. Vivienne's quirky mannerisms and wacky rants made her more recognisable to the general public.

Adding to her notoriety, Vivienne was voted 'Britain's most influential designer' for two years straight, in 1991 and 1992.

The brand Vivienne Westwood now had a viable annual turnover, though it was still substantially less than her fashion house counterparts.

She hired John Rowley, a Liverpudlian expert in marketing, to help turn her brand into a household name. Rowley was responsible for some of Vivienne Westwood's most memorable and surprising business collaborations, including the release of two limited-edition watch collections called 'Orb' and 'Putti', for the Swiss company Swatch. Perhaps the most unusual business partnership was the label's advertising deal with the carpet company Brintons.

When the campaign launched, the demand for Vivienne Westwood carpets was exceptionally high. Hillary Clinton even chose Brintons carpet to refurbish the living quarters of the white house.

Vivienne made her way into the homes of people, making her a familiar face even amongst those not involved in fashion.

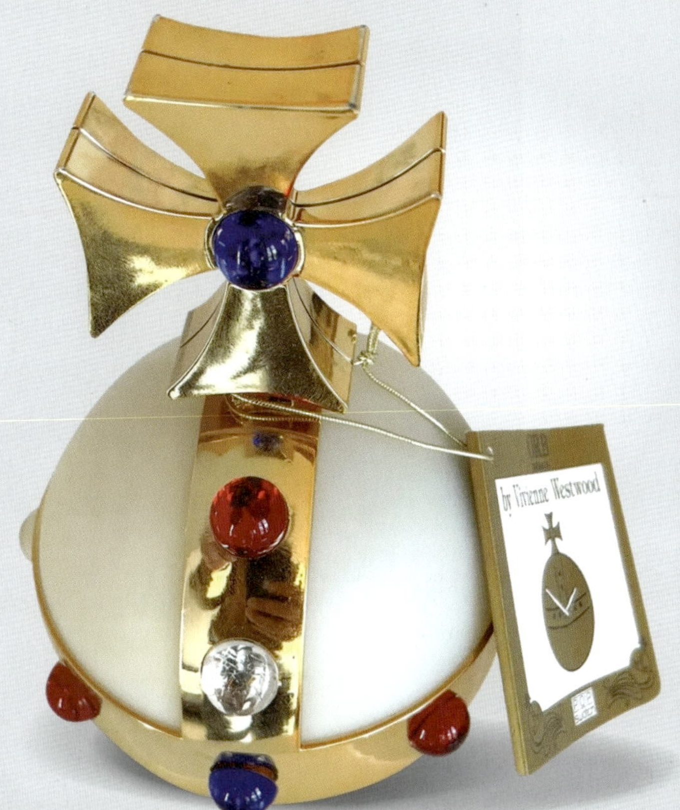

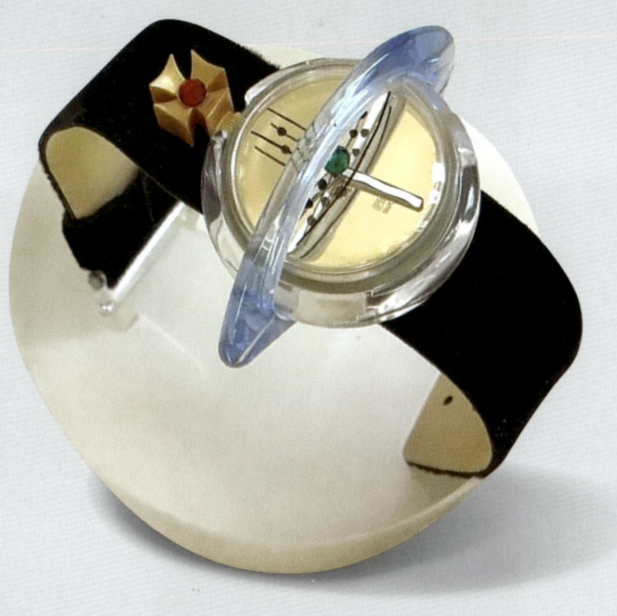

OPP PAGE: The iconic corset seen during a media preview of '1001 Remarkable Objects' at Powerhouse Museum in 2023

ABOVE: Swatch Orb Vivienne Westwood watch and case

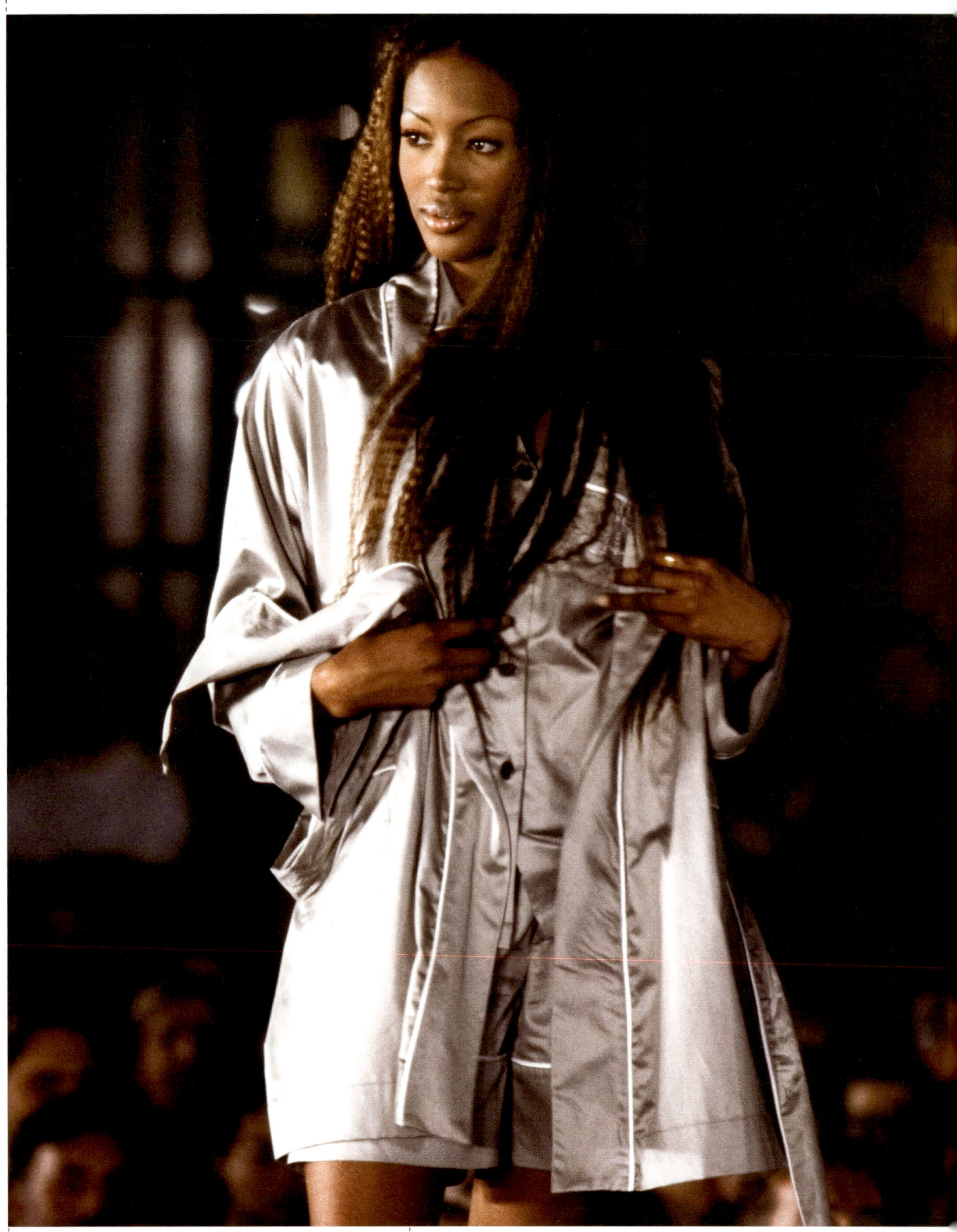

ABOVE: Naomi Campbell walks the runway at the Vivienne Westwood Spring/Summer 1992-1993 fashion show
OPP PAGE: Vivienne Westwood after receiving her OBE, at Buckingham Palace

THE QUEEN OF PUNK MEETS THE QUEEN OF ENGLAND

In 1992, she received an OBE from Queen Elizabeth. Vivienne showed up at Buckingham palace wearing a smart grey suit, however she seemed to have forgotten to wear any underwear.

Members of the royal family famously have strict style protocols to abide by, and the unspoken rule is that visitors should follow the same standards, but after receiving her OBE from the Queen, Vivienne celebrated her achievement by taking a twirl around one of the courtyards of Buckingham Palace in front of a crowd of paparazzi.

In true Vivienne style, the fashion rebel was famously snapped in all her commando glory.

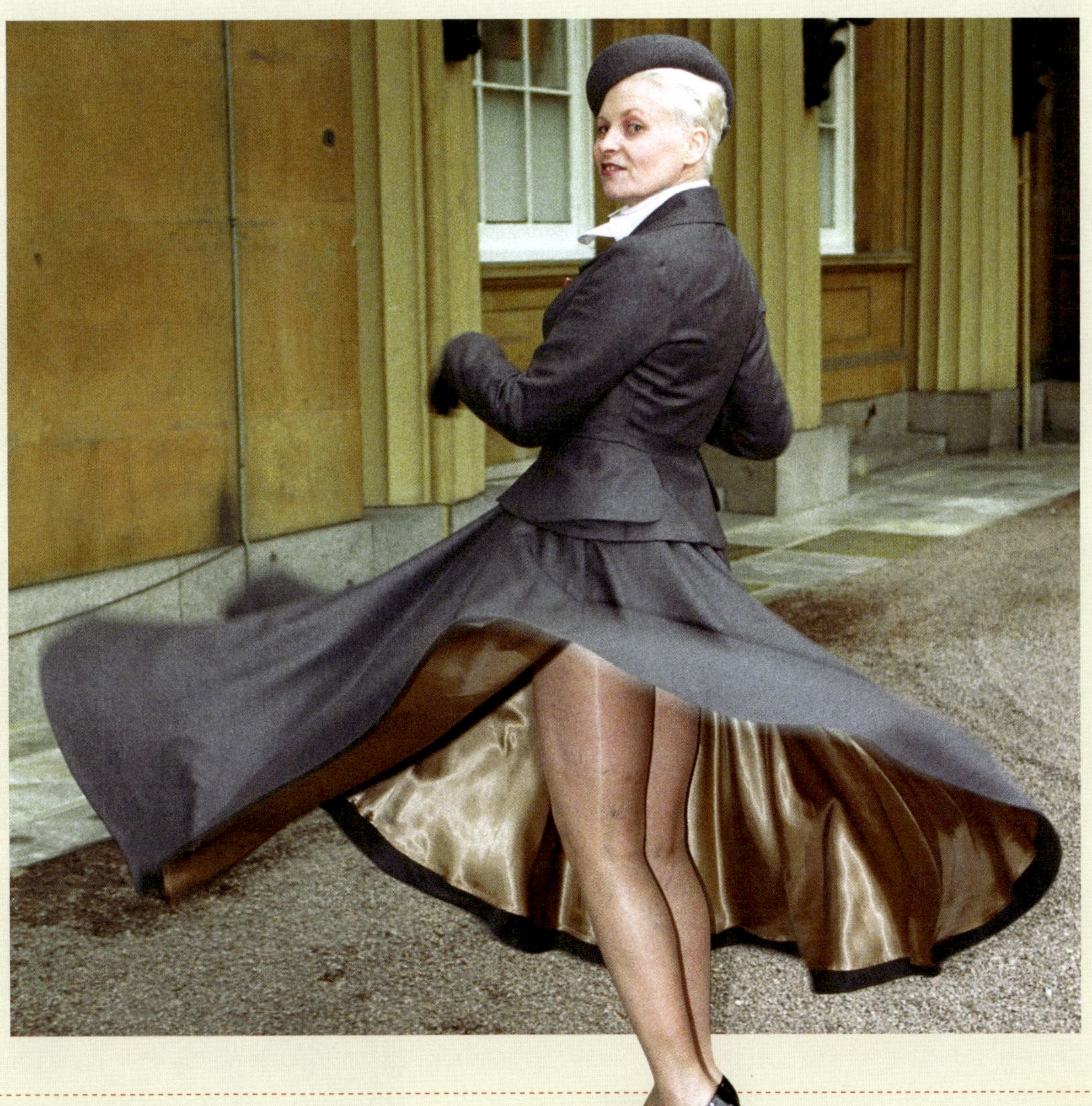

THE END OF THE ROAD

1994-2000

"Fashion is very important. It is life-enhancing and, like everything that gives pleasure, it is worth doing well."

Vivienne Westwood

By the mid-1990s, Vivienne had ceded most of her designer responsibilities to her husband Andreas. Though all the clothes still bore the Vivienne Westwood tag, without the original designer at the helm of the brand, the clothes felt devoid of their usual originality. Vivienne's brand became formulaic, and based on reinterpretations of her archived looks. Following the release of the 'Salon' collection, most subsequent fashion lines were composed of the same articles of clothing, just redesigned for every show and made from different fabrics.

Vivienne firmly believed that Andreas brought an element of grandeur to the Vivienne Westwood brand, but her deep love for him often clouded her senses. Many people from her entourage were aware

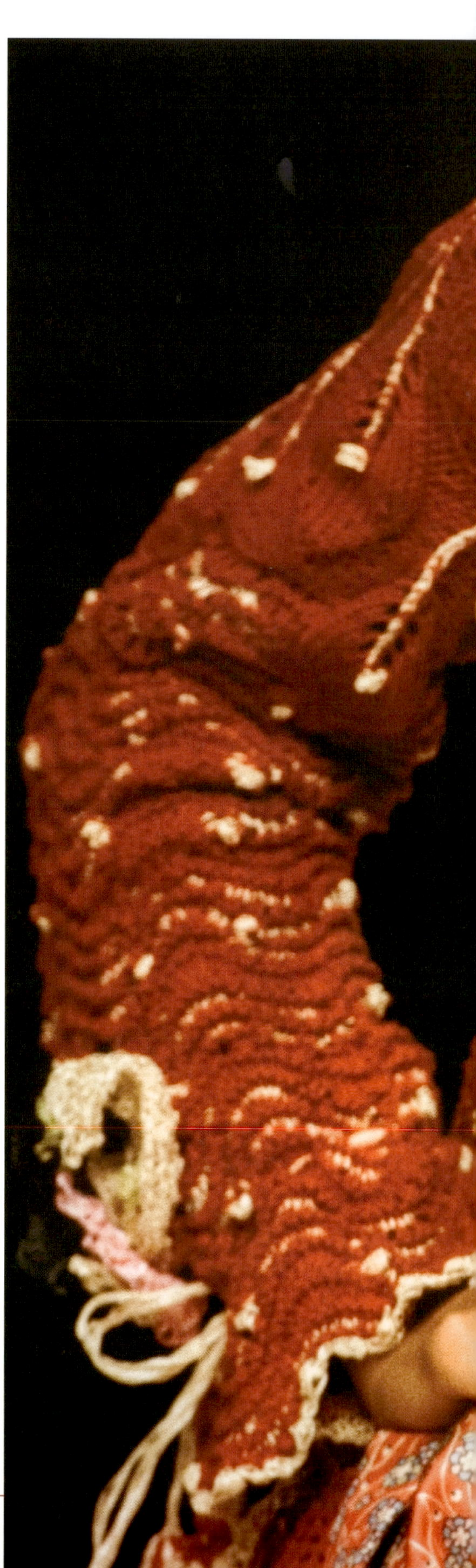

RIGHT: From the 1995 Ready-to-wear collection

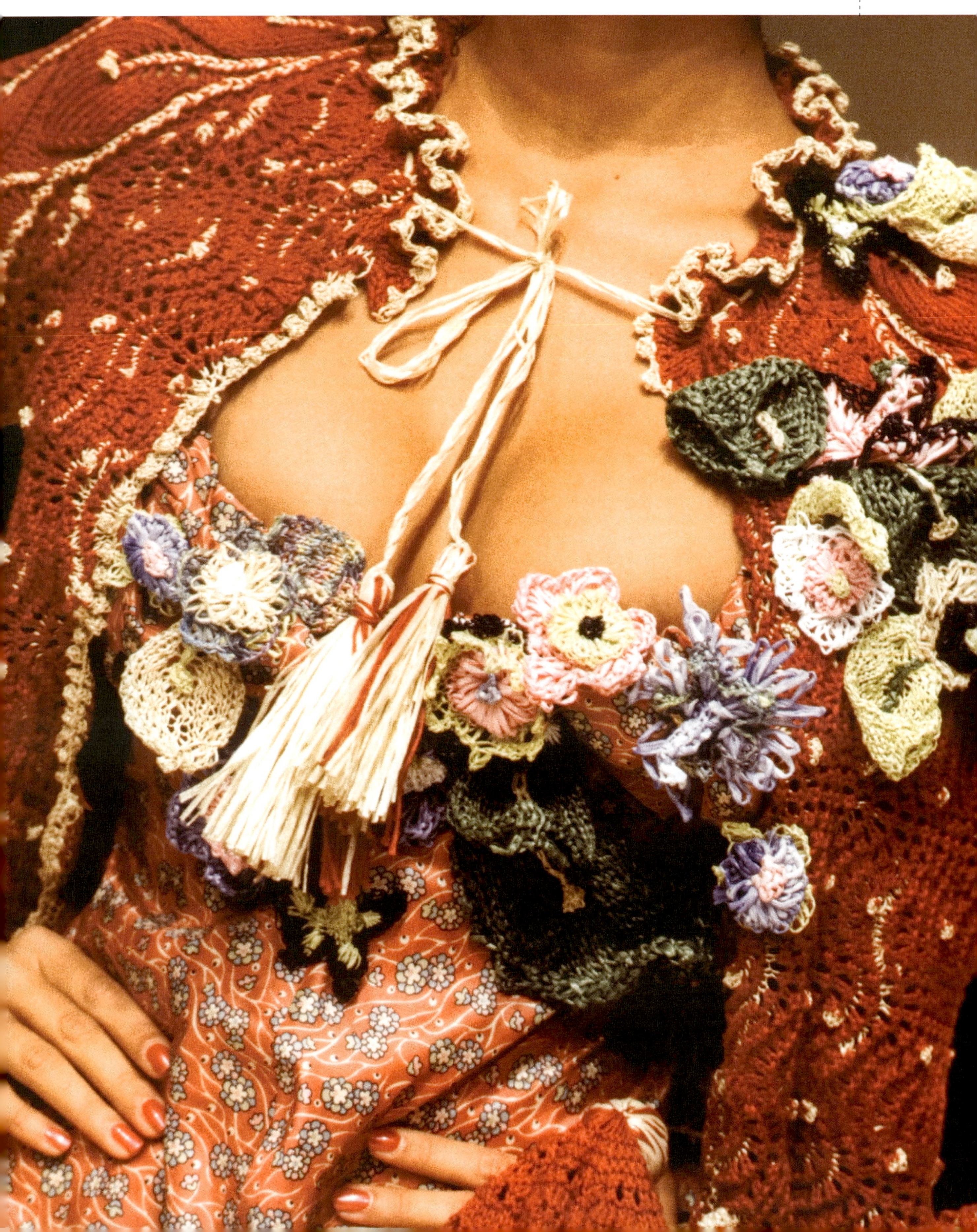

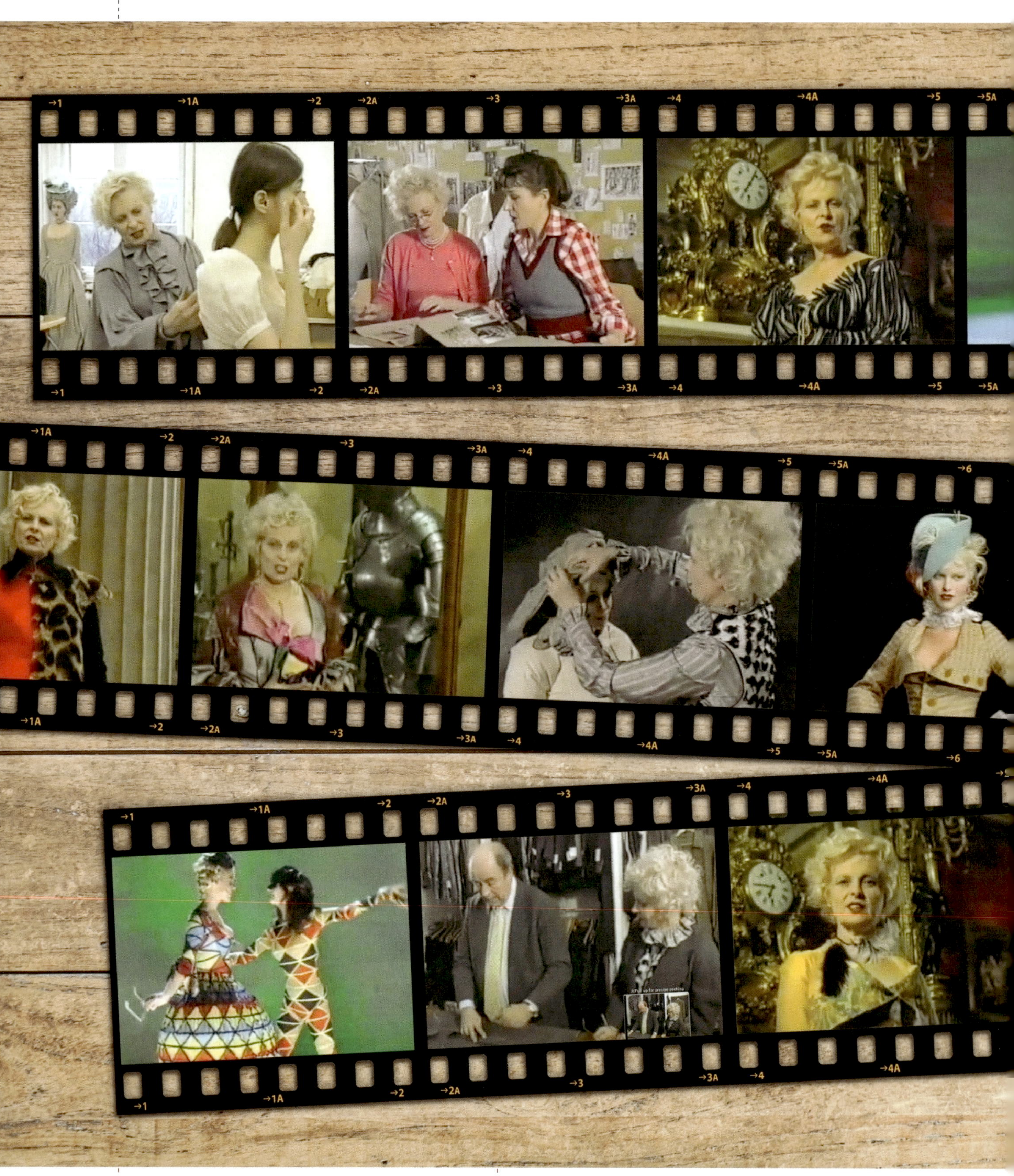

ABOVE: Stills from the 'Painted Ladies' TV series by
Channel 4

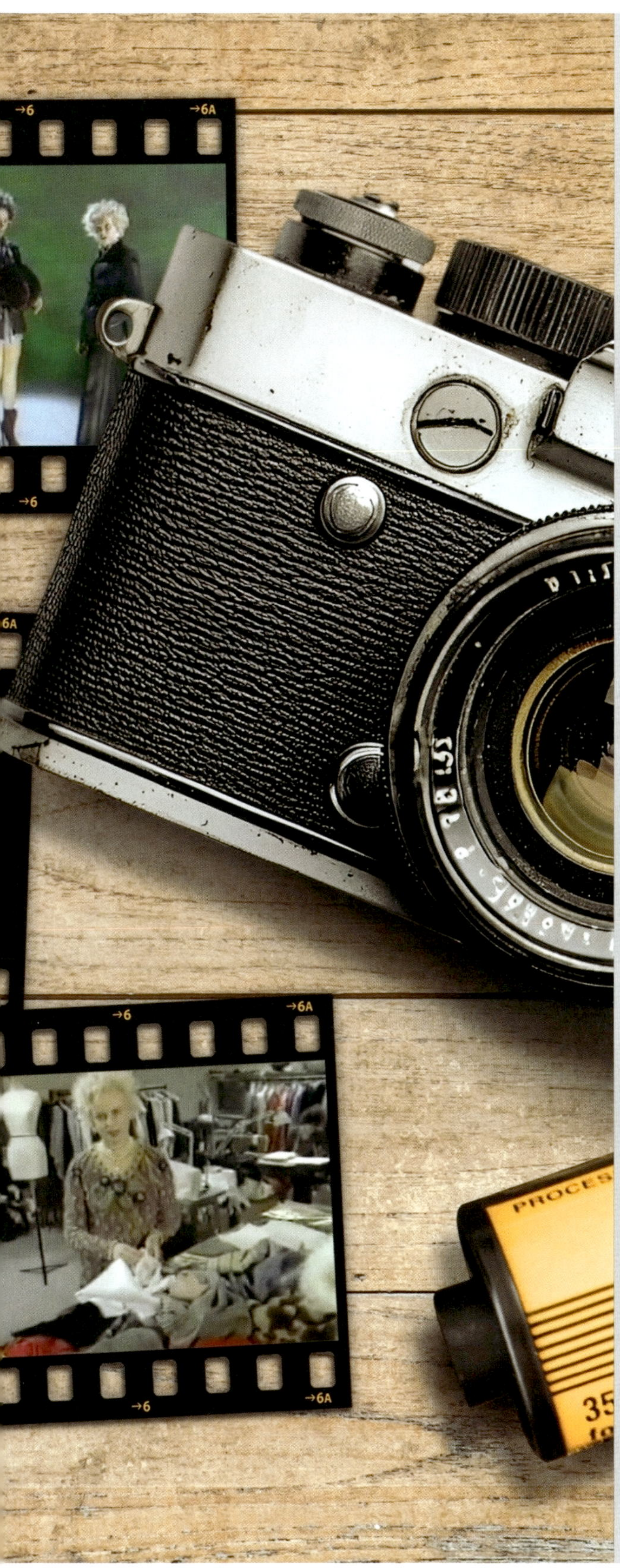

of Andreas' growing influence over Vivienne and her brand, but they hadn't expected her to be so far removed from the design process. The designer was so disconnected from her fashion that when a friend of hers asked what would feature in her upcoming collection, Vivienne simply replied with "I don't know, Andreas is doing it". At the time, the public wasn't aware that Vivienne had stepped away from her label.

Without her usual workload, Vivienne spent most of her abundant free time making media appearances. Vivienne relished in her role as a public persona and was often asked to comment on subjects both in connection to her job and not. She also gave lectures in universities, including the prestigious Cambridge University, and worked in Museums such as the Leiden Museum in Amsterdam.

During the Spring/Summer 1995-1996 season, Vivienne wasn't even present at her own fashion show. She was off working on a three-part television series called 'Painted Ladies' with her brother Gordon and his wife. The show was for Channel 4, and explored the link between fashion and art.

By the end of 1995, Vivienne publicly admitted to delegating creative control to her husband. Though her brand would continue to flourish, even under the guidance of Andreas, the original rebellious spirit built upon by Vivienne and Malcolm had now come to an end.

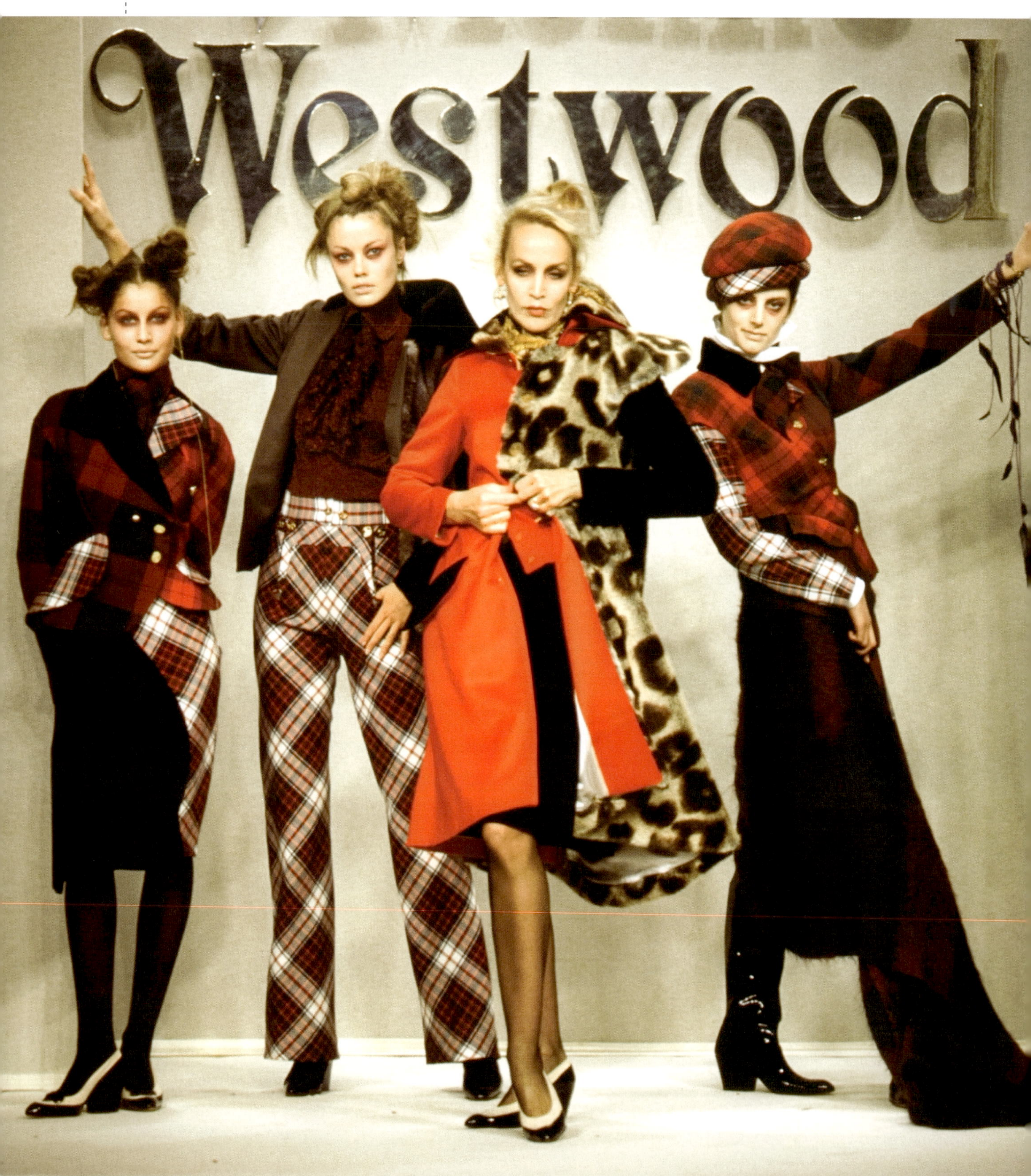

ABOVE: Ready-to-wear Autumn/Winter 1996/97 collection
OPP PAGE LEFT: Vivienne and Andreas in 1997
OPP PAGE RIGHT: A pair of Vivienne Westwood designed
Linen Pirate Boots from 1998

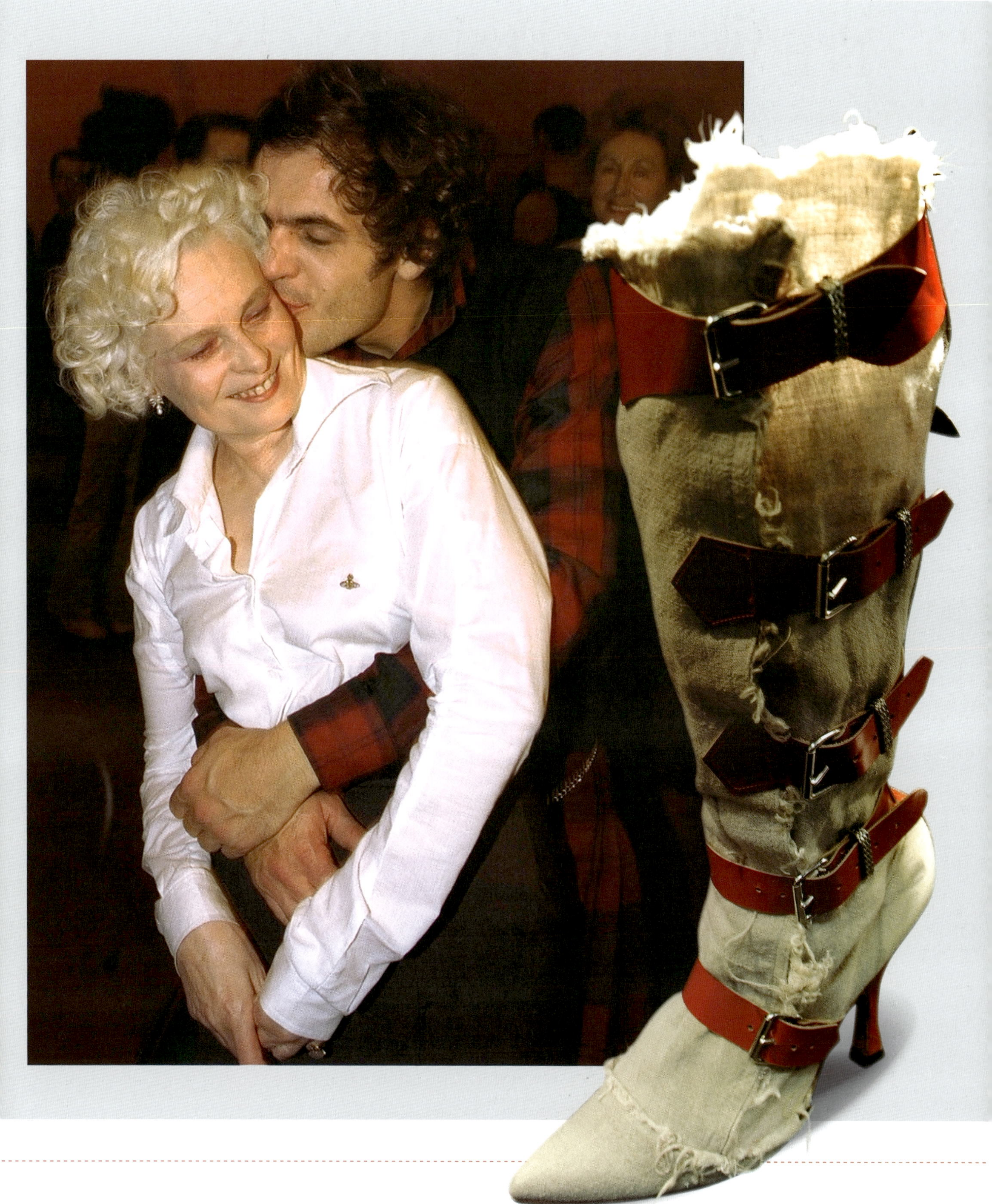

NEW BEGINNINGS

2000-2005

"All activists were driven by the same motive. We cannot stand human suffering. We can't stand the mismanagement of the world."
Vivienne Westwood

Although Vivienne was no longer the executer of the designs for the Vivienne Westwood label, she still lent her voice to the brand and continued to use the runway as a platform for political commentary and positive activism.

The early 2000s was a period marked by Vivienne's growing preoccupation with sustainability and the climate crisis, causes that would dominate much of her later career. The British designer became a vociferous critic of fast fashion, and began championing the mantra, "Buy less, choose well, make it last," encouraging consumers to invest in timeless, quality pieces instead of indulging in the rapid turnover of mass-market fashion.

However, fashion and over-consumption are intrinsically linked, and the irony of campaigning for climate action through a commercial fashion brand was not lost on Vivienne. The brand owns up to the fact that they are not perfect, but has taken strides to minimise their environmental impact. All of Vivienne's Ready-To-Wear collections are made from 90% lower impact fabrics with plastic-free packaging, and she also reduced the overall size of her collections so that her brand can produce less. Without the power of her global fashion empire, there is no doubt that

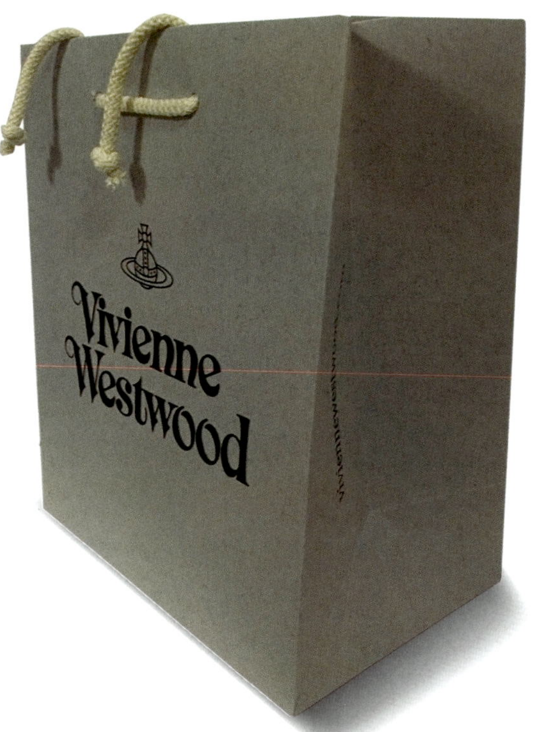

ABOVE: Plastic-free packaging
OPP PAGE: Vivienne Westwood, at a retrospective dedicated to her work at the Victoria & Albert Museum, London 2005

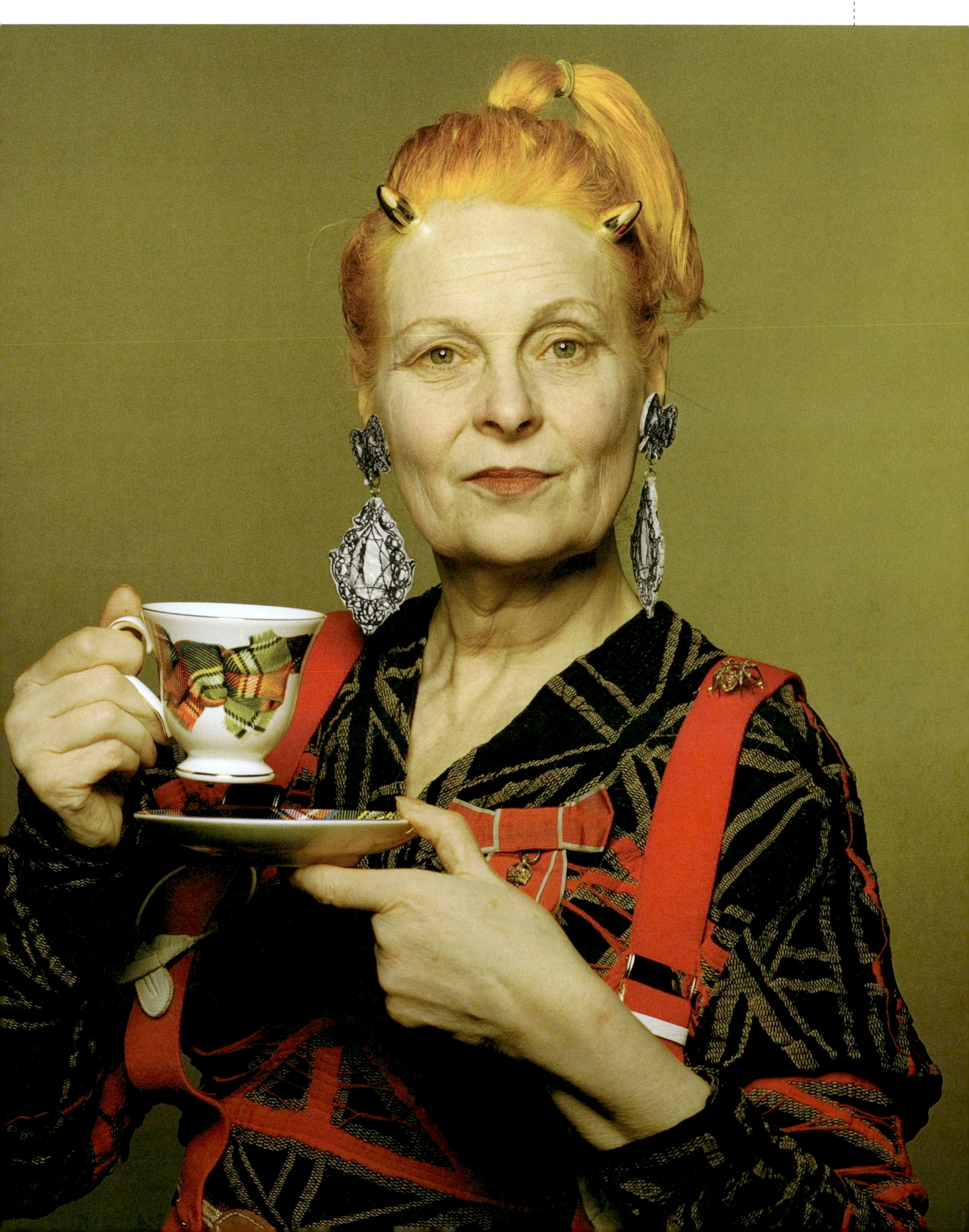

Vivienne's ecological crusade would have reached fewer people.

Vivienne compared the dire situation to battle: "It's a war for the very existence of the human race. And that of the planet. The most important weapon we have is public opinion: go to art galleries, start to understand the world you live in. You're a freedom fighter as soon as you start doing that."

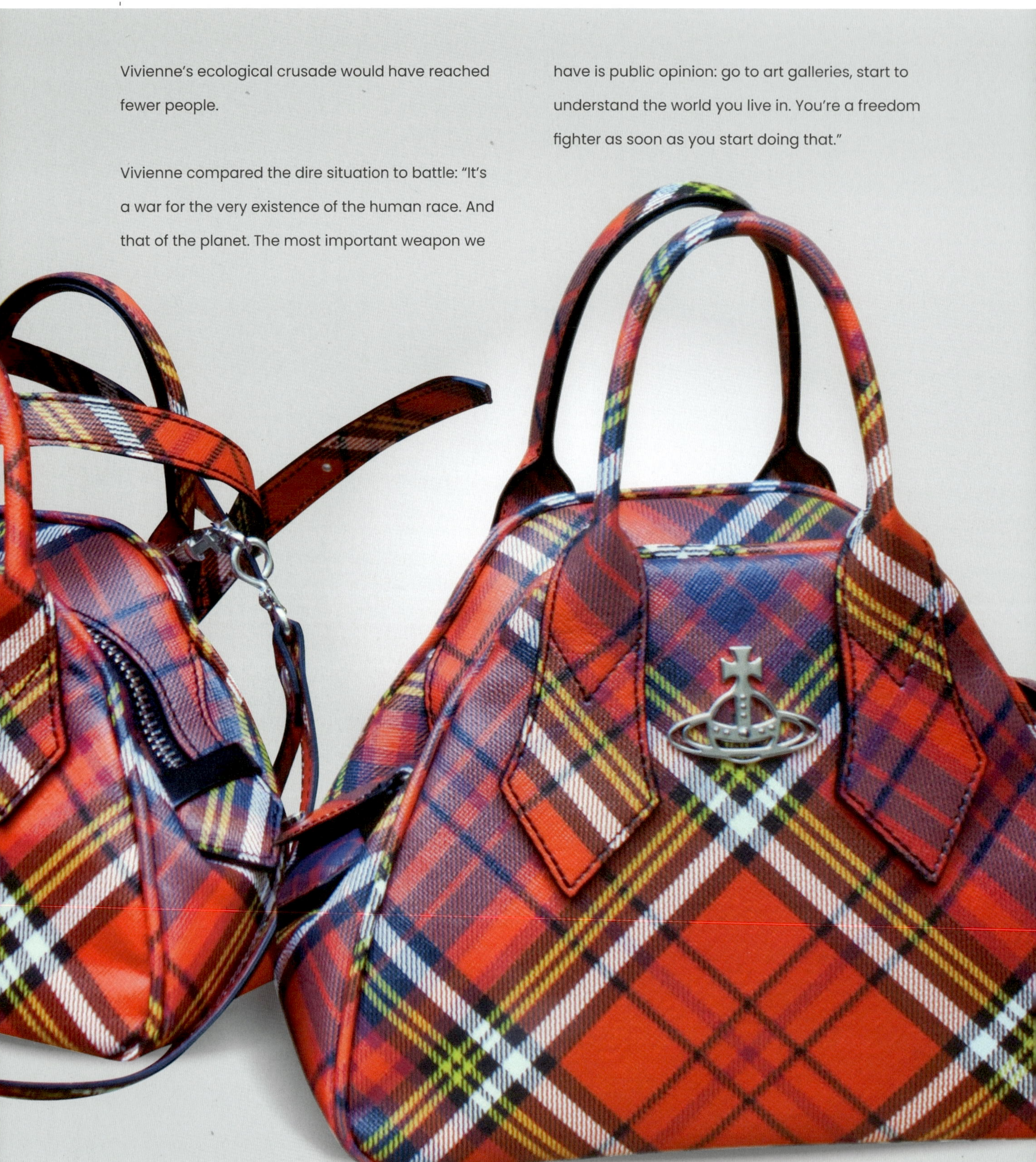

ABOVE: Vivienne Westwood Yasmine derby bags
OPP PAGE: A selection of outfits at the Vivienne Westwood: 34 Years in Fashion exhibition

'VIVIENNE WESTWOOD: 34 YEARS IN FASHION'

In 2004, the retrospective 'Vivienne Westwood: 34 Years in Fashion' opened its doors on the 12th of November at the Victoria and Albert Museum in London. This exhibition featured a highly accessible and visual exploration of fashion culture from the 1970s onwards through Vivienne's lens, as well as reflecting on her significant contributions to fashion, from the early punk years to the historicism of her more recent work.

Key exhibits included examples of punk clothing worn by members of the Sex Pistols in the 1970s, items from the revolutionary 'Mini-Crini' and 'Pirate' collections of the 1980s and the infamous shoes in which Naomi Campbell toppled over in on the catwalk in 1993. The exhibition also displayed major pieces worn by Sarah Jessica Parker as the style icon Carrie Bradshaw in the television series Sex and the City, as well as a dress worn by Cameron Diaz at the 59th annual Golden Globe awards in January 2002.

'Vivienne Westwood: 34 Years in Fashion' was the largest exhibition the museum has ever dedicated to a designer, proving her importance in shaping British culture.

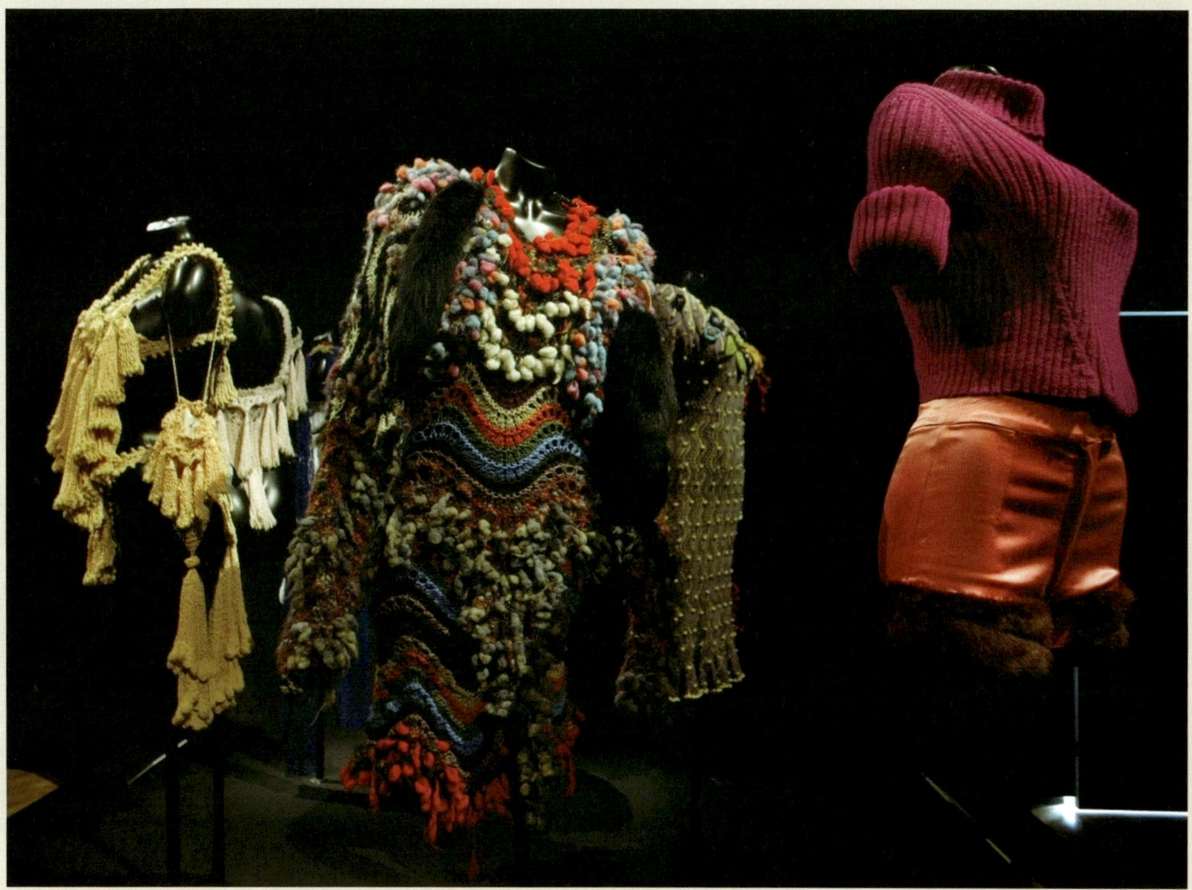

"I AM NOT A TERRORIST"

Vivienne collaborated with the civil rights group Liberty to denounce the UK government's anti-terror legislation, and created one of her most impactful slogan tees to date. The words "I AM NOT A TERRORIST, please don't arrest me" were sprawled in childlike writing next to a red heart. The T-shirt was originally created in 2005, following the murder of innocent man Jean Charles de Menezes, who was falsely suspected of terrorism by the London Met police. All profits went to charity.

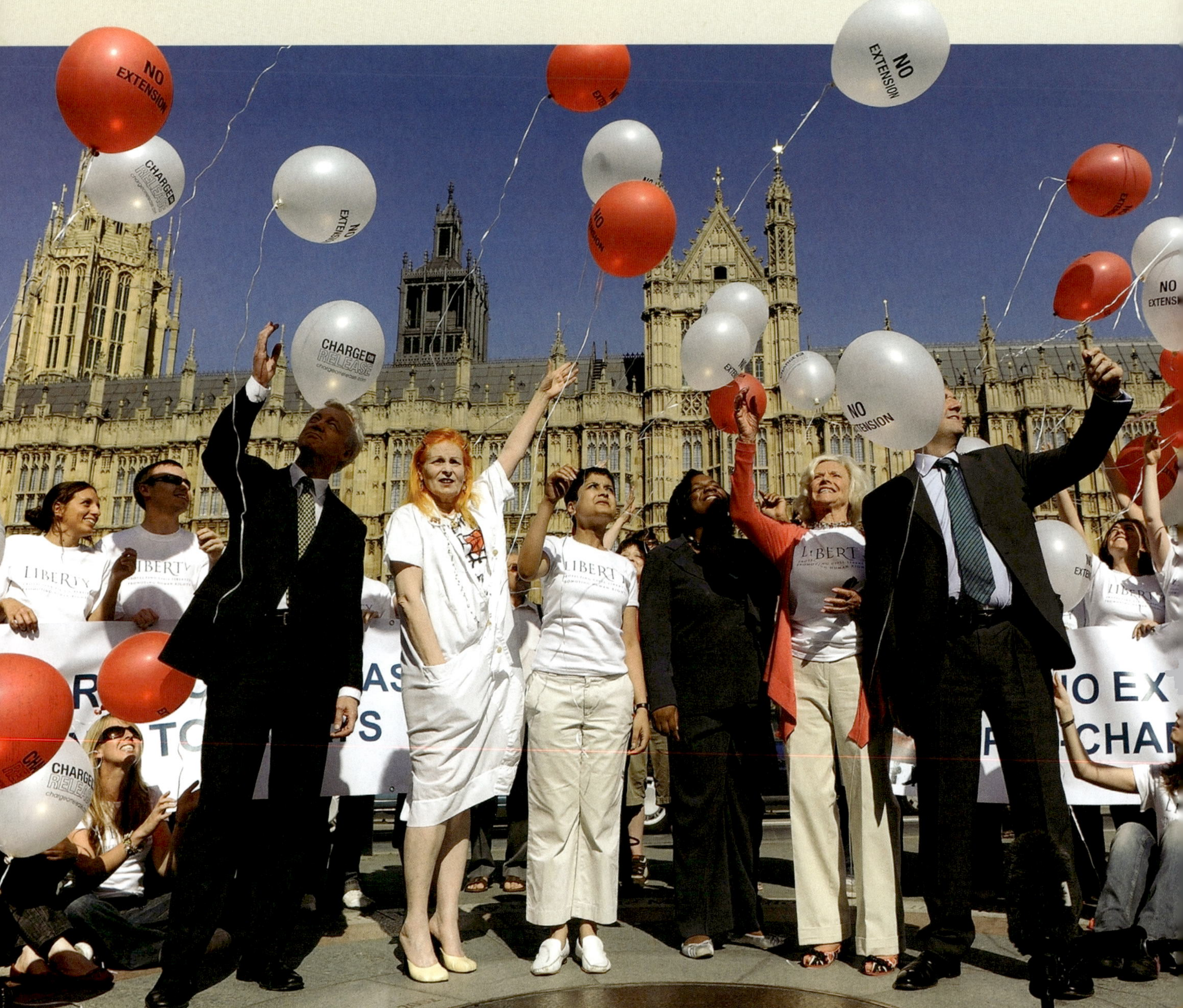

ABOVE: Vivienne takes part in the Liberty balloon protest
OPP PAGE: Vivienne launches her exclusive Liberty design T-shirt, 28 September, 2005, in London

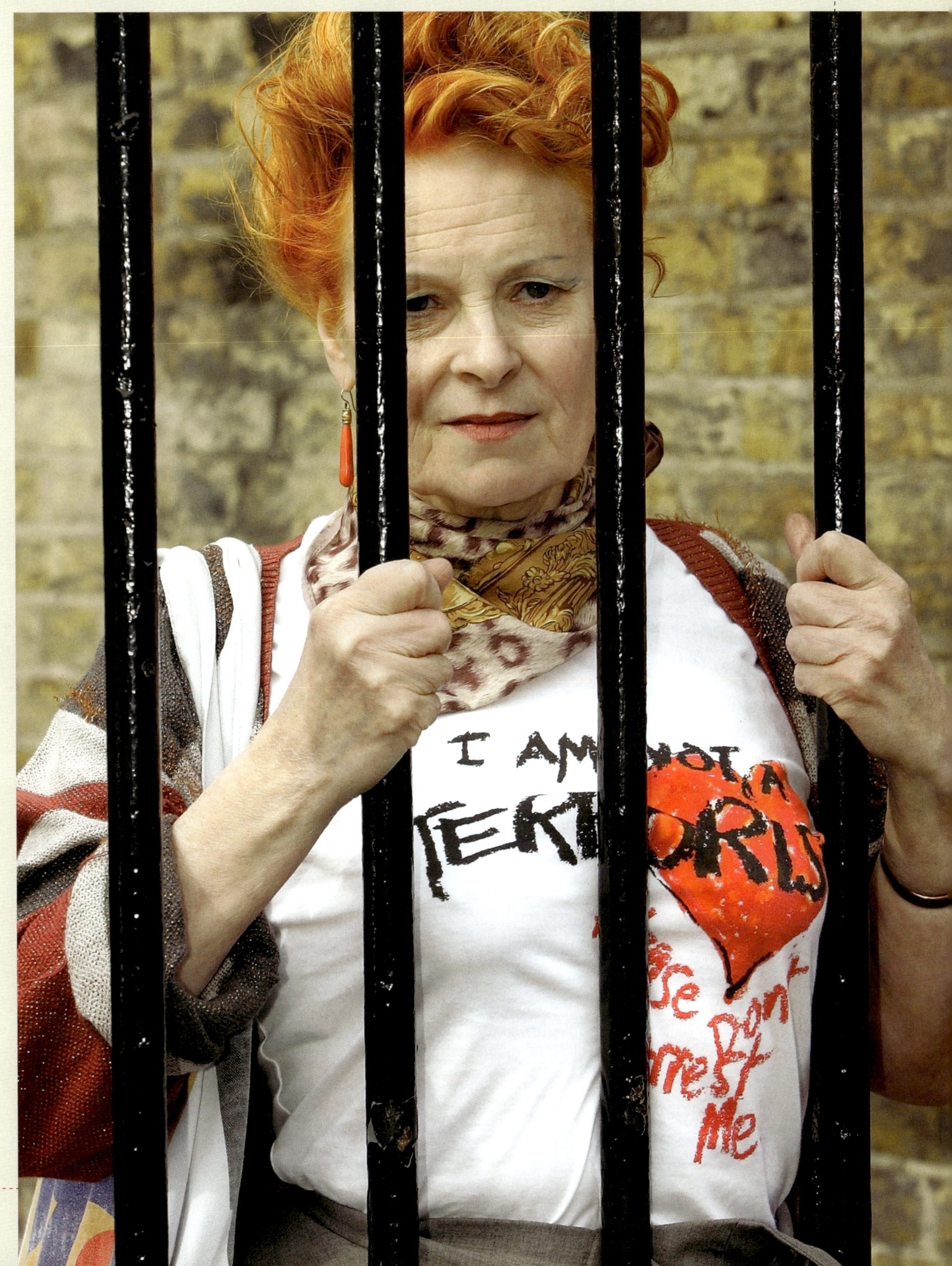
I AM NOT A
TERRORIST
lease Don't
arrest
Me

JACK OF
ALL TRADES
2006-2010

"I reach people — people who read fashion magazines for instance – who would never have heard about some of this otherwise. My main point, though, is quality rather than quantity. What I'm always trying to say is: buy less, choose well, make it last; though sometimes I might as well say, 'buy Vivienne Westwood'!"

Vivienne Westwood

Despite Vivienne's earlier blunder upon receiving her OBE, famously without underwear, the Queen was apparently not offended by the spectacle. Exactly twelve years later, in 2006, Vivienne was invited back to Buckingham Palace to receive the even more auspicious designation of Dame Commander of the British Empire — a female equivalent of a knighthood. Vivienne had finally earned her place at the top of the fashion food chain, and was being rewarded in the highest way possible.

Vivienne continued to tackle different projects left and right. In 2007, she was approached by the Chair of King's College London, Patricia Rawlings, to design an academic gown for the college after it had successfully petitioned the Privy Council for the right to award degrees. A year later, the dresses Vivienne Westwood designed for King's College were unveiled. In true Vivienne style, she imbued the gowns with meaning, commenting, "Through my reworking of the traditional robe I tried to link the past, the present and the future. We are what we know."

Vivienne continued to make contributions to pop culture, though this time, through the medium of the silver screen.

OPP PAGE: Vivenne Westwood after receiving the Dame Commander of the British Empire

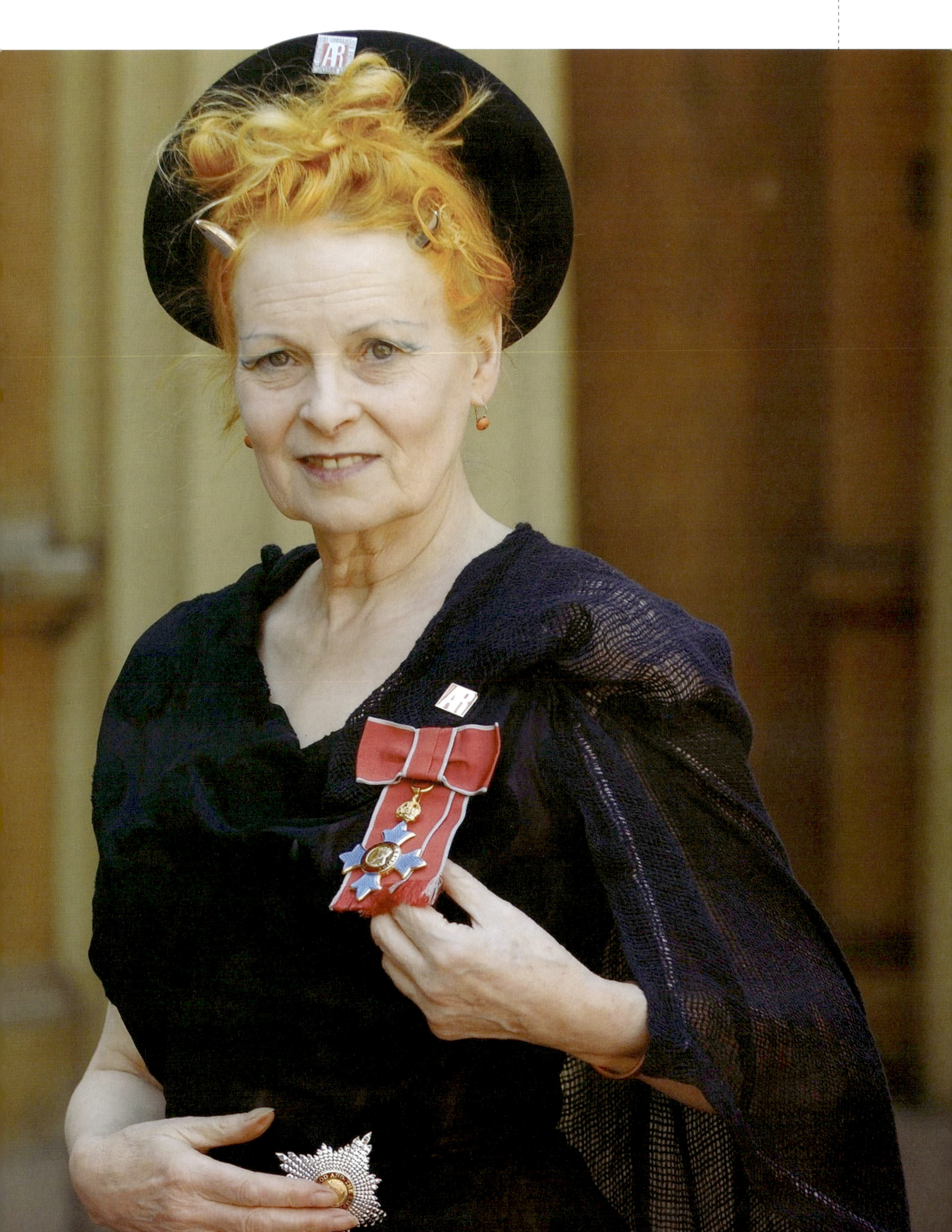
AR

SEX AND THE CITY

The hit show 'Sex and The City' aired from 1998 to 2004, featured numerous Vivienne Westwood looks worn by sex columnist Carrie Bradshaw, played by Sarah Jessica Parker. From her iconic 'Anarchy in the U.K.' T-shirt dating back all the way to 'Seditionaries', to her satin feathery skirt from Vivienne's 1994 Spring/Summer collection, Vivienne's designs were favourites in the show.

Vivienne's designs also featured in the 2008 film adaptation of the television series. In the film, Carrie Bradshaw becomes engaged to long-term lover Mr. Big. Being a writer at Vogue, she is invited by her editor to model wedding dresses, including a design made by Vivienne. The appearance of the wedding dress is largely considered the most iconic fashion moment in the movie and a version of the dress was subsequently made available for purchase on the Net-a-Porter website, though it sold in a matter of hours. Despite 'Sex and the City's' reverence for Vivienne's designs, the designer wasn't particulary a fan of the movie saying, "I thought 'Sex And The City' was supposed to be about cutting-edge fashion and there was nothing remotely memorable or interesting about what I saw".

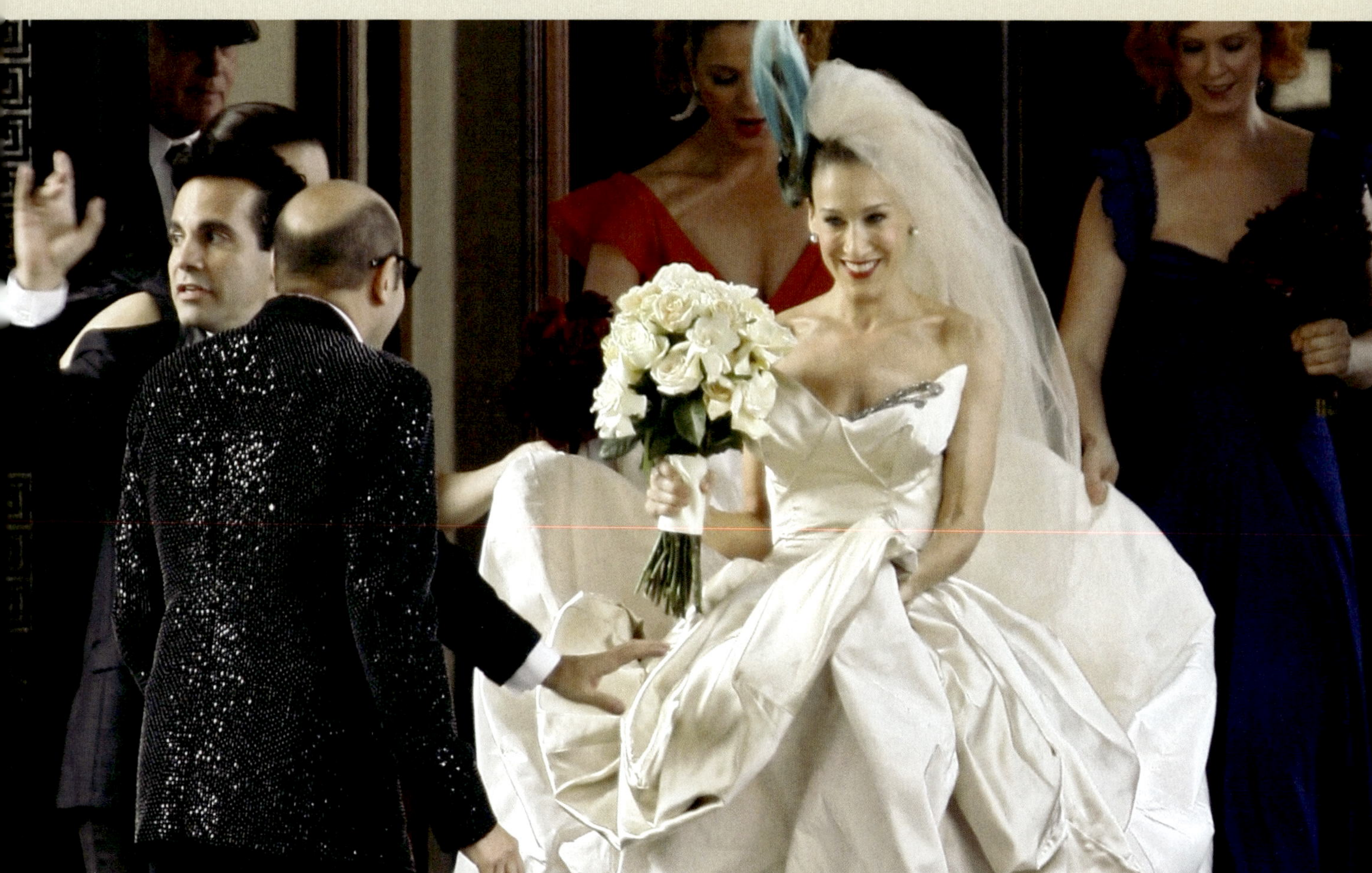

ABOVE: Sarah Jessica Parker wearing a Vivienne Westwood wedding dress in the 'Sex and The City' film

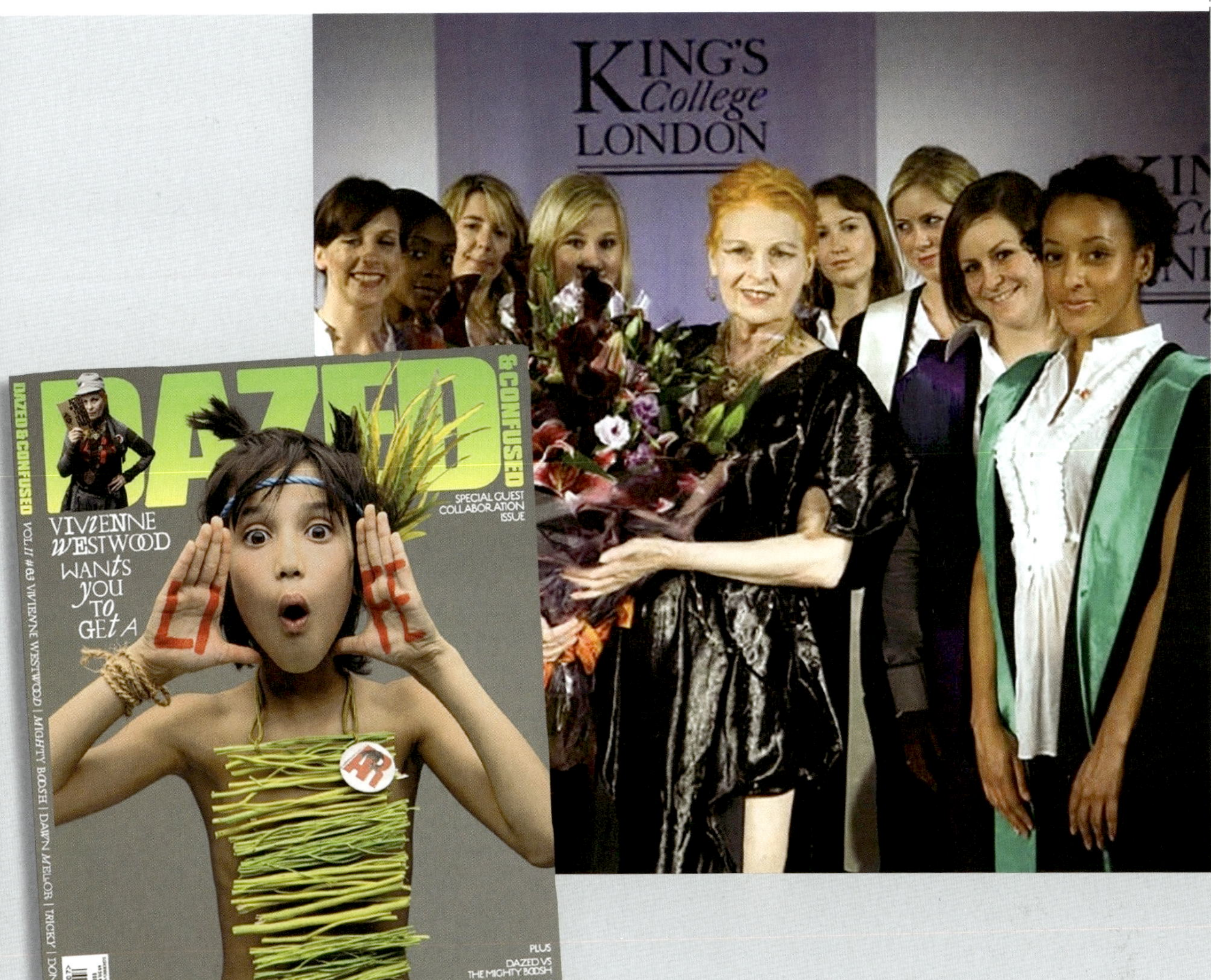

and history. The article was all about challenging the status quo, and becoming what Vivienne would call a "freedom fighter" in the process.

In 2008, Vivienne brushed up on her writing skills, as she took over the reins of *Dazed* magazine's special 'Active Resistance' edition for July. Fronted by a child eco-warrior cover star, Vivienne told readers to "Get a Life", as she addressed many of the political concerns nearest and dearest to her heart. She discussed the climate crisis and rising sea levels, whilst also expressing her love for higher culture such as art

Following her publishing debut, Vivienne decided to show her loyalty to the climate change cause and shaved her head. Later, the designer-turned-activist was seen sporting a shower cap and little else for a PETA ad campaign to promote World Water Day and vegetarianism, drawing attention to the meat industry's water consumption.

VIVIENNE WESTWOOD X
2014-2021

"You have a better life if you wear impressive clothes."
Vivienne Westwood

After taking a long sabbatical to focus on her activism, Vivienne came back to her fashion roots and started designing independently again. In 2014, it was announced that Vivienne Westwood had redesigned the full range of uniforms for the 7500 members of staff working on Richard Branson's airline. The British billionaire, known for his own maverick spirit and rebellious stunts, unsurprisingly chose Vivienne as the first choice to design the next Virgin Atlantic uniform. A representative from Virgin Atlantic commented on the decision, stating, "Original design and sustainability are vital to both Virgin Atlantic and Vivienne Westwood".

The uniform for the female cabin crew featured a bright red jacket with a nipped-in waist and high collar detail, paired with a pencil skirt. The outfit came with a matching red double-breasted coat with an oversized collar, gathered at the waist for the colder climates. The uniform is then completed with a red shoes, incorporating Vivienne's signature hourglass

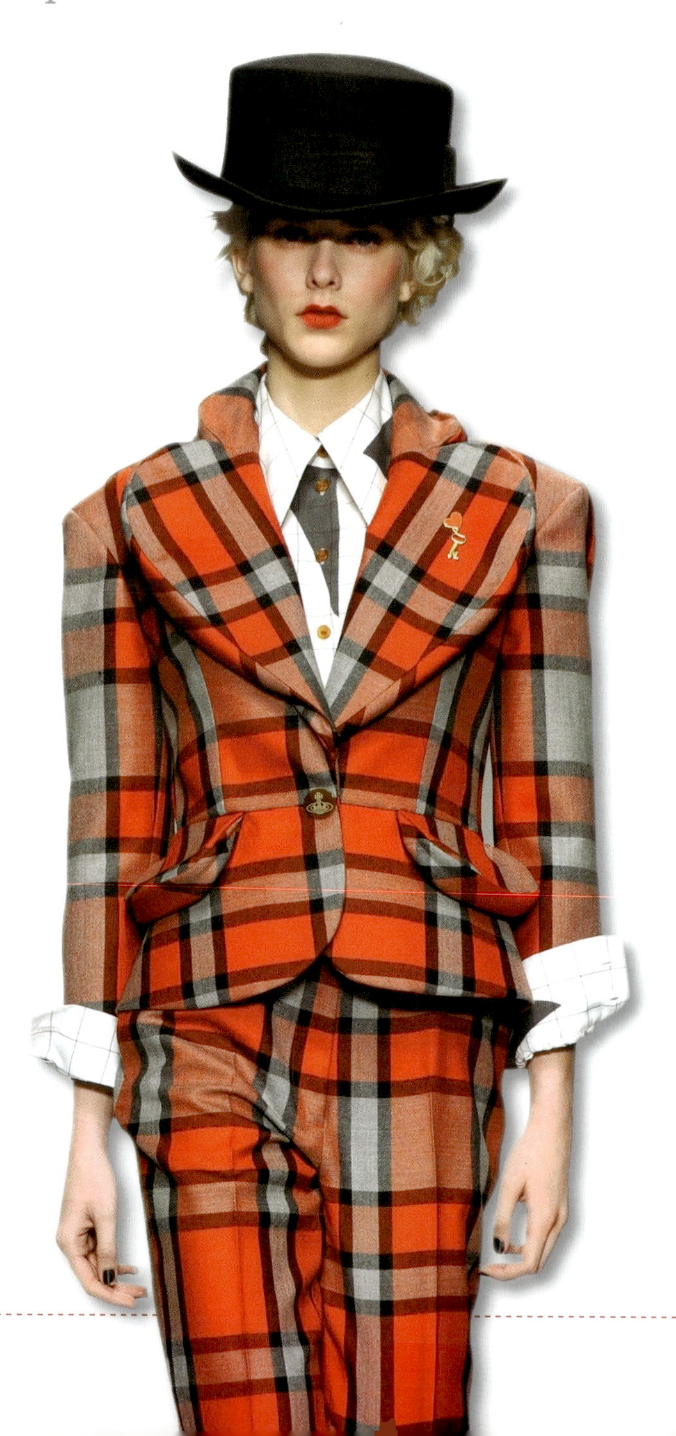

RIGHT: A model wears a Vivienne Westwood design at London Fashion Week, Autumn/ Winter 2014
OPP PAGE: Virgin Atlantic crew attend the launch party to celebrate Virgin Atlantic's new Vivienne Westwood uniform collection at Village Underground on 1 July, 2014

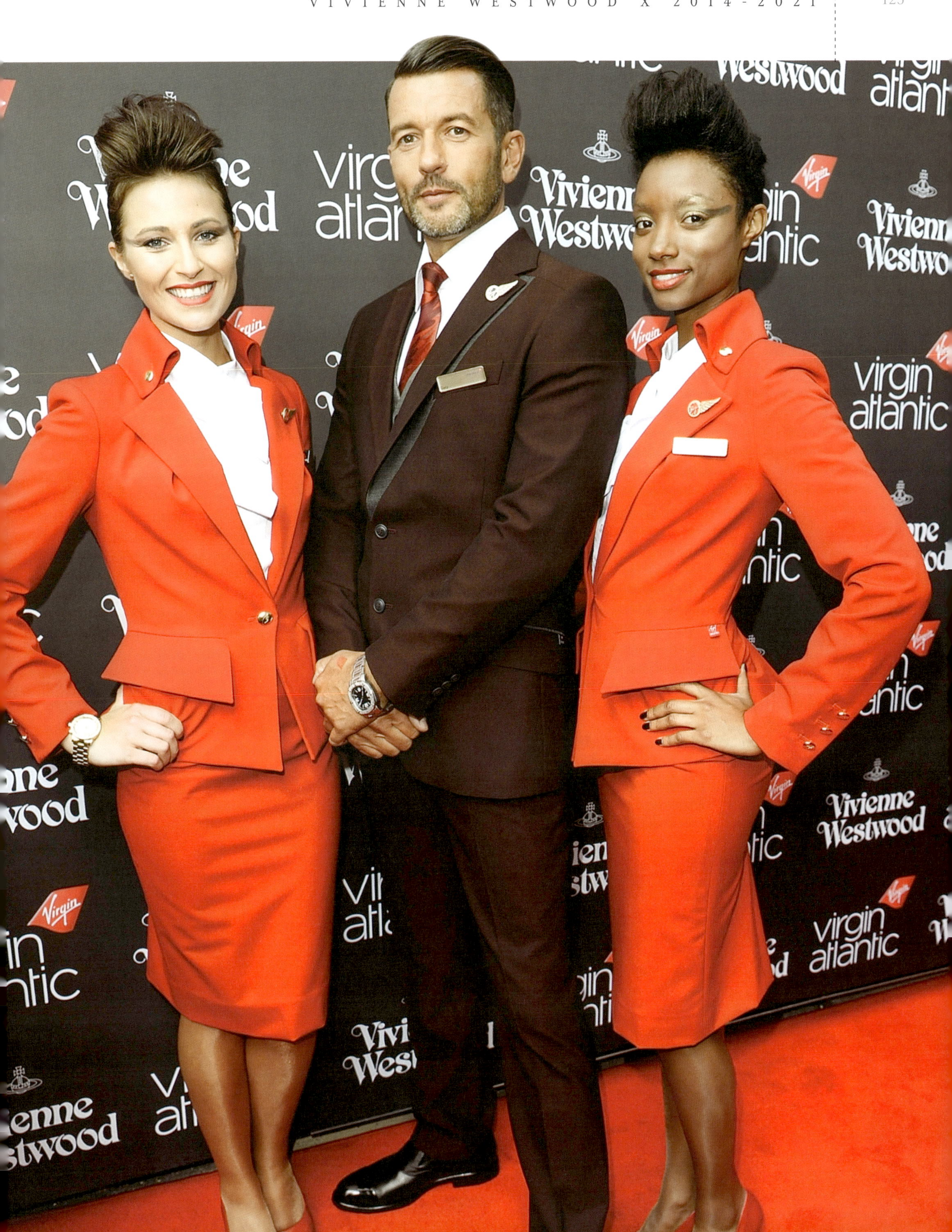

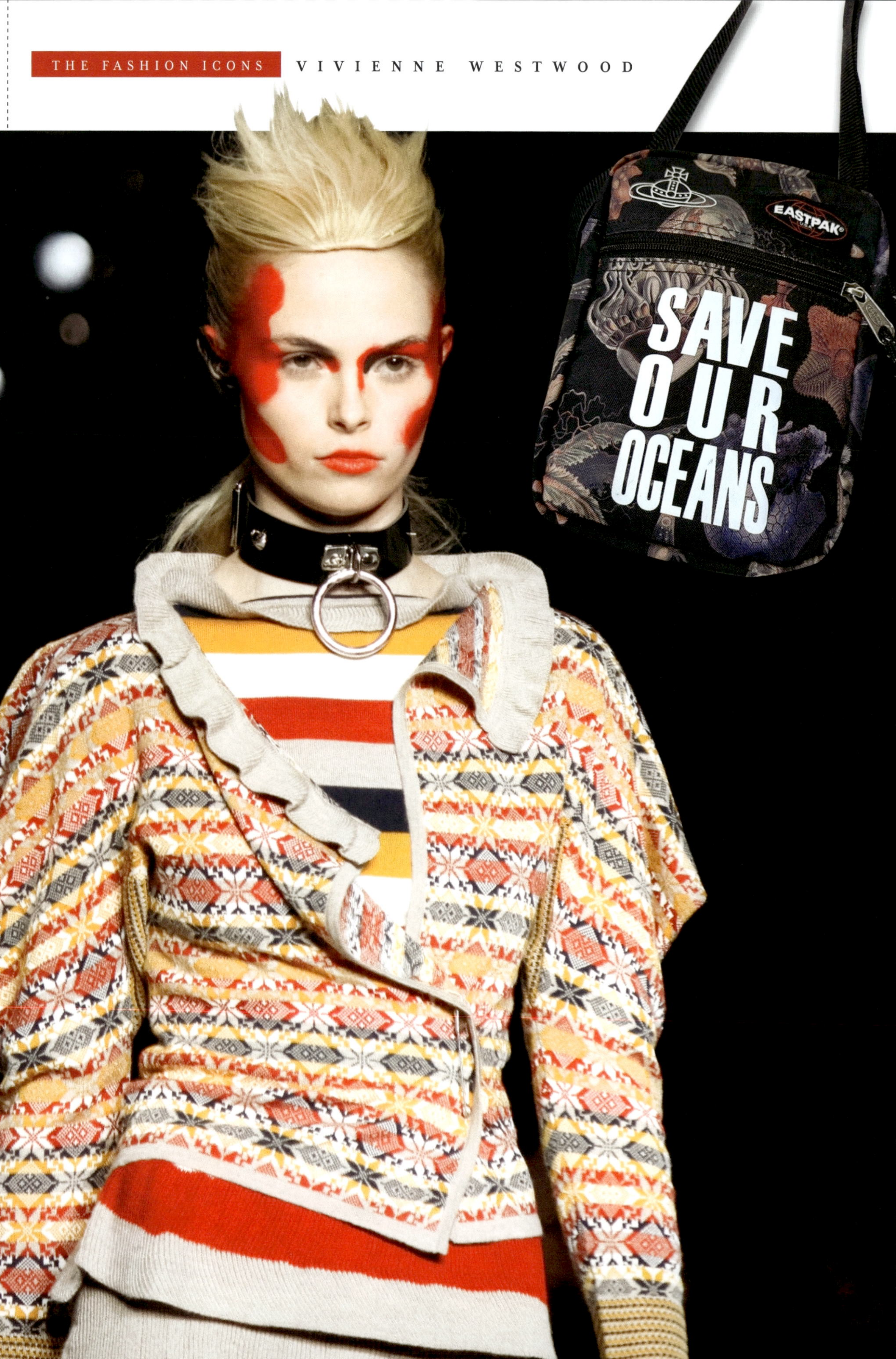
EASTPAK
SAVE
OUR
OCEANS

heel, and a red leather bag that featured diamond-shaped handles.

The menswear, on the other hand, featured a three-piece suit made of deep burgundy Oxford weave wool, worn over a white shirt with a wide collar.

The entire collection of uniforms from beginning to end was steeped in Vivienne's inimitable style, and consistently referenced her archival looks. Following her successful collaboration with Virgin, Vivienne embarked on a streak of various different collaborations with Asics, Vans, and Eastpak.

Vivienne's collaboration with Asics was one of the most surprising and innovative partnerships of her career. Asics, known primarily for its performance-focused athletic footwear, forced Vivienne to strike a balance between high functionality and high fashion. The partnership launched in 2019, and featured a reimagining of several classic Asics silhouettes, including the Gel-Kayano and the Gel-Mai, two of the brand's most iconic sneaker styles. The collection incorporated Vivienne's adoration of historical references, now a staple of her brand, while also embracing the futuristic and athletic roots of Asics. One of the most eye-catching elements of the designs was Westwood's use of Renaissance-inspired prints.

Vivienne's partnership with Vans, the legendary skate wear brand, on the other hand, was a natural fit. The Vans brand is known for its association with youth culture, rebellion, and skateboarding, and so the collaboration brought her back to her punk roots.

The collection featured several of Vans' classic sneaker models, including the Sk8-Hi, Slip-On, and Old Skool, all reinterpreted with Vivienne's signature motifs, such as tartan patterns, graffiti-style graphics, and her iconic orb logo. Some of the shoes featured handwritten notes and postmarks, a nod to earlier work.

One of the standout pieces in the collection was the Sk8-Hi Platform, which combined Vans' iconic high-top silhouette with Vivienne's penchant for elevated platform shoes. This collaboration was the perfect example of how two brands can bridge the gap between street culture and high fashion.

Lastly, in 2020 Vivienne worked with the American backpack company Eastpak, to create an eco-conscious collection with a focus on practical, durable products. The partnership resulted in a range of backpacks and luggage, featuring eco-friendly materials such as organic cotton and recycled fabrics, including a backpack adorned with Vivienne's signature 'Save the Planet' graphics. The collection aimed to encourage consumers to make more thoughtful, sustainable choices when it came to fashion, aligning with Vivienne's long-standing campaign for ethical consumption.

Though it had been over a decade since Vivienne had properly participated in her brand's clothing line, her collaboration with different brands proved she was still one of the greatest designers to ever exist.

OPP PAGE MAIN: Vivienne Westwood London Fashion Week, Autumn/Winter 2015 collection
OPP PAGE RIGHT: Eastpak bag designed by Vivienne Westwood, showcasing her 'Save the Planet' graphics

DO NOT BUY A BOMB

On the 8th April 2021, Vivienne turned 80. To celebrate this milestone, Westwood was commissioned by the Cultural Institute of Radical Contemporary Arts (CIRCA) to make a video message, marking the special occasion. Live from Piccadilly Circus, Vivienne presented her ten-minute film, created with her brother, entitled 'Do Not Buy A Bomb'. She performed a rewritten rendition of 'Without You' from 'My Fair Lady' to offer a stark warning of societal indifference to the looming environmental catastrophe.

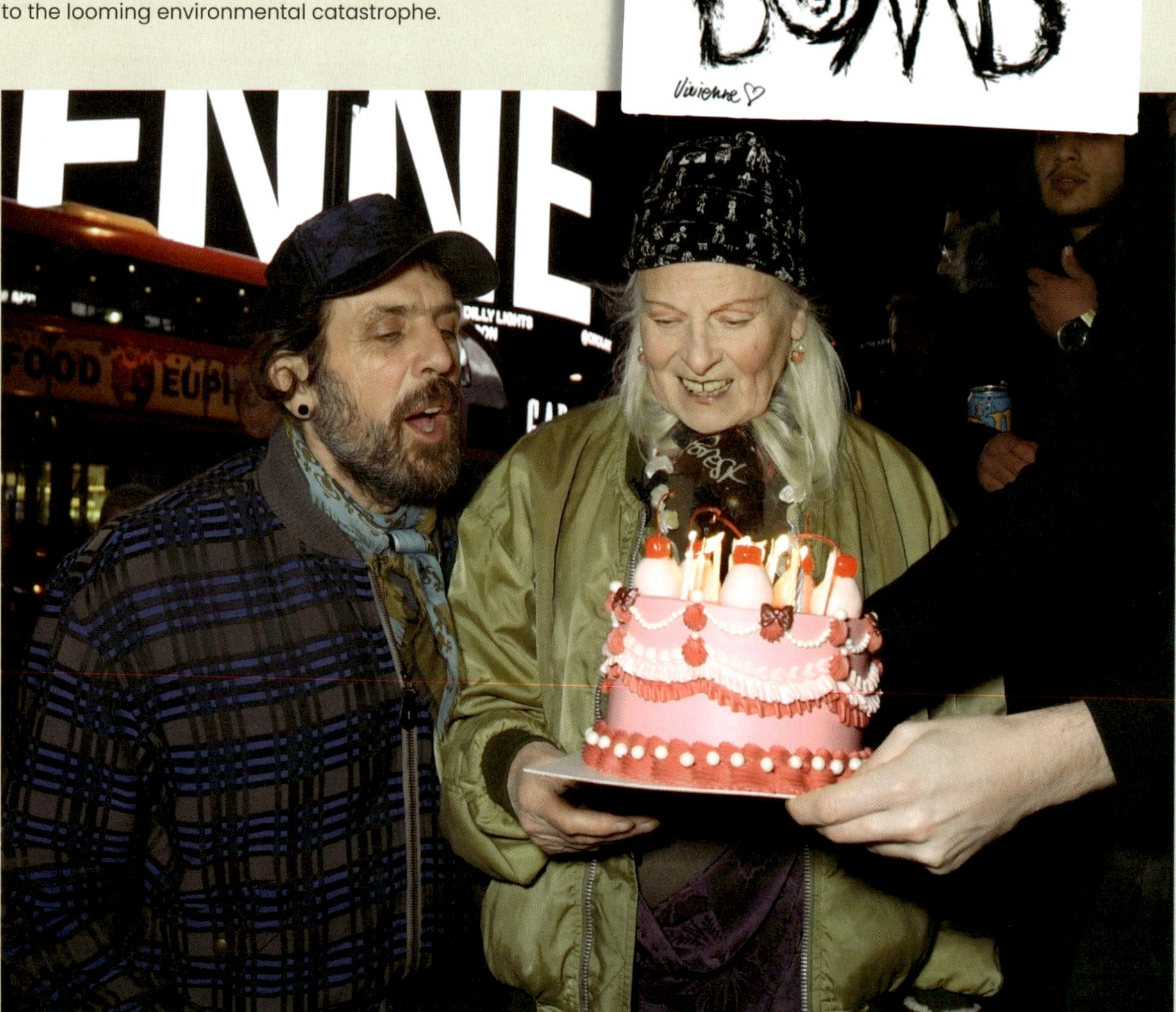

TOP: Graphic designed by Vivienne to support the 'Do Not Buy a Bomb' campaign
ABOVE: Andreas Kronthaler and Dame Vivienne Westwood attend a short film screening to celebrate Dame Vivienne Westwood's 80th birthday 8 April 2021

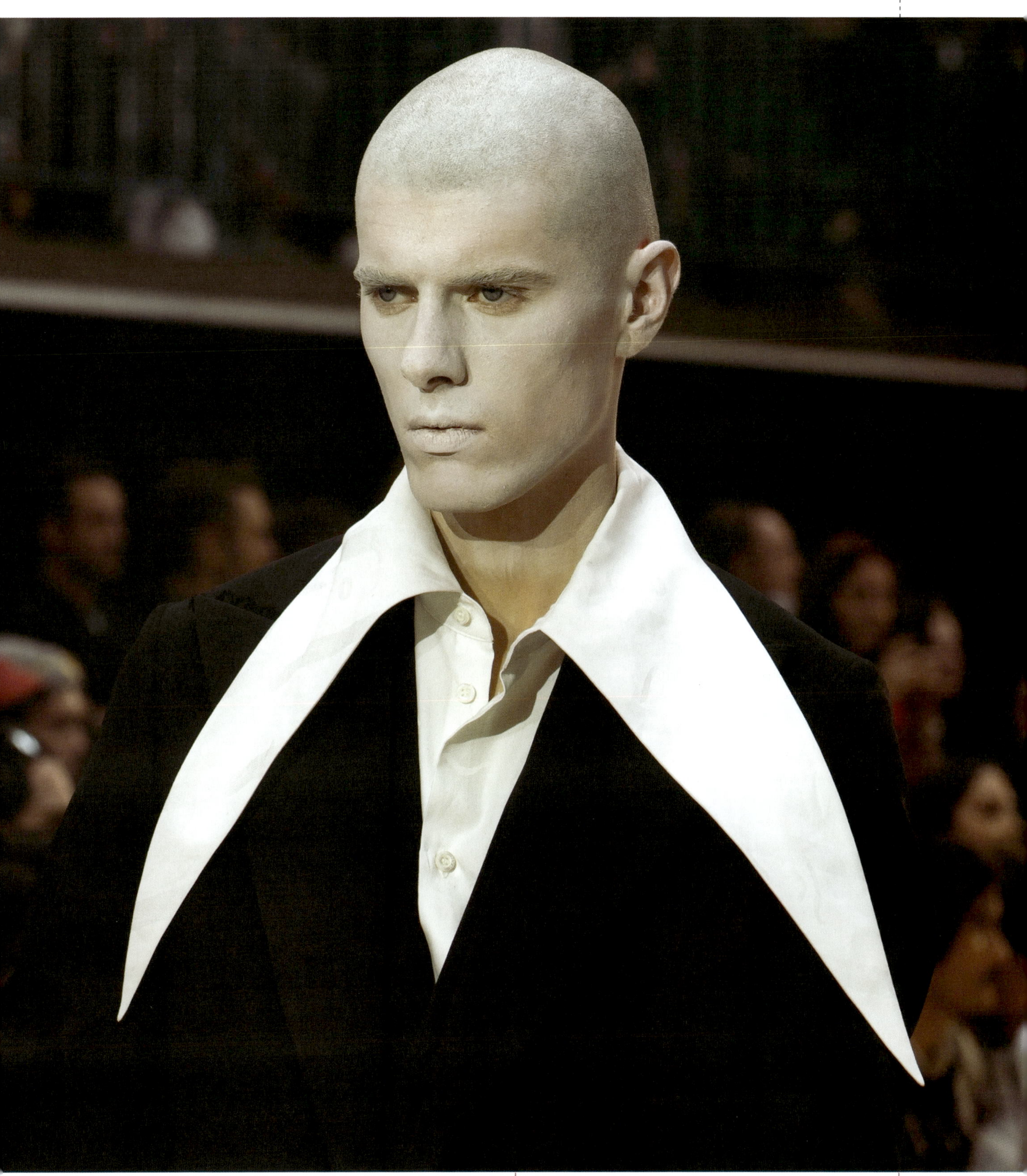

ABOVE: A model walks the runway at the Vivienne
Westwood show during the London Fashion Week, 2017

LONG LIVE THE QUEEN

2022

"Vivienne is gone and the world is already a less interesting place."
Chrissie Hynde

On December 29th, 2022, Vivienne Westwood, one of the most influential and revolutionary figures in fashion, passed away at the age of 81. She died peacefully in her home in Clapham, South London, surrounded by her family and loved ones. In January 2023, a private funeral was held at Christ Church in Tintwistle, Derbyshire, the village where Vivienne had grown up. The church was decorated with 45 metres of MacLeod Harris Tweed tartan in honour of the designer, and a memorial service was held, at Southwark Cathedral in London, on the 16th February 2023.

Following the announcement of her passing, social media was flooded with tributes to Vivienne and her work. Former Sex Pistols guitarist Glen Matlock wrote on Twitter that it was "a privilege to have rubbed shoulders with her in the mid-70s at the birth of punk

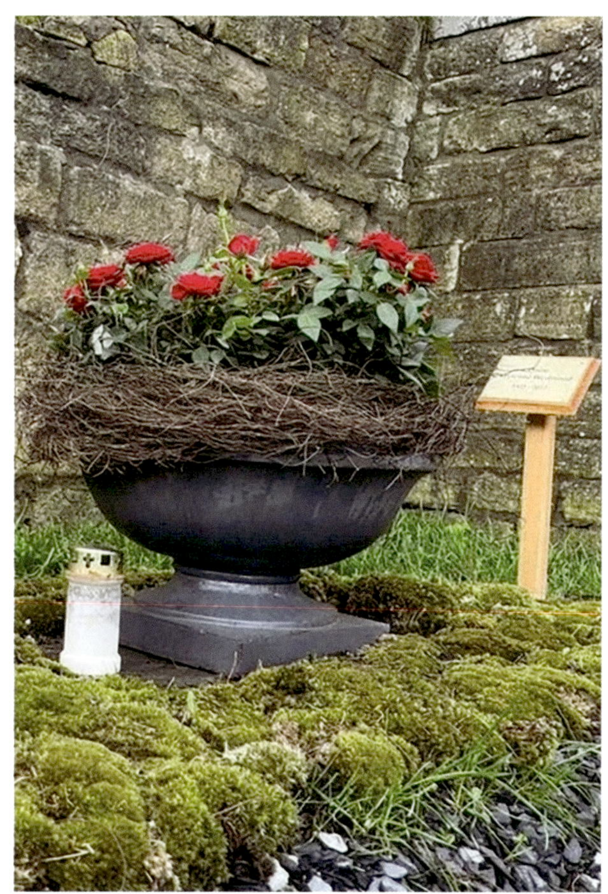

RIGHT: Her place of rest in the Tintwistle cemetery
OPP PAGE: Vivienne Westwood at her Worlds End Chelsea Store, 1987, wearing her iconic Harris Tweed crown

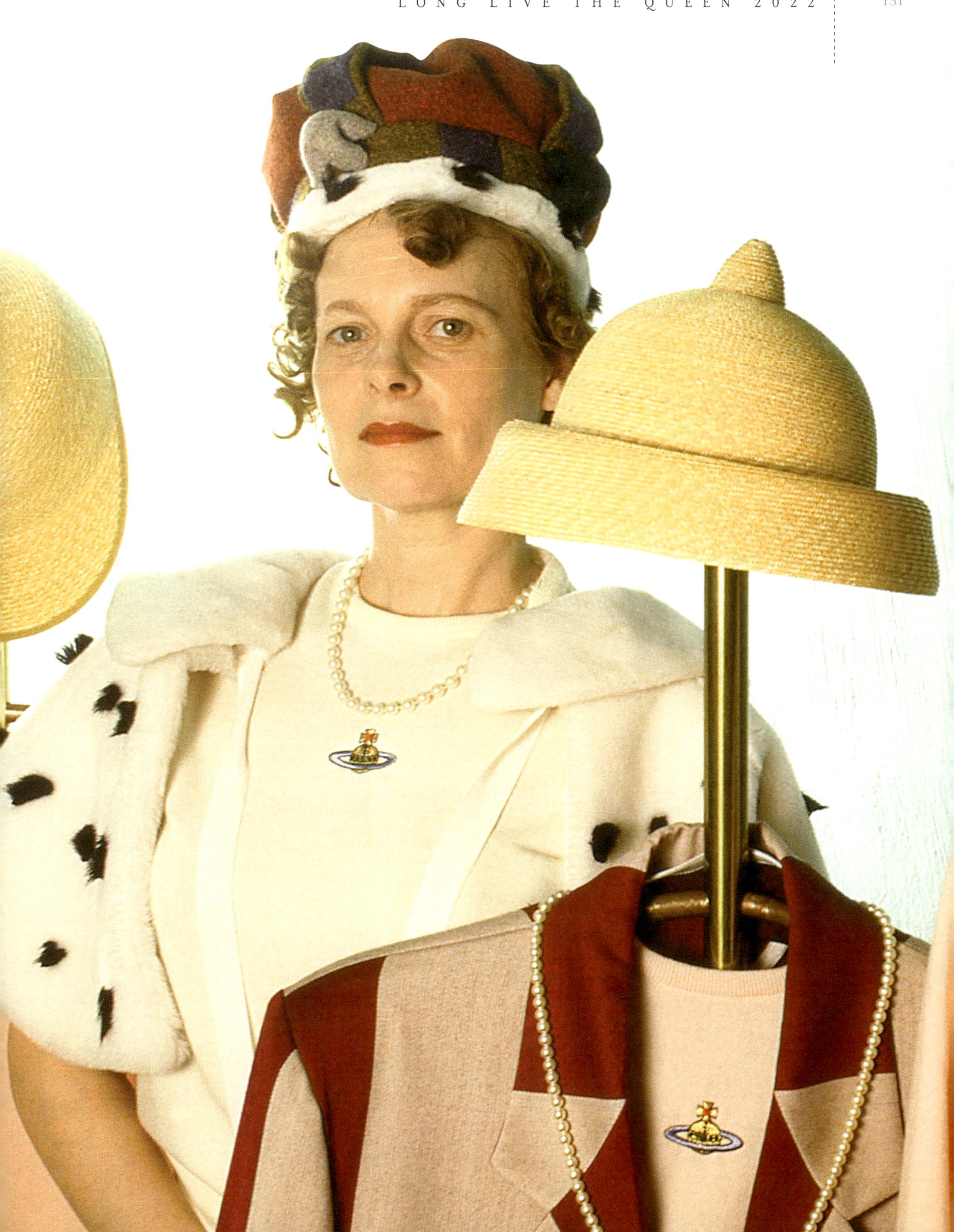

and the waves it created that still resound today for the disaffected". Singer Simon Le Bon from Duran Duran, Boy George, former Frankie Goes to Hollywood member Holly Johnson, Yoko Ono, Paul McCartney, and the fashion house Alexander McQueen all paid homage to the recently departed designer.

Her death marked the end of an era for both the fashion world and culture in general. Vivienne was a pioneering force, whose designs, ideas, and activism redefined what fashion could be and how it could speak to the world.

Vivienne's career spanned over five decades, during which she continually challenged conventions and pushed boundaries. From her early days in the 1970s, co-creating the punk movement alongside Malcolm McLaren, to her later years as a staunch advocate against climate change and consumerism, the iconic British designer always used her platform to question authority and speak truth to power. She was more than a fashion designer—she was a cultural provocateur, a political activist, and a champion of individuality and self-expression.

Her radical approach to design, which blended historical references with subversive, anarchic elements, influenced not only fashion, but also music, art, and broader pop culture.

As for the future, the Vivienne Westwood fashion house was left to her husband and long-time

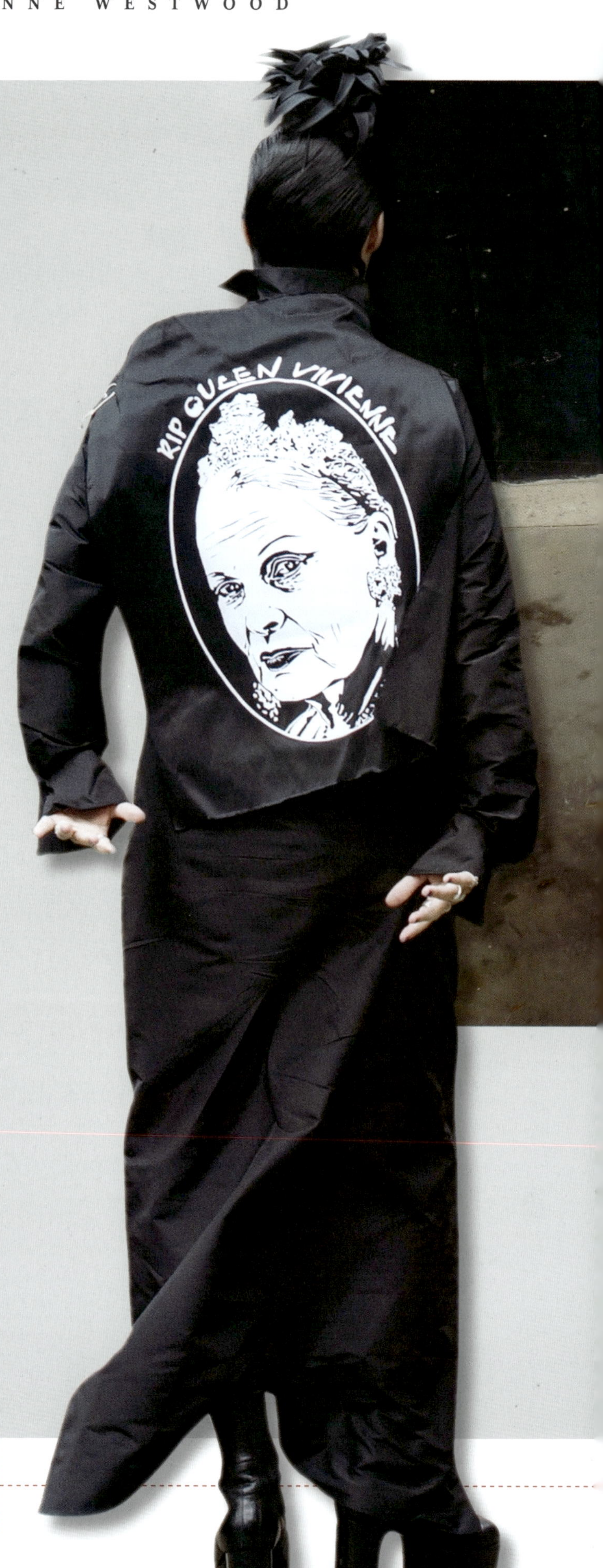

RIGHT: A mourner arriving at the memorial service wears a coat adorned with a Vivienne's face
OPP PAGE: Flowers were placed outside her famous shop at 430 King's Road, Chelsea, London, 30 Dec, 2022

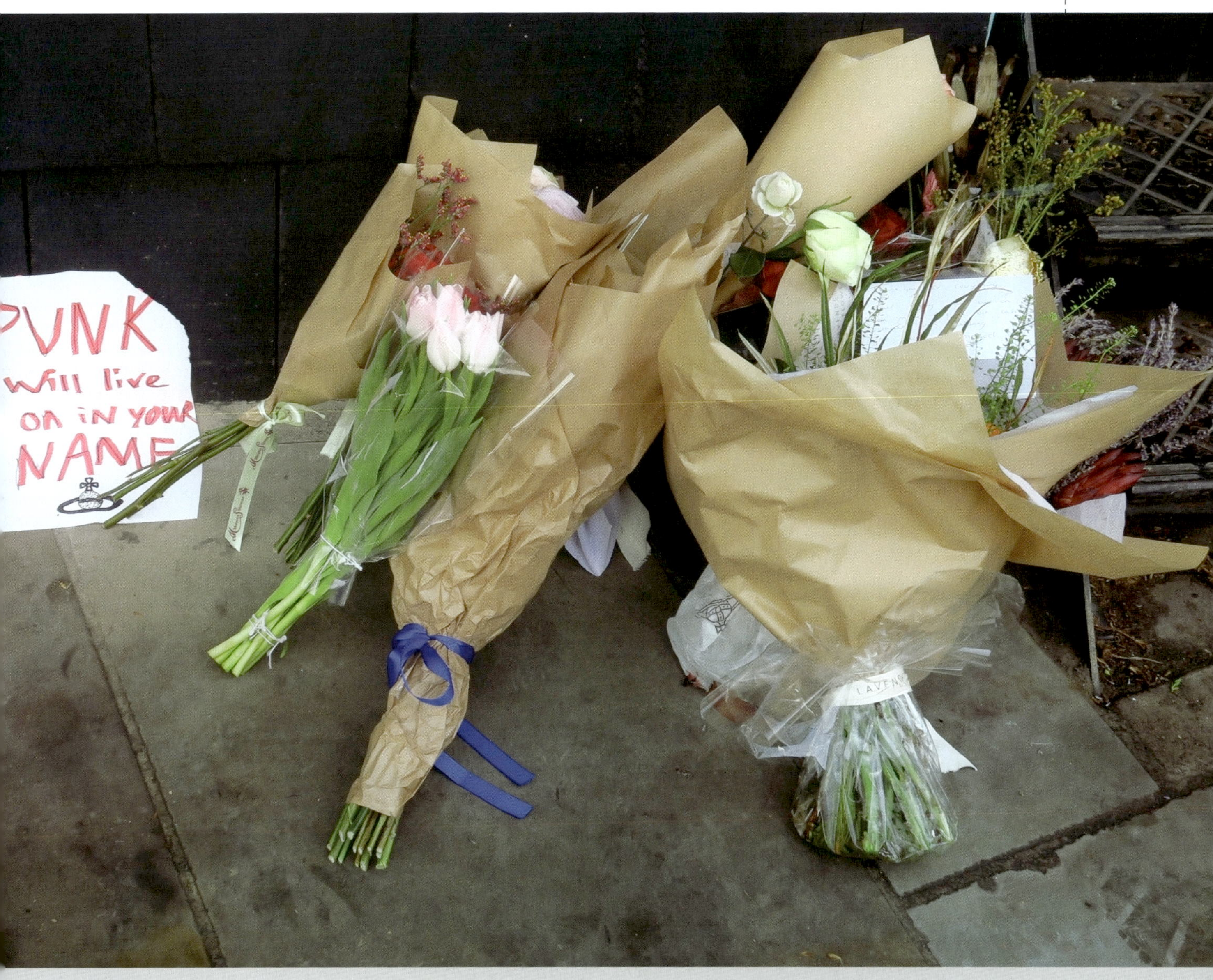

collaborator Andreas. Kronthaler is expected to continue Westwood's legacy, steering the brand in her honour while maintaining the rebellious and avant-garde spirit that defined her work.

In her later years, Westwood openly reflected on her life's work and the impact she hoped it would leave. Her message, always clear and uncompromising, was about freedom, truth, and responsibility—values that will continue to shape her brand and inspire future generations.

As the fashion world continues to evolve, Vivienne's contributions will remain a vital part of its foundation, and her legacy will continue to inspire those who seek to disrupt, innovate, and create in the years to come.

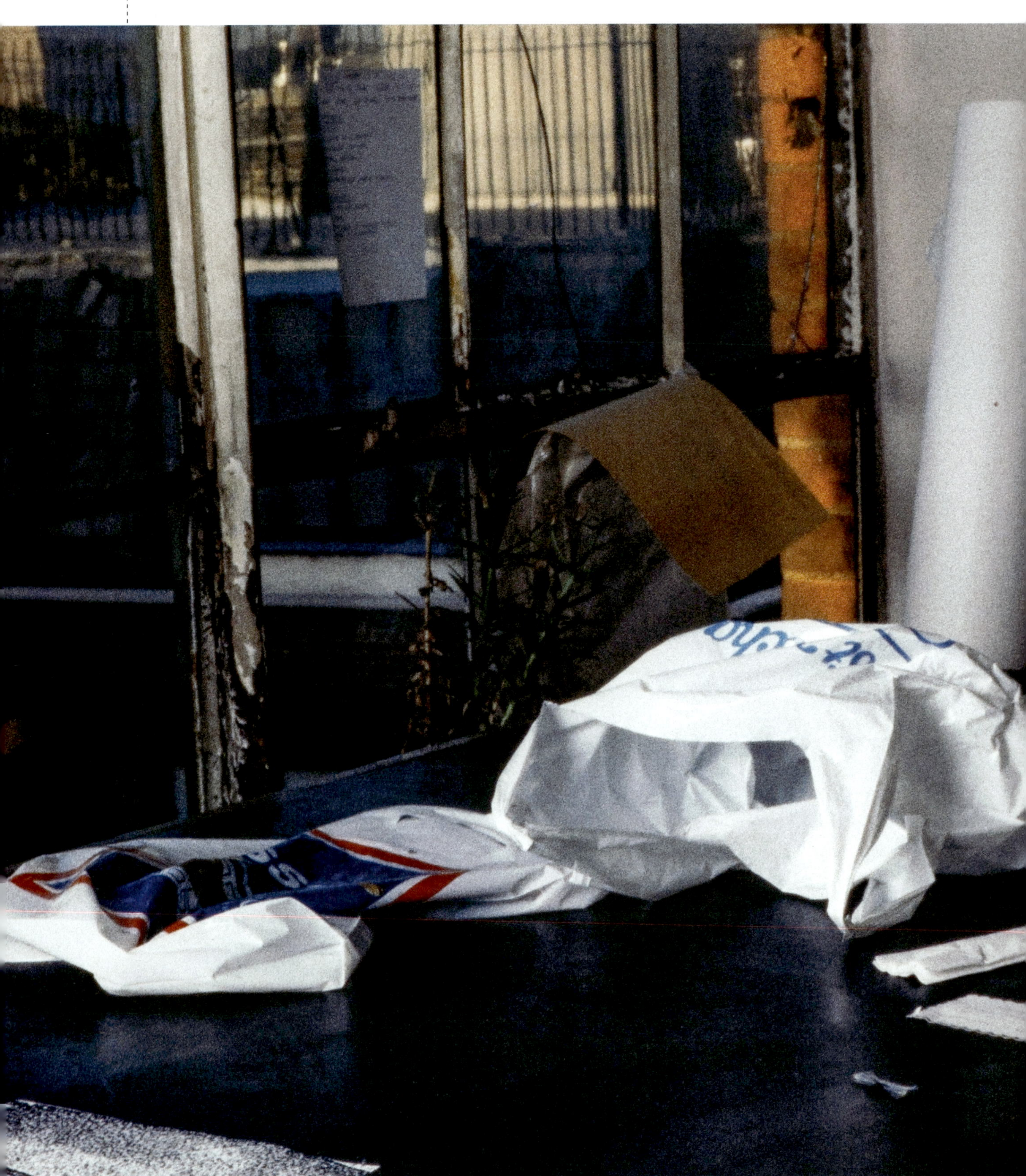

ABOVE: Vivienne Westwood photographed in her studio in Camden Town after winning another award for her cutting-edge work, 10 October, 1990

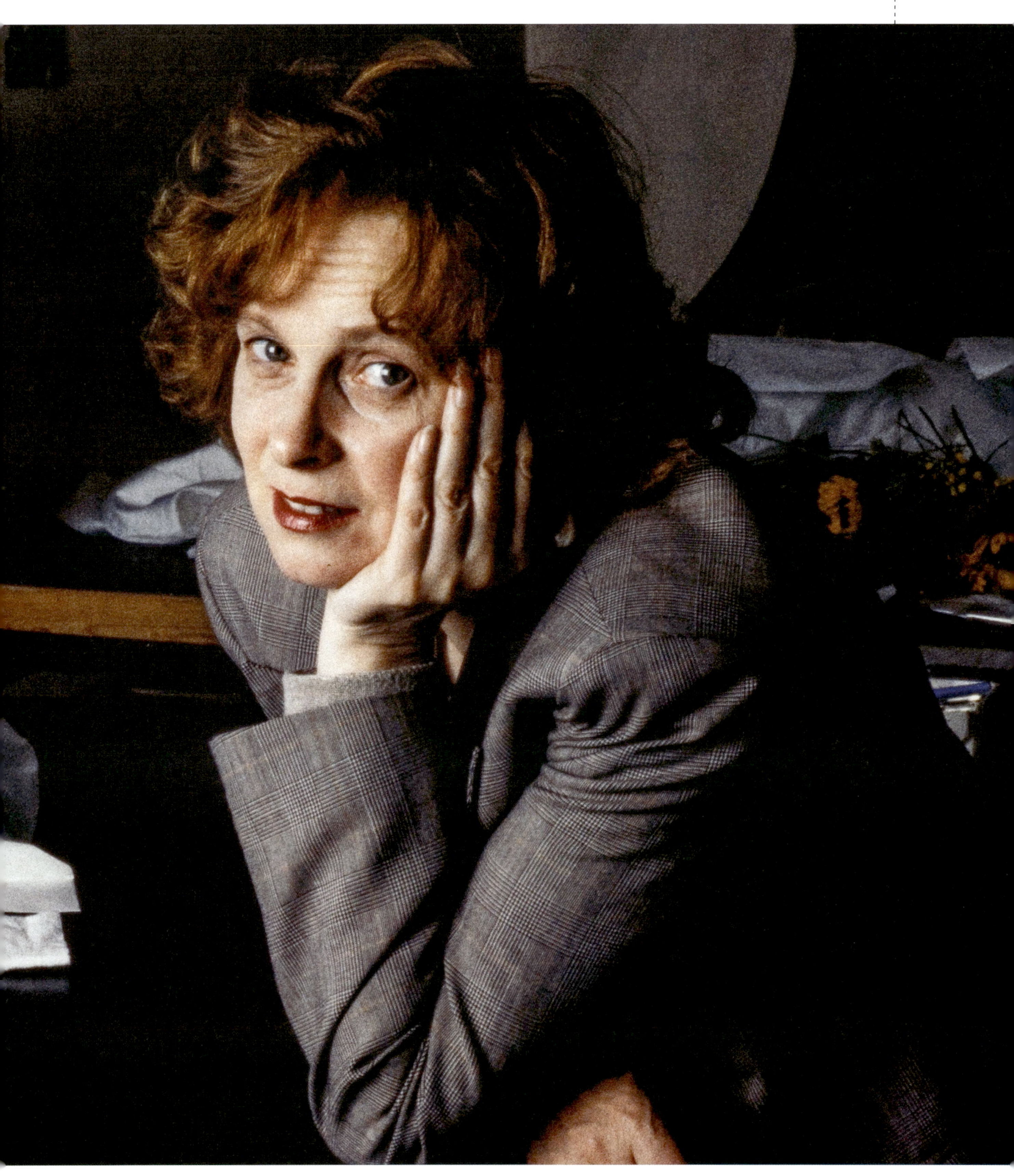

A LIFE IN DATES

"Fashion is about eventually being naked."
Vivienne Westwood

1941

Vivienne was **born in Tintwistle**, U.K.

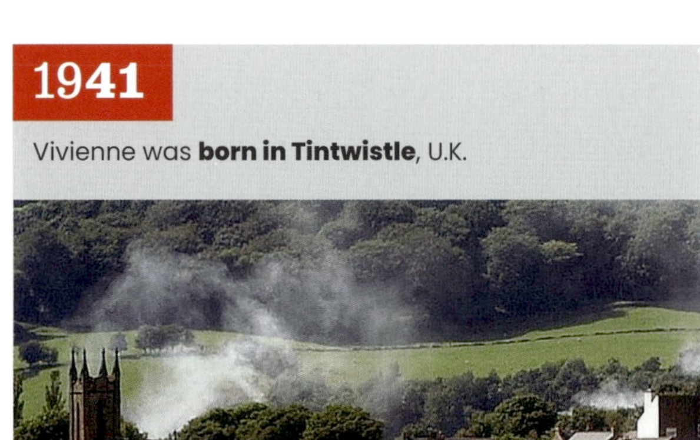

1966

Vivienne and **Malcolm** **meet**.

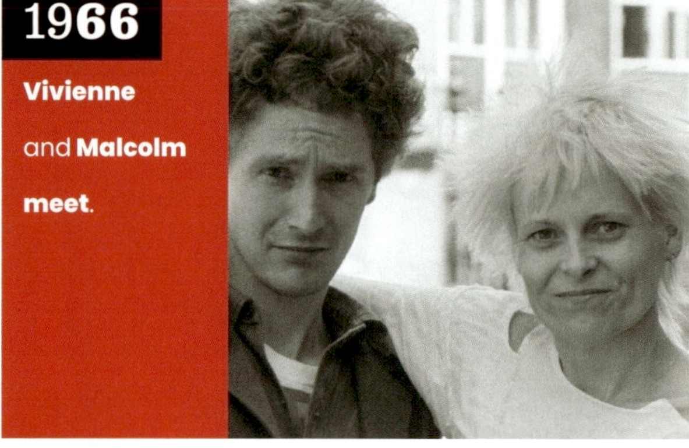

1967

The couple welcome their **son Joseph**.

1971

Together with Malcolm, she **founded her first boutique** 'Let it Rock' at 430 King's Road in London.

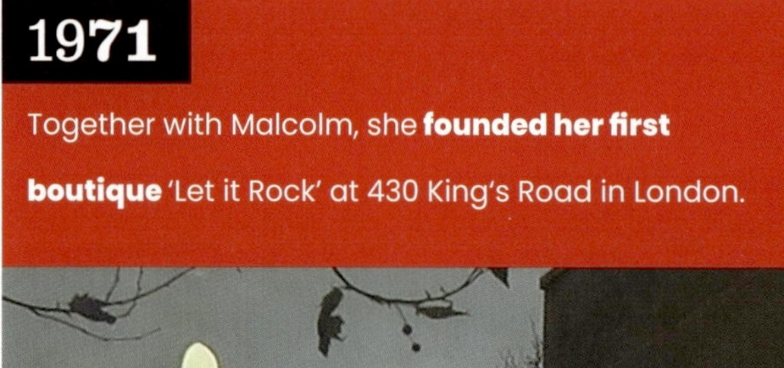

1962

She **married Derek Westwood**.

1963

Vivienne **gives birth to their first son Ben**, but soon after, the couple separated.

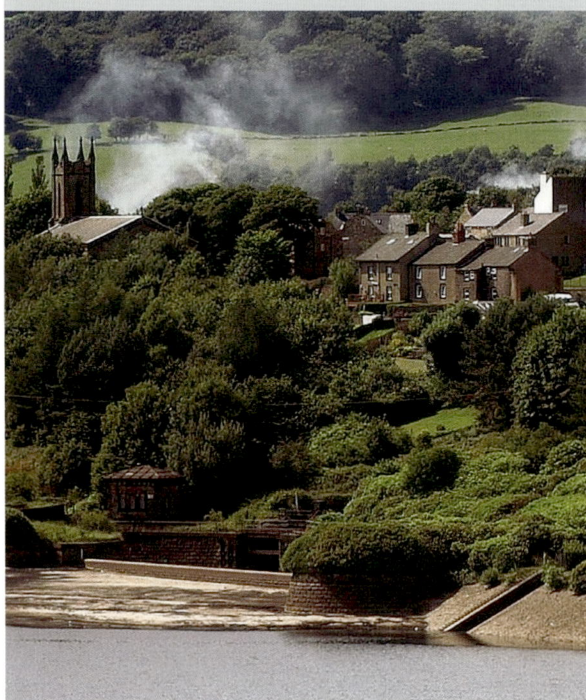

1973

A new product range brings a **new name for the store:** 'Too Fast To Live, Too Young To Die'.

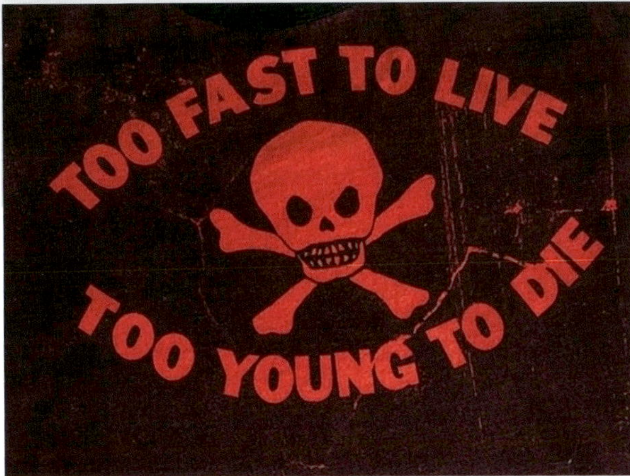

1974

The store has reopened with the name 'SEX', and **the product range changed to erotic lingerie and SM articles.** During this time, the first touch-points with the Sex Pistols can be identified, for whose outfits Westwood is largely responsible.

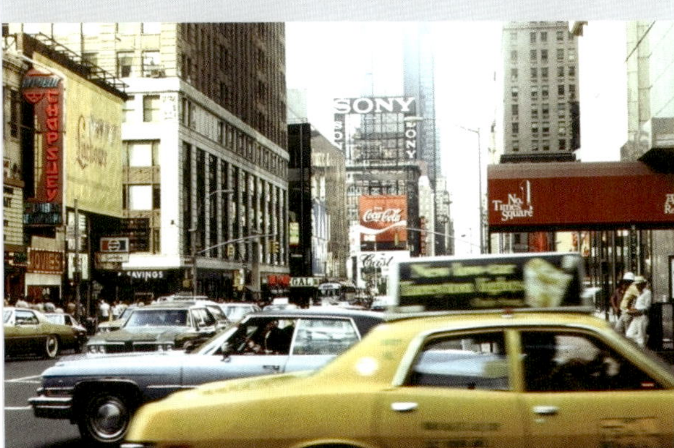

Vivienne and Malcolm **visited New York to try to promote their business,** and Malcolm was hooked on the music scene.

1975

The Sex Pistols were created and **managed by Malcolm**.

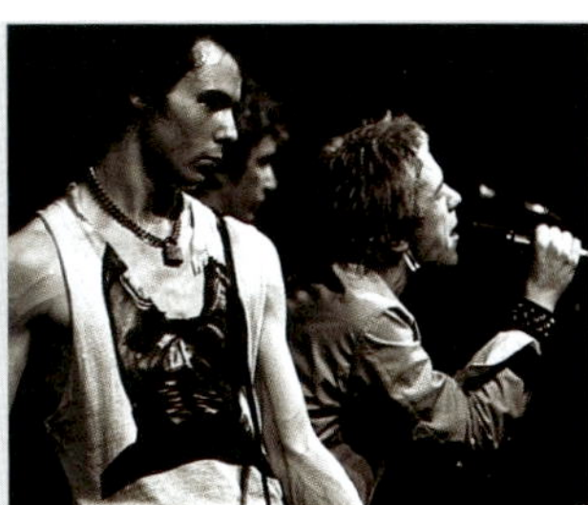

1979

After another renaming ('Seditionaries — Clothes for Heroes'), **Westwood's boutique receives its name 'World's End'**, which it remains today.

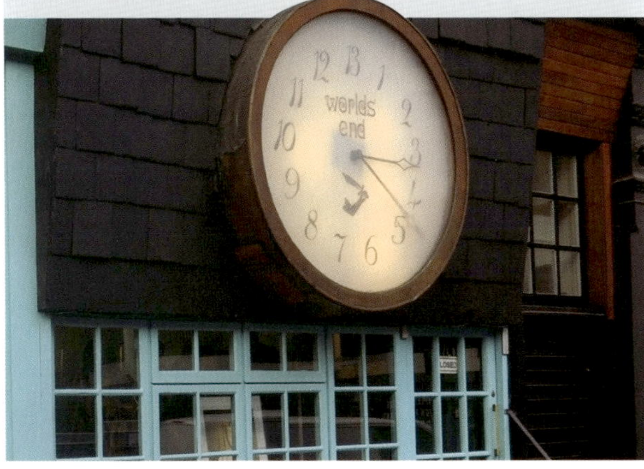

1981

Westwood presents her first fashion collection 'Pirates', followed in 1982 by 'Savage', a collection inspired by Wild West motifs. Both are part of the runway fashion shows of the London Designers Collection at the Olympia Exhibition Hall.

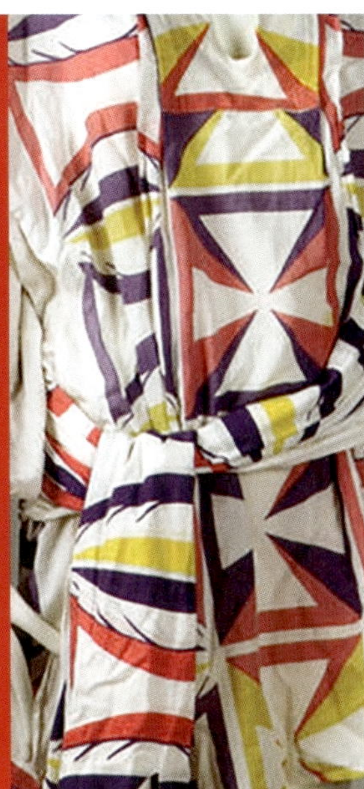

1982

Westwood introduces her collections in Paris, the first British fashion designer to do so since **Mary Quant**, the inventor of the miniskirt.

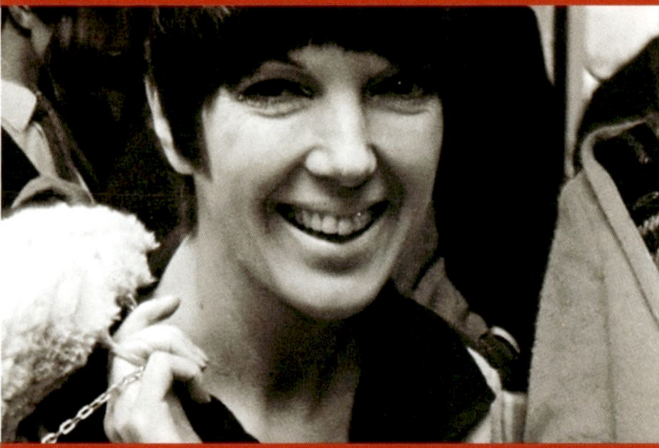

Westwood and McLaren operate a **second store at St. Christopher's Place in London**.

1983

The separation from McLaren leads the Westwood brand to financial crisis, from which a **licensing agreement with Giorgio Armani emerges in 1984** (dissolved in 1987).

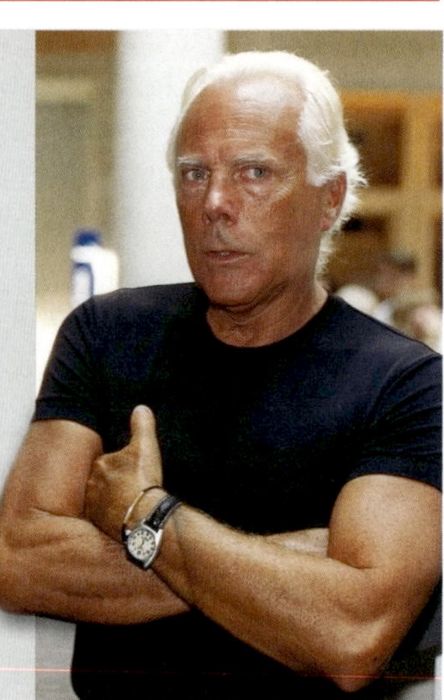

1985

Her **Petrushka-inspired collection 'Mini-Crini'**, still famous today, is created.

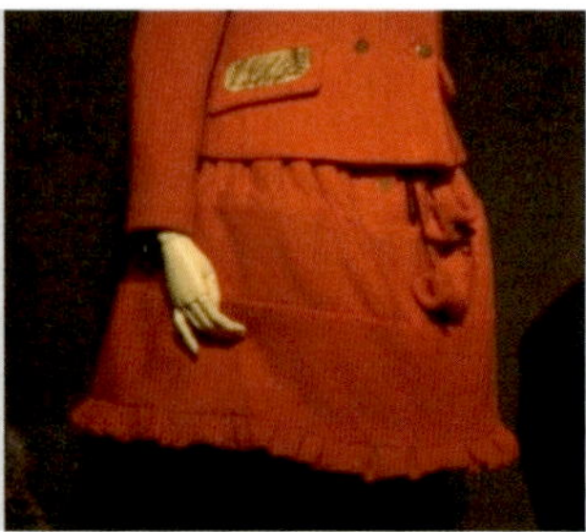

1987

Westwood creates another classic with the **'Harris Tweed' collection**, marking a successful turning point in her career as a designer.

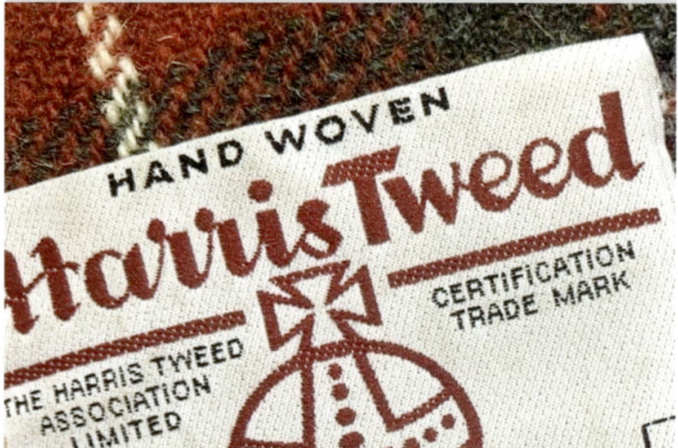

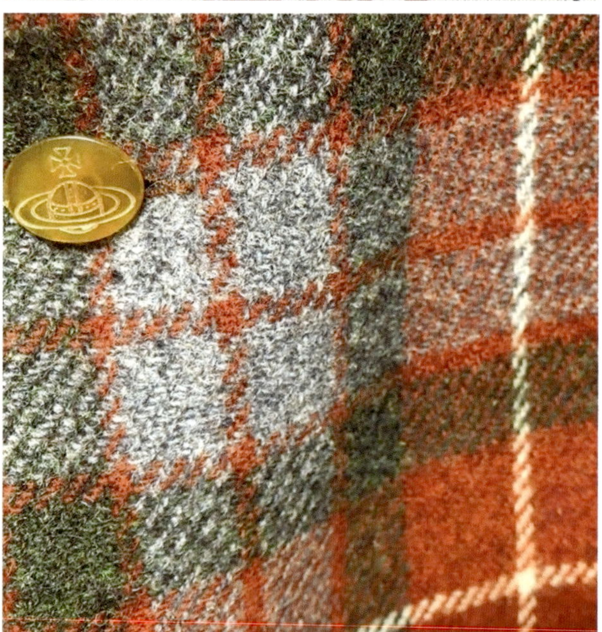

1992

Westwood was awarded the **Order of the British Empire**.

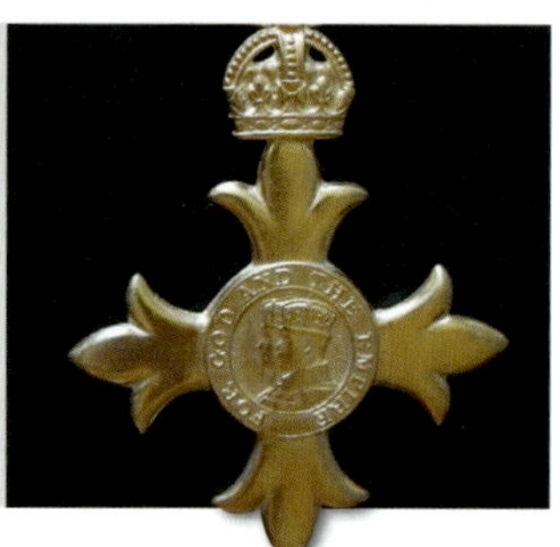

1989-2005

Westwood holds teaching positions at the University of Applied Arts Vienna and the Berlin University of the Arts. **In Vienna, she also met Andreas Kronthaler, a student, whom she married in 1992.** He continues to work for her company as a designer to this day.

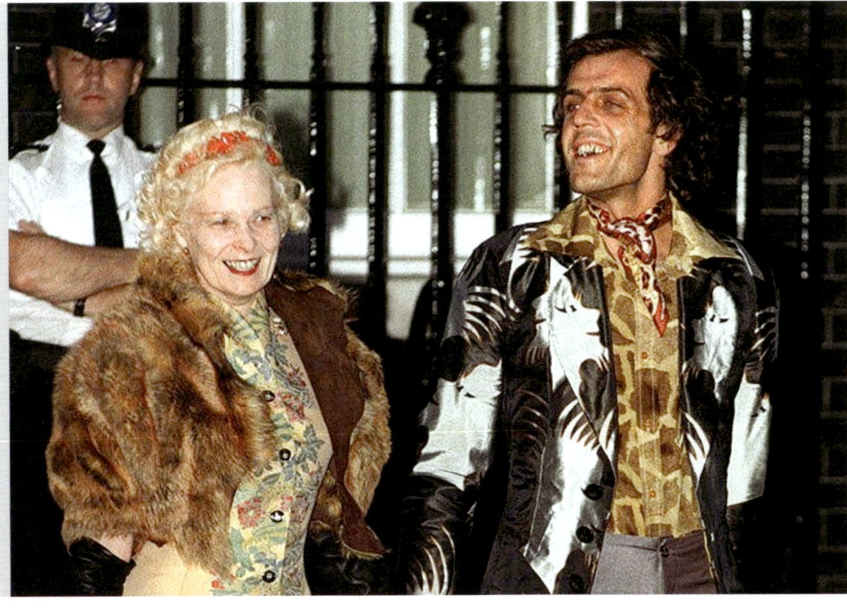

2004

The retrospective **'Vivienne Westwood: 34 Years in Fashion'** is held at **the Victoria and Albert Museum in London.** It is the largest exhibition the museum has ever dedicated to a designer.

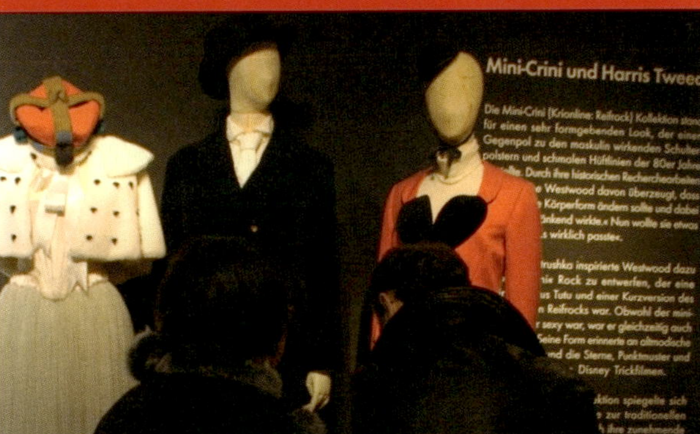

2006

Westwood received the **Dame Commander of the Order of the British Empire (DBE) award.**

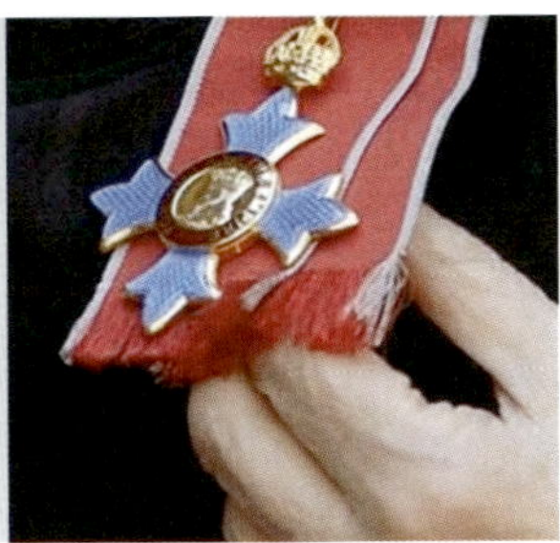

2014

Westwood designs **uniforms for the British airline Virgin Atlantic.**

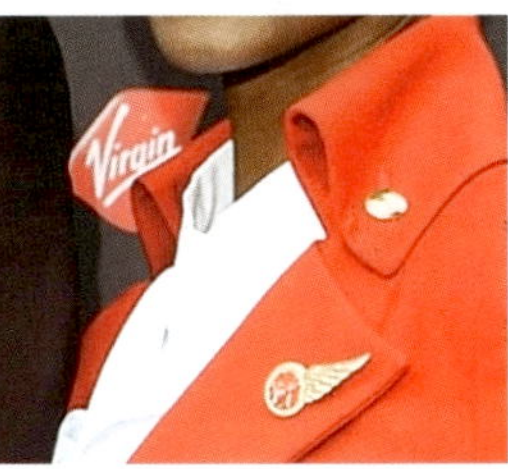

2019

Launch of **various collaborations** with Asics, Vans, and Buffalo, as well as Eastpak.

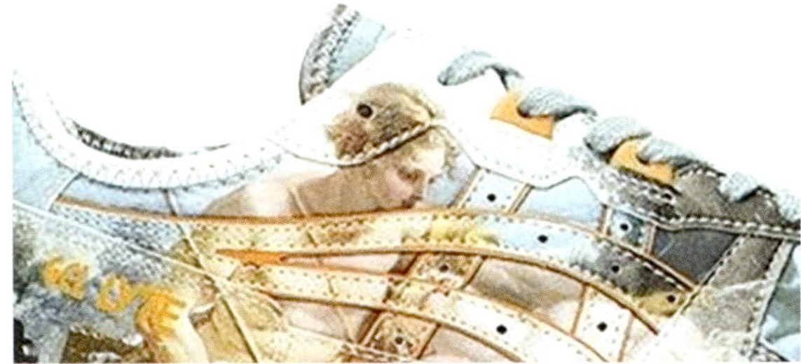

2022

Vivienne Westwood **passes away at the age of 81.**

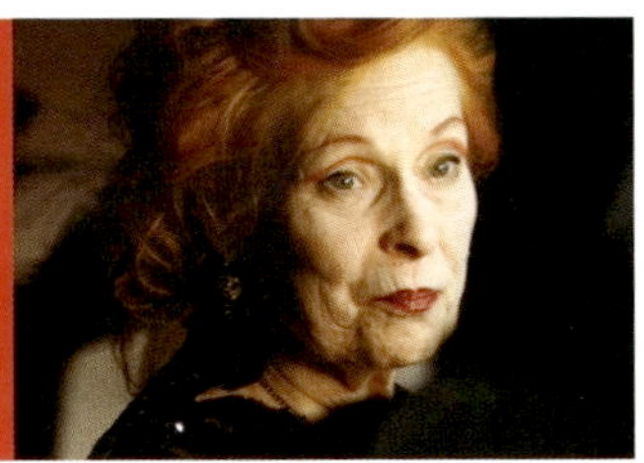

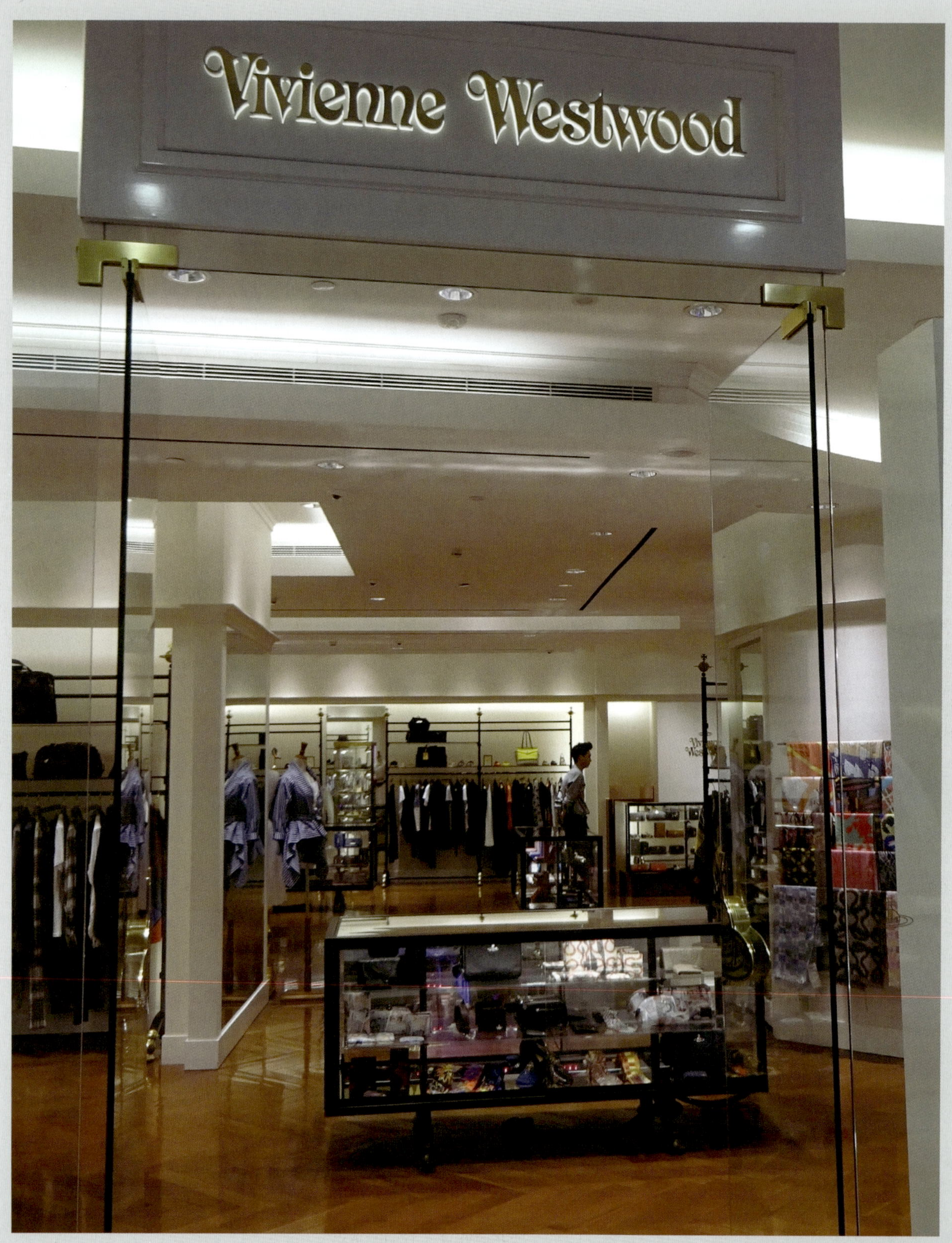

ABOVE: Westwood worldwide. This shop is in Shenzhen, China–Vivienne made it a long way from her Tintwistle beginnings!

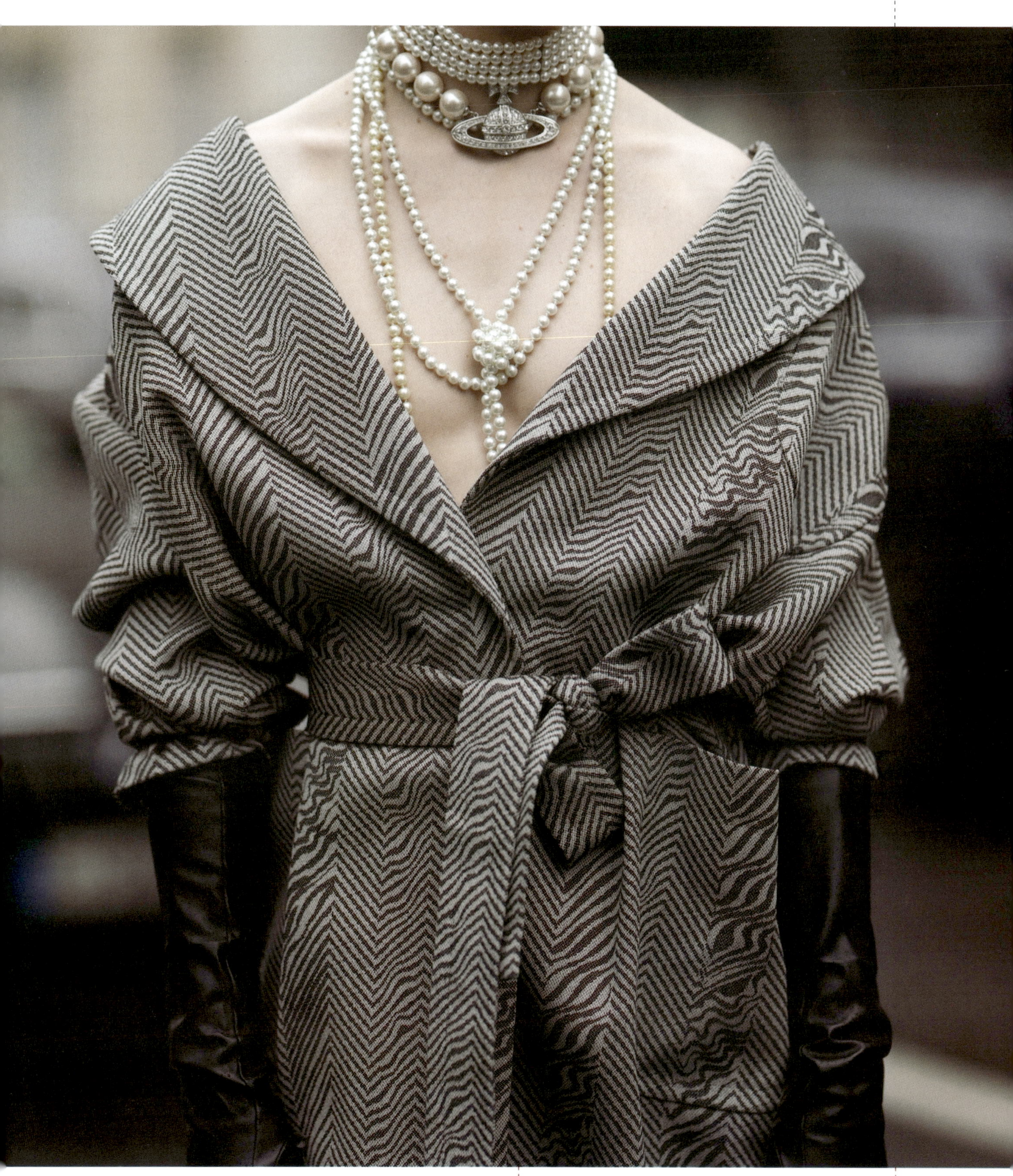

ABOVE: Black and grey patterned wool coat with V-neck and bow, long black leather gloves and pearl necklaces by Vivienne Westwood during the Vivienne Westwood Show, Fall/Winter 2024/25 at Paris Fashion Week

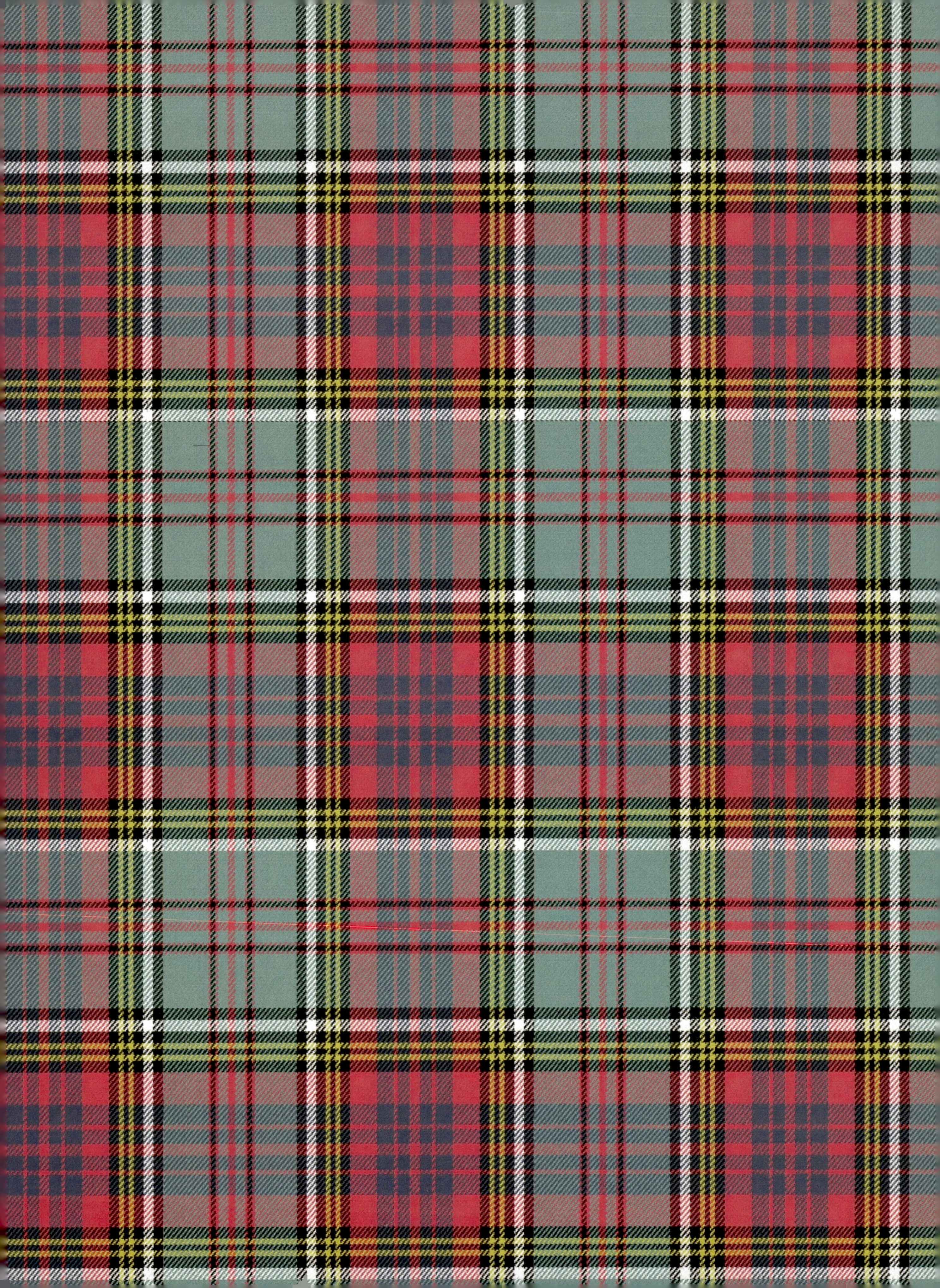